SMUGGLING AND TRAFFICKING IN HUMAN BEINGS

SMUGGLING AND TRAFFICKING IN HUMAN BEINGS

All Roads Lead to America

Sheldon X. Zhang

 PRAEGER

Westport, Connecticut
London

Library of Congress Cataloging-in-Publication Data

Zhang, Sheldon.
  Smuggling and trafficking in human beings : all roads lead to America /
Sheldon X. Zhang.
     p. cm.
  Includes bibliographical references and index.
  ISBN 978-0-275-98951-4 (alk. paper)
  1. Human trafficking—United States. 2. Human smuggling—United States.
I. Title
  HQ281.Z53 2007
  364.1'3—dc22   2007016225

British Library Cataloguing in Publication Data is available.

Library of Congress Catalog Card Number: 2007016225
ISBN-13: 978-0-275-98951-4
ISBN-10: 0-275-98951-8

First published in 2007

Praeger Publishers, 88 Post Road West, Westport, CT 06881
An imprint of Greenwood Publishing Group, Inc.
www.praeger.com

Printed in the United States of America

The paper used in this book complies with the
Permanent Paper Standard issued by the National
Information Standards Organization (Z39.48-1984).

10 9 8 7 6 5 4 3 2 1

Table of Contents

Tables and Figures

Preface

As night falls on Altar, a dusty Mexican border town, scores of migrants begin to emerge from rickety guest houses and motels and converge on several gathering grounds littered with garbage. Passenger vans and pickups with camper tops pull up to the roadside. A brisk business ensues. Migrants and their *polleros* (Mexican slang for human smugglers) mingle and discuss the night's excursion across the desert. For a price anywhere from $200 to $2,000, these migrants from the interior of Mexico, Latin America, and elsewhere in the world pack into passenger vans, fifteen to twenty at a time, and head to the staging ground in nearby Sasabe. The Buenos Aires National Wildlife Refuge to the north and the Tohono O'odham Reservation to the west offer vast and perilous environments where these migrants walk, run, huddle, and hide, for hours and days, while dodging sensors and the Border Patrol agents. Many make it through uneventfully. Others are arrested and turned back by the U.S. Border Patrol. Still others succumb to the scorching heat or freezing cold of the desert.

Farther to the west along the border between San Diego and Tijuana, enterprising agents charge $5,000 to $9,000 to fly eastern Europeans out of Warsaw and Amsterdam to Mexico City and then transport them overland to Tijuana, where these illegal immigrants from Russia, Lithuania, Ukraine, and Poland change into American-looking clothes and pose as U.S. citizens to cross immigration checkpoints in expensive cars.[1]

Halfway around the world in Southern China, dozens of lightly packed passengers ride in a bus heading toward a coastal village, taking breaks together and eating identical meals at the same restaurants. Upon arrival, they are quickly gathered by local *snakeheads* (Chinese human smugglers) onto a dock where small boats will ferry them in small groups to the mother ship moored in the distance, awaiting the night's several uploads before its transpacific journey. For a price of up to $65,000, these Chinese nationals are among the world's highest-paying migrants to be smuggled into the United States.

Human smuggling is a booming business along the U.S.-Mexican border, attracting groups of entrepreneurs who provide transportation services for a fee. Distinctive ethnic groups and enterprising agents (e.g., the Mexican *coyotes* and the Chinese *snakeheads*) in recent decades have increasingly engaged in cooperative activities with great efficiency to deliver their clients to their destinations inside the United States. These smuggling organizations exploit legal loopholes as well as established commercial venues to transport foreign nationals by sea, by air, and by land. No one knows exactly how many foreign nationals enter the United States illegally. U.S. Border Patrol agents arrest about 1 million illegal immigrants each year along the southern border. *Time* magazine estimated that about 3 million illegal immigrants enter the United States each year—"enough to fill 22,000 Boeing 737-700 airliners, or 60 flights every day for a year."[2] Guided by their smugglers, thousands of illegal immigrants walk across the border between the United States and Mexico without the knowledge of any law enforcement agencies. Many have made trips back and forth on established routes for years.

Many smuggling methods have been developed to circumvent U.S. immigration control. Human smugglers as a group are well connected and resourceful. Although the United States remains a primary destination for transnational human smuggling and trafficking activities, many other Western countries are also facing an influx of illegal immigrants.

Although most human smuggling activities involve transporting willing migrants in search of better economic opportunities, a few are in it for a far more sinister purpose—trafficking in women and children for sexual purposes and involuntary servitude. In recent decades, criminal gangs in eastern Europe have developed schemes to recruit and transport young women with promises of lucrative jobs overseas, only to force them into prostitution or servitude. Some of these women wind up in the United States. Although the trafficked victims have traditionally come from Southeast Asia and Latin America, in recent years they are increasingly from central and eastern Europe. Many of these women are forced into sweatshop labor and domestic servitude. The rest are forced into prostitution and the sex industry or, in the case of young children, sold for adoption. Although many victims begin their journeys willingly, few are aware of the terms and conditions placed upon them by their handlers. Many end up in cities in New York, Florida, North Carolina, and California. However, law enforcement agencies across the United States have noticed the migration of trafficking activities to smaller cities and suburbs.

According to a recent U.S. State Department intelligence report, between 45,000 and 50,000 women and children are trafficked into the United States each year by criminal organizations and loosely connected criminal networks. Another State Department report puts the annual figure at 18,000 to 20,000. Although these numbers are small relative to those involved in human smuggling, the exploitative and predatory nature of trafficking in women and children has caused grave concerns to the U.S. government and law enforcement agencies. Both the Clinton and Bush administrations and the U.S. Congress have taken steps to strengthen government-wide antitrafficking measures in prevention, in protection and support for victims, and in the prosecution of traffickers.

The United States has struggled for many years to effectively control its borders and to decide how best to handle the influx of foreign nationals. The rise of organized crime in transnational human smuggling or trafficking activities in recent decades further complicates this problem and bears significant political, social, and economic consequences. Improved global commerce, travel, and telecommunication infrastructures will only expand such criminal opportunities.

With the increased dominance of one country (Mexico) and one region (Latin America) in the U.S. immigrant population, public discourse has shifted more toward suppression and control and less toward integration and assimilation. On the other hand, although poverty in immigrant households continues to be a serious problem, most other social indicators (e.g., English-language acquisition and upward mobility of subsequent generations) suggest that these recent immigrants are not much different from their predecessors of a few generations ago.

The events of September 11, 2001, have fundamentally altered the way the United States views and approaches illegal immigration. Once treated as a nuisance, human smuggling and unauthorized entry by illegal immigrants are now linked to terrorism and national security. The U.S. immigration and border patrol agencies are often criticized for having repeatedly failed to protect the nation's borders and screen out undesirable elements from the masses of foreign visitors. Although critics and policy makers on both sides of the debate call for different measures to overhaul or improve the nation's border control functions, human smuggling and trafficking activities appear to continue unabated.

Although human smuggling and trafficking are illegal activities and oftentimes exploitive and violent in nature, the causes of these activities are complex. The vast majority of illegal immigrants seeking entry into the United States are doing so voluntarily. The social and international environments that initiate and sustain transnational migration and smuggling activities are rife with conflicting economic and political demands, a problem for which there are no obvious solutions. One can think of few legislative or policy measures taken by the U.S. government in recent history that have proved to be effective in managing the nation's borders. A number of books have been written in recent years on the topics of immigration and transnational migration in the United States, and the policy debates have intensified in all possible arenas by politicians, the public, news media, and academics. Much has been said and published about these debates.

This book instead presents only how smuggling and trafficking activities are carried out and explores policy challenges in combating the problem. Illegal immigrants have been accused of many things in the United States—including straining the social and economic resources of the host countries, contributing to rising crime (and the resulting anti-immigrant sentiment), suppressing the wages and worsening the working conditions of native-born workers and legal immigrants, and increasing health and safety risks to the workforce. Much has been written on these topics, although much more research is needed to deal with these complex social issues. Instead of arguing the political ramifications of illegal immigration, this book is oriented toward a criminological analysis of the illicit venues and strategies employed by groups of entrepreneurs as well as criminal organizations in gaining unauthorized entry into the United States. Although illegal immigration and illegal immigrants themselves are part of the discussion, this book focuses on smuggling and trafficking activities, their organizational profiles, and their operational patterns. The emphasis here is on the *organized* and *business* nature of unauthorized entries facilitated by enterprising agents.

It is a daunting task to engage in a book project of this nature without appearing biased toward one side of the political debate or the other. This book strives to achieve a balanced look at the problem of human smuggling and trafficking. The purpose is to compile and synthesize the most current research findings to shed light on the complexity of how human smuggling and trafficking activities are carried out and how the players operate in this illicit enterprise. There are various options as to what we can and should do to stop or minimize this illicit business. The challenge is not just gathering enough political will and resources but also anticipating unintended consequences and deciding to what extent and at what price we as a nation are willing to withstand the problem.

Data sources include published governmental and nongovernmental agency reports, academic studies, news media reports, and personal interviews with illegal immigrants and human smugglers, as well as with law enforcement representatives.

Acknowledgments

Many individuals have contributed to this book project. First and foremost, I want to thank my editor, Suzanne Staszak-Silva at Greenwood, for approaching me with the challenge of assembling the most current research on U.S.-bound human smuggling and trafficking activities and of making the material accessible to a wider audience than just the academics and government agencies. Her sustained encouragement and support provided much-needed impetus to keep this project on track.

I want to thank the anonymous reviewers whose insightful comments and suggestions have sharpened my focus and enhanced the quality of the finished product.

My contacts within U.S. law enforcement agencies have continued to keep me informed about the trends of and measures to combat human smuggling and trafficking activities along the borders and ports of entry—most notably Darwin Tchen of U.S. Immigration and Customs Enforcement (ICE); Michael Wheat, U.S. attorney in San Diego; Larry Lambert of the Orange County District Attorney's Office; Brian Schlosser of the Los Angeles County Sheriff's Department, and Ken Sanz of Florida State Law Enforcement Intelligence. Your continued support and friendship are much appreciated.

Much gratitude is due to the illegal immigrants and human smugglers who trusted me with their personal stories and expected that I would not reveal their identities.

I am particularly thankful to Donnamarie Cruickshank, who spent much time in proofreading and editing earlier drafts of this manuscript. Her friendship and wordsmithery are greatly appreciated.

Last and most important, I thank my wife, Susan, and my children, Amanda, Jacob, and Sarah, for blessing me with a loving environment that keeps me recharged, and for tolerating the intrusion of this prolonged writing project. I also want to thank my in-laws Iva, Ken, and Sue for providing much-needed child care while I was in the field conducting interviews and observing human smuggling activities.

Portions of this manuscript have been presented at professional conferences and published in academic outlets.

Chapter 1

Human Smuggling and Irregular Population Migration

WHAT IS HUMAN SMUGGLING?

In a narrow sense, human smuggling is the act of assisting or facilitating, often for a fee, the unauthorized entry of a foreign national into another country. Such characterization applies to most smuggling activities, but there are exceptions to this definition. Human smuggling conjures up different images to different people, and different definitions may lead to different understandings and conclusions about the same activity. For example, must one charge a fee for transporting migrants before the process is considered smuggling?

Although most human smugglers charge a fee for their services, there are also those who claim to be doing their relatives or friends a favor and charge only enough to cover the actual costs. Illegal Mexicans as well as Chinese in the United States often send for family members or relatives to join them. They actively participate in the smuggling process and work with the smugglers closely. Oftentimes, they pay for the smuggling expenses. Financial gains are apparently not the motive for these individuals who orchestrate the smuggling operations of their own relatives.

Once inside the United States, these newcomers typically repay the expenses that their relatives incurred, sometimes with interest and other times not. In these cases, should these relatives in the United States be considered human smugglers? Or should the definition apply only to individuals who participate in human smuggling activities solely for the purpose of making money? Both scenarios make sense: (1) smuggling by friends and relatives for personal reasons, and (2) smuggling for profits.

In either case, the act is the same—getting people into another country in a deliberate attempt to evade normal immigration procedures.

Not all human smugglers gather along the borders and guide fee-paying clients across the desert, although those who do attract much media attention. It would seem easy to simply define human smuggling as the surreptitious entry of people into the United States facilitated by a third party. However, many smugglers take perfectly legal venues to send their clients into the United States by exploiting legal loopholes in certain visa-waiver programs and the asylum system. Human smuggling is a far more complex sociopolitical as well as economic phenomenon than the one commonly portrayed in the news media or even in government reports.

Transnational migration has always been a part of human history as people move away from their ancestral villages and townships in search of better economic opportunities or living environments. For most of history, few paid attention to where people moved and where they chose to settle until, of course, those already settled came to view the newcomers as competitors for limited resources (be it land, water, pastures, or jobs). Over the centuries, communication problems and difficulties in travel restricted human migration to relatively small geographical regions. Except for a few countries, such as the United States and the United Kingdom, out-migration and in-migration for most countries up until very recently remained largely unregulated. In fact, the concept of immigration control did not enter any public discourse and government policies until a few decades ago.

As long as the scale of migration was small and migration channels limited, there was little need for formalized commercial assistance (i.e., human smuggling activities); therefore the term *human smuggling* did not enter the contemporary vocabulary until very recently when migrants received coordinated and systematic assistance from organized gangs and groups of entrepreneurs in North America and many Western European countries. To explore the phenomenon of human smuggling, one must understand some of the fundamentals behind transnational population movement when legitimate channels are either blocked or inadequate, thus creating a demand and an unauthorized market where transportation and other logistical services are sought and purchased.

GLOBALIZATION, POPULATION MIGRATION, AND HUMAN SMUGGLING

Transnational population migration has become a global phenomenon that affects practically all nations. In the past century the general trends have shifted from outflows of Europeans to their overseas colonies to emigrations from developing nations in Africa, Asia, and Latin America to industrialized countries in North America and Europe. The expanding global commerce in the latter half of the twentieth century ushered in an unprecedented era of international exchanges of goods and services, as well as the movement of laborers in response to employment opportunities. International migration has exploded since the 1980s, with people from developing countries and countries in the former Soviet Union seeking opportunities elsewhere, mostly in the West.[1]

Global population migration has reached unprecedented levels in the past two decades. According to the United Nations, around 175 million persons currently live outside their native countries (roughly 3 percent of the world's population), and almost 10 percent of the populations in developed nations are made up of foreign-born immigrants.[2] Migration patterns in the past few decades have remained largely the same, with more-developed regions receiving migrants from less-developed regions, currently at the rate of about 2.3 million a year. In the past thirty years or so, the number of migrants throughout the world has more than doubled, with the majority of them living in developed countries. North America led the world in absorbing large numbers of immigrants, at a rate of 1.4 million annually, followed by Europe with an annual net gain of 0.8 million.[3] At the country level, the United States has the largest number of immigrants, with 35 million, followed by the Russian Federation with 13 million and Germany with 7 million.[4]

During the 1990s, according to a report by the United Nations Commission on Population and Development, the European Union saw a sharp increase in non-EU foreign labor population, mostly from the former Yugoslavia and the eastern European states, Turkey, and the Maghreb.[5] Transnational migration also affected these eastern European countries in significant ways. In Hungary, some 50,000 work permits were issued annually for jobs not being filled by native Hungarians. Some 300,000 to 500,000 foreigners were in the Russian Federation, many of whom came from the former Soviet republics and China, either illegally employed or in transit to other destinations.[6] Currently legal and illegal migrants account for 15 percent of the populations in some fifty countries, and the percentage is likely to grow well into the foreseeable future.[7] Figures 1.1 and 1.2 illustrate the magnitude and size of immigrant populations in the top ten countries (i.e., international migrant stock).[8]

To keep these figures in perspective, one should note that the United States, although having the largest number of immigrants, is nowhere close to many other countries in terms of the proportion of foreign-born residents in the total population. In fact, the United States is not even in the top twenty nations with the highest percentage of foreign-born residents among the population.[9]

In the decades after World War II, trends in transnational migration took on two main characteristics. First, there was a reversal of population flows where former sending (mostly colonial) countries became receiving

Figure 1.1 Countries with largest foreign-born populations in 2000 (in millions).

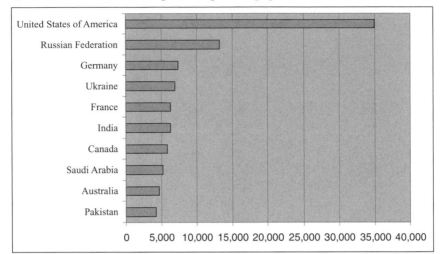

Source: United Nations International Migration Report, 2002.

countries.[10] Europeans used to be the typical migrants, going overseas in search of a better life. Now most European countries are drawing large numbers of migrants from around the world.[11] Historical immigrant countries such as the United States, Canada, and Australia continue to be strong magnets for international migration. The list of receiving countries has expanded to include Asia, the Middle East, and the Pacific Rim. Second, unlike the European migrants in earlier decades, who were received as essential for nation building, receiving countries today are wary of and often hostile toward new immigrants. Restrictive policies and procedures have been implemented to reduce and restrict the entry of immigrants.[12]

Increased global commercial activities and easier access to other parts of the world have made people in developing countries more aware of their adverse living conditions, thus intensifying the push-and-pull factors that drive migrants' desires to seek opportunities abroad. Drastic differences in wages and living standards have continued to draw unprecedented numbers of migrants from developing countries in Asia, Africa, South America, and eastern Europe to developed countries in western Europe, Australia, and North America. Despite the continued reliance on cheap labor, developed countries have become more selective in the type of and skills of their desired labor force in recent decades. Legislative efforts and government policies in receiving countries have therefore been primarily aimed at restricting low-skilled manual laborers.

When the United Nations first tracked views and perceptions toward international migration in 1976, most member states showed little interest, considering it a topic of secondary concern.[13] Countries with explicit

Figure 1.2 Countries with highest percentage of foreign-born residents in 2000.

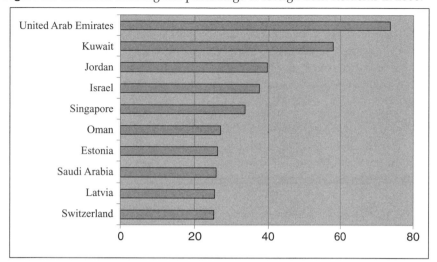

Source: United Nations International Migration Report, 2002.

migration policies were decidedly a minority. By 1995, 40 percent of the UN member states had developed policies specifically regulating levels of immigration. In the past two decades, the number of governments adopting measures to restrict the flow of immigrants continued to grow.[14] It was interesting to note that although developed countries have been most eager to restrict the level of immigration, developing countries are also following suit. Countries such as China, Thailand, and South Korea have in recent years adopted restrictive procedures and policies to regulate foreigners from seeking employment or residency. Even countries with a long history of admitting large numbers of foreign nationals for permanent settlement (namely Australia, Canada, New Zealand, and the United States) are moving toward giving greater preference and priority to those with valuable skills.[15]

The United States has for decades remained the number one destination country in international migration, legal or illegal. It is home to 33.5 million foreign-born persons as of 2003, representing 11 percent of the total population.[16] Of those foreign-born residents, more than half came from Latin America—18.6 million. Mexico alone accounted for more than half of these immigrants from Latin America.[17] Immigrants from Latin America are the fastest-growing ethnic group in the United States, and Hispanics, already the largest ethnic minority, are projected to make up 29.8 percent of the U.S. population by 2050.[18] Coastal states continue to have the largest number of foreign born residents in the nation, as shown in Table 1.1.

Table 1.1 Top Ten States with Most Foreign-Born Residents

		2000		1990		
Rank	State	Total Number	% of Population	Total Number	% of Population	% Change
1	California	8,864,255	26.2	6,458,825	21.7	37.2
2	New York	3,868,133	20.4	2,851,861	15.9	35.6
3	Texas	2,899,642	13.9	1,524,436	9.0	90.2
4	Florida	2,670,828	16.7	1,662,601	12.9	60.6
5	Illinois	1,529,058	12.3	952,272	8.3	60.6
6	New Jersey	1,476,327	17.5	966,610	12.5	52.7
7	Massachusetts	772,983	12.2	573,733	9.5	34.7
8	Arizona	656,183	12.8	278,205	7.6	135.9
9	Washington	614,457	10.4	322,144	6.6	90.7
10	Georgia	577,273	7.1	173,126	2.7	233.4
	United States	31,107,889	11.1	19,767,316	7.9	57.4

Source: Data abstracted from *Demographic Profiles: 1990 and 2000 Comparison Tables* published by the U.S. Census Bureau, available at http://www.census.gov/Press-Release/www/2002/dp_comptables.html.

According to the last two U.S. censuses (i.e., 1990 and 2000), the total number of foreign-born residents (irrespective of their legal status) saw a steady and significant increase throughout the country. Although states such as California, New York, Texas, and Florida continued to lead in the number of foreign-born residents, states in the Midwest and the South, where the numbers of immigrants were historically low, showed the most rapid growths over the ten-year span between the two censuses.[19] Unlike New York, Los Angeles, Chicago, and San Francisco, where socioeconomic systems as well as political establishments are used to dealing with large numbers of immigrants of diverse backgrounds, the new settlements in the heartland of America have created integration challenges and social stress for governmental and nongovernmental agencies not accustomed to their presence and their needs for services.[20]

The continued breakdown of barriers in the global economy will continue to encourage labor movement, which in turn drives illegal immigration and its by-product—human smuggling. Illegal immigrants in the United States have drawn much attention from the news media, the public, and the political establishment for years. Despite greater concerns over the nation's border integrity and significant reinforcement following the events of September 11, 2001, the volume of illegal immigrants entering the United States does not appear to have decreased much.

Although it is difficult to provide accurate figures on the number of illegal immigrants residing in the United States, or how many are entering the country illegally, researchers have used various strategies to try to provide some estimates for specific years. In a 2004 study, based on data from the U.S. Census Bureau and the Department of Labor, the Pew Hispanic Center, a private research group in Washington, drew some profiles on the size and characteristics of the illegal immigration population residing in the United States. The main findings are as follows:[21]

- The illegal immigrant population in the United States had been on a steady growth path for several years, averaging about 500,000 per year.
- At the same growth rate as observed in recent years, the illegal immigrant population can reach 11.5 to 12 million, 40 percent of which have lived in the country five years or less.
- More than half of the illegal population in the United States came from Mexico, numbering about 6.2 million.
- Since the mid-1990s, the most rapid growth in the number of undocumented migrants has been in states that previously had relatively small foreign-born populations. As a result, Arizona and North Carolina are now among the states with the largest numbers of undocumented immigrants.
- Although most undocumented migrants are young adults, there is also a sizable young population. About 16 percent of the undocumented population, about 1.8 million, are under eighteen years of age. Furthermore, two-thirds of all children residing in illegal immigrant families are U.S. citizens by birth.

The Pew Hispanic Center study pointed to two main characteristics of the illegal population in the United States: (1) Mexicans make up the largest group of illegal immigrants, at about 57 percent as of March 2004, and an additional 24 percent, or 2.5 million illegal immigrants, are from other Latin American countries; and (2) states historically low in foreign-born populations have witnessed the greatest growth. The increasing immigrant populations in general have been attributed to the growing employment opportunities in such industries as construction, hospitality, agriculture, and food processing plants.[22]

Within Mexico, the majority of illegal migrants have traditionally come from the central-western states such as Michoacan, Guanajuato, and Jalisco. However, migrants from Oaxaca and Guerrero have also increased rapidly in recent years.[23] According to one estimate, the majority of the migrants from Mexico came from about 5 percent of its *municipios* (counties).[24]

EXPLAINING TRANSNATIONAL MIGRATION

There have been many theories explaining human migration, most of which address two levels of factors.[25] At the micro or personal level, disparities in earnings draw individuals from poor countries toward countries with prospects for greater personal or family wealth. Wage differences between sending and receiving countries are the most important factor in people's decisions to move.[26] At the macro level, countries with a shortage in labor attempt to recruit workers from abroad to fill the demand of the economy. As the economy expands or contracts, the labor market fluctuates, and countries in need of labor thus respond by encouraging or discouraging immigration. Individual laborers, on the other hand, adjust and adapt to the cycles of economy. A state of equilibrium is thus achieved through periodic redistributions of labor through migration.[27] International migration thus becomes an equalizing mechanism to balance the distribution of economic resources across countries.[28]

Labor markets in many postindustrial nations have become bifurcated, with high pay and steady jobs on one end and low pay and unstable jobs on the other. Such dual labor markets can be found in cities such as Los Angeles and New York, where managerial, administrative, financial, and technical jobs have reached high levels of concentration among segments of the urban populations. At the same time, these high-paying jobs have also created high demands for low-wage services. Such a bifurcated labor market structurally depends on a steady supply of cheap labor to sustain itself.[29] In other words, poor economic conditions in developing countries are insufficient to cause massive outward migration. There must be a corresponding demand in developed countries to create the pull factor.

A few other theories focus on the family or clan rather than on individuals as the starting point. Families send their members to distant places in search of jobs to increase or ensure the overall financial well-being of the family. These sojourners effectively become an insurance policy for the aging parents and other family members against crop failure, market crash, and a host of other adverse economic conditions at home. In return, families with members working overseas can increase their resources to deal with current and future financial uncertainties. Migration therefore is a collective act to maximize a family's income, to minimize risks, and to deal with a variety of economic failures.[30]

Migrants therefore are rational actors who calculate social and personal costs against potential profits in their decision-making and move to a foreign country where they can expect positive financial returns. Wage differences are not the only incentive that motivates people to move, and migration decisions are not made by isolated actors. They are taken within the family or household and sometimes within a clan or even an entire community.[31]

Still other scholars argue that transnational migration of labor forces reflects the penetration and expansion of the competitive market economy advocated and promoted by the few postindustrial countries. This world system perspective perceives the global marketplace as being dominated by a few core nations that command vast amounts of capital and resources. As a result, the global economic system is moving toward greater interdependence, with other countries on the periphery supplying not only labor but also consumer markets. The global expansion of the market economy causes disruptions to the traditional economic systems and livelihoods in developing countries, which in turn stimulate population migration.[32] Therefore, migration does not necessarily represent a lack of economic development in the sending countries but rather disruptive development itself, because historically it has not been the poorest countries that came to dominate international migration but countries that experienced an economic expansion.

Although these theories attempt to explain the same phenomenon from different angles, they all share a few consistent themes.

The Poverty Factor

Poverty is probably the most cited factor in explaining transnational migration. People migrate for many reasons (e.g., famine, wars, job opportunities, family reunion); however, the search for economic opportunities and security appears to remain constant for most people who choose to uproot from their native land and transplant themselves in a foreign country. In other words, people move because of the prospect of a better life somewhere other than their current geographical location.

Economic opportunities and earning differentials remain a fundamental driving force behind transnational population migration. Income disparities between developed and developing countries have widened in recent decades as a result of a globalized economy in which the production of goods and market transactions can take place in the most efficient manner. Technological advances in transportation and communication have produced unprecedented wealth. The shrinking of the world economy and marketplace, however, has also produced unprecedented inequality between the rich and the poor. Half of the current world population, nearly 3 billion people, lives on less than $2 a day.[33] The income of the richest fifth of the world population in 1999 was seventy-four times that of the poorest fifth; in 1960 the difference was only thirty times.[34]

Mexico, the country that sends the most illegal immigrants to the United States, contrasts sharply in wage differences, and the disparities in earnings remain the main impetus for cross-border migration.[35] According to the World Bank, half of the 104 million residents in Mexico live in poverty and one-fifth in extreme poverty (defined as living on less than $1 a day). Mexico's economy was seriously weakened during the financial meltdown of 1994–95. In 2002 the extreme poverty rate was only one percentage point below the level prior to the 1994 financial crisis.[36] Despite Mexico's proximity to the world's largest economy and consumer market, between 4 and 9 percent of its population in 2002 was living on less than $1 a day, a level close to that found in some of the world's poorest countries.[37] In other words, Mexico had made little economic progress in elevating its poorest for seventeen years.

The remittances from overseas allow immigrant families back in their native countries to make major purchases, such as building houses or buying farmland. Having a family member in the United States is similar to creating a private pension system that minimizes the risk of poverty in old age. Higher wages and diversified opportunities for making a living abroad have thus been a core explanation for transnational migration. For instance, in the Chinese context, the prospect of accumulating more wealth than one can ever dream of making presents a powerful incentive for would-be migrants and their families to pool resources to pay the sky-high smuggling fees to come to the United States. An illegal Chinese immigrant, who came by way of Mexico, explained his motive in the following way:[38]

> Back in China, even if you want to work hard, there is no place for you to work, because there are so many people out of jobs and waiting for employment. If you work in a restaurant in the United States, you can make $1,500 to $2,000 a month. Here in this restaurant, the owner provides food and lodging. I have practically no other expenses of my own. So I can save all my money each month and send it home. One year's work in the United States equals ten years of work in China. The main problem in China is that there is no safety net. When there is no safety net, people are afraid of spending money. Once you are out of money, you are out of luck. The government is not going to save you when you have no money. The main reason people in the United States spend a lot of money is that they have a safety net. This is important. People in China have no sense of financial security. No one knows what's going to happen when they get old. If I work here for a few years, and even if my application for political asylum is not granted, I can still return to China with enough money to last the rest of my life.

Although sending countries in general are in worse economic conditions than receiving countries, those who decide to migrate are not necessarily among the poorest. Poverty is relative in this context. The actual economic condition of a prospective migrant is less important than how it is perceived. An incentive to migrate is typically formed by the discrepancy between what people expect to obtain in life and the opportunities in their present surroundings. The greater the perceived discrepancy, the stronger the motivation to migrate.

The new economics of migration, a theory gaining popularity in recent years, emphasizes this perceived discrepancy in its explanation of causes of transnational migration. Households send their members abroad to improve their financial situations relative to some reference group, that is, the income of the community with which these families are comparing themselves.[39] Therefore the mere availability of local jobs or opportunities to make a living in one's home country does not necessarily influence people's decision to migrate. The Pew Hispanic Center found in a recent survey that the vast majority, some 95 percent, of migrants from Mexico had been gainfully employed at home prior to their arrival in the United States, and many were able to find jobs in the same or similar industries as they did back home (namely agriculture, construction, manufacturing, and hospitality).[40] Therefore, these Mexican nationals migrated north not because they were unemployed or were about to starve but because they could do better financially in the United States than in their own country.

Labor Shortage

The demand for cheap labor has long been a magnet to draw people from developing countries to the developed ones, much the same way as laborers migrate from rural to urban areas in many parts of the world, particularly in China, where an expanding economy is fueling a massive internal migrant population in excess of 150 million.[41] When such migration takes place within a country such as China, it is not only considered legal but also imperative to sustain the rapid economic growth in coastal provinces and other major urban centers.

The U.S. economy also has its own uneven labor force distribution problems. In some sectors the shortage has been chronic for decades. Much of the U.S. meatpacking and agricultural industries have become heavily dependent on foreign-born (and many illegal) workers for processing slaughterhouse products, harvesting fruits and vegetables in Florida and California, milking cows on dairy farms in Wisconsin and Oregon, and packing potatoes in Idaho. It is no secret that business owners and politicians recognize the importance of the labor provided by illegal immigrants in many industries. According to U.S. government sources, there are about 1 million farm laborers at any one time. Nearly 40 percent of them are illegal. About one-quarter of the meatpacking labor force in the Midwest is probably illegal also.[42]

In California, for instance, agriculture is big business at $32 billion a year. The combined crop value from three California counties—Fresno, Tulare, and Kern—is worth more than that of many states.[43] More than 250 agricultural commodities are staggered over different seasons, making the demand for manual labor virtually year-round. Most farm laborers in California are Latinos.[44] In the late 1990s and early 2000s, booming real estate across the country has weakened the supply of farm laborers because of higher-paid jobs in construction. Growers are complaining that their farm workers are leaving in droves to take better-paid, less strenuous jobs in construction and landscaping. The pay differences can be as much as 30 to 40 percent.[45] Furthermore, whereas most farm workers must follow the crop season and work from farm to farm, construction work is less seasonal.

Recent buildup along the U.S.-Mexican border is not helping the matter either. Restricted flows of illegal immigrants reduce the number of available farmhands during busy harvesting seasons. Although illegal immigrants still manage to cross into the United States, they are more likely to make the entry farther east in the high deserts of Arizona. This change in border crossing means that prospective illegal immigrants must travel greater distances to work on Californian farms.

Low Fertility and Aging Population

A shortage in labor can be attributed to many factors. A low fertility rate and long life expectancy are some of the main contributors. A low fertility rate in the developed world means that the existing labor market must be replenished with imported labor in order to sustain the economic growth required to keep up with the demand of the existing system of social benefits.[46] Most developed countries are struggling to deal with the challenge of supporting a graying population that is already out of the workforce but continues to strain publicly funded benefits. Many governments in western Europe, long known for their progressive social policies and generous welfare benefits, are considering drastic measures to curtail the escalating costs as people live longer and have fewer children. The British government, for instance, recently announced that it would consider raising the retirement age to as high as sixty-nine to ward off a looming funding crisis in the state pension system.[47] Italy has raised the age for full pension benefits from fifty-seven to sixty. Germany is proposing to raise the retirement age from sixty-five to sixty-seven. The United States has already postponed the retirement age to sixty-seven for full Social Security benefits.[48]

An aging population poses many financial challenges. First, the population retiring from the workforce must be replenished by fresh labor in order to sustain the production of goods and services. If the nation's childbearing population cannot produce enough for replacement purposes, labor must be imported from abroad, which is a major reason for the high rate of immigration for most developed countries.

Second, an aging population creates downward pressure for subsistence (i.e., funding of state-run pensions, health care, and other social welfare benefits). The bigger the aging population, the greater the pressure on the younger generations. In the United States, Social Security is facing the possibility of insolvency in the not-too-distant future unless drastic measures are taken. Although politicians and interest groups are debating courses of action to take, the basic facts remain irrefutable. Baby boomers are retiring at an accelerating rate, and 78 million of them will begin retiring in 2008. In about thirty years, there will be twice as many older Americans as there are today.[49]

People live longer and collect Social Security benefits well beyond the years anticipated by the program when it was first envisioned in 1935. At the same time, the number of workers it takes to support one person on Social Security will drop from 3.3 in 2007 to about 2.1 in 2031. In 1940 the ratio of workers to Social Security beneficiaries was 159.4 to 1. During the early years most workers were contributing to rather than benefiting from the Social Security program because about half of them worked till they died. Other than raising retirement age and taxes, there are few alternatives. Massive importation of young foreign labor would be one way to increase the workers-to-beneficiary ratio.

The United States is not alone in this respect. Worldwide, the proportion of the population aged sixty years or older tripled over the last fifty years, and it will probably triple again over the next fifty years.[50] Unlike many developing nations, where multiple generations may reside in the same household, older people in the United States in general prefer independent living arrangements. Senior citizens living apart from their children in the United States are the norm, and 25 percent of Americans aged sixty years or older live alone.[51] With the increase in the aging population comes the increase in the demand for unskilled labor. Older people simply have increased needs for domestic services such as nursing care, housekeeping, maid services, and assistance in aspects of life that are not covered in any retirement or insurance plans.

Rising Education Attainments and Employment Aspirations

Current debate on issues of human smuggling rarely examines the fact that, even though unemployment continues to plague a small segment of the U.S. native population, many jobs go unfilled. In fact, jobs are so abundant and easy to find that few illegal immigrants go unemployed for any extended period of time. According to a recent survey conducted by the Pew Hispanic Center, illegal immigrants from Mexico had few problems finding jobs in the United States, particularly those who had been living in the country for at least six months.[52] Their low education levels, poor English-language skills, and lack of legal paperwork did not pose barriers to employment. Few of these illegal migrants work at minimum wages because most labor-intensive industries such as agriculture and construction that employ large numbers of illegal immigrants are paying higher than legally mandated wages. Outright exploitation and slave labor are not common in these industries. Why then, one may ask, must employers hire undocumented workers?

Many have pointed fingers at corporations such as Wal-Mart as epitomizing the race to the bottom. Fixing the blame on Corporate America for its relentless pursuit of profit through outsourcing or hiring illegal immigrants tends to oversimplify the problem. In a competitive market environment, consumers strive to maintain or even expand their purchasing power by demanding lower prices. If Tyson Foods were to pay $40 an hour to its workers in poultry processing plants, chicken would become an expensive delicacy that most Americans could hope to savor only on special occasions or holidays.

When Tyson Foods, one of the world's largest poultry processors, was indicted on December 19, 2001, by a grand jury in Tennessee on thirty-six counts of recruiting illegal workers from Mexico and transporting them to its poultry processing plants in the Midwest and the South,[53] the uproar in the news media focused on the greed of Corporate America. The Tyson case was used to exemplify a corporate culture that condones the use of cheap illegal labor in its pursuit of profits. Others, however, lamented that the meatpacking and agricultural businesses only reflect the fact that the nation has become dependent on illegal workers for its food production, so much so that their absence would cause serious disruptions to the nation's food supply. Profit is only part of the story. It is not the pay that is too low. Only two decades ago, meatpacking plants in the United States were staffed mostly by unionized workers who earned the equivalent of today's $18 an hour.[54] Many entry-level white-collar jobs pay less and are just as monotonous and repetitive if not as backbreaking.

Shifts in popular culture, brought about by rising levels of education and concomitant career aspirations, have made most, if not all, Americans look down upon agricultural or construction jobs as the bottom of the social and occupational hierarchy with few avenues for upward mobility. The great American education system has significantly elevated literacy standards of the general populace. It also has contributed to depleting the pool of domestic workers willing to take the least desirable jobs.

High schools these days are preoccupied with preparing students for college or for other postsecondary educational programs. The percentage of graduates entering college is a basic benchmark for ranking the performance of all high schools. The U.S. college is certainly not interested in cultivating students' intellectual abilities in preparation for jobs at construction sites or in farm fields. People do not work just for money. They also work for social status. Children are taught to believe that college is the normative goal for everyone entering high school. Parents warn their children of a bleak future if they cannot get into college, a future of backbreaking labor in a tomato field. Children are encouraged to pursue more education and higher education in order to secure higher standards of living. Prolonged education has turned a large section of the U.S. population away from menial and labor-intensive occupations. Even the basic primary education curriculum is preparing students, who by law must attend school, for a life away from agriculture, construction, and food processing.

Education, as an American ethos, has acquired great authority through formality and credentialism in conferring social status and assigning career options, because the levels of formal education are consistently linked to people's earning potentials and occupational prestige. Farm labor or hospitality work requires few special skills and little formal education, which effectively falls outside the realm of formal education, and therefore can be relegated only to the bottom of the labor market and excluded from any hope of upward movement. To fill these bottom-tier jobs, employers must turn to immigrants, legal and illegal, whose point of reference is not in the receiving country but at home, and whose goal in life is not striving for status and prestige in the United States, but earning enough money to build a house and buy consumer goods to improve their financial and social standings in their home countries.[55]

Beyond the Earning Disparity Factor

Although relative deprivation and the prospect of elevating one's family status and financial standing in the sending country provide a strong incentive for people to migrate, it is not a sufficient condition. Far more people in developing countries are aware of the earning differentials and dream of a life in a Western country than those who actually take the journey. The fact that not more people from developing countries participate in transnational migration indicates that the decision to migrate involves more than monetary factors.

The picture of transnational migration is a complex one. Although most migrants would cite economic reasons as the main motive for leaving their home countries, the actual configuration of how and why migration takes places goes beyond merely changing residences for the sake of a better lot in life. International migration typically started with a few pioneers who landed in a foreign country, either fortuitously or deliberately, in search of better economic opportunities. These pioneers, once settled, became a recruiting depot for labor and business partners from their home countries.

Kinship and community ties, legal barriers and human smugglers, airlines, railways and shipping companies, and even law firms, human rights groups, and anti-immigration activists all become part of this complex picture, each group playing out some roles that directly or indirectly affect the flow and direction of legal as well as illegal migration.[56] In practice, most migrants follow existing networks to particular destinations rather than simply moving to the country where the most money can be made. This is particularly the case for illegal immigrants from Mexico, who rely on their family and social networks. Their migratory decisions and paths hew closely to their existing social networks in the United States.

Finding jobs and choosing places to settle are a result of consultation with friends and family members in the United States. The same is true for Chinese immigrants. Emigrants from Zhejian Province favor Spain and Italy, whereas most from Fujian Province would rather be smuggled to New York City. Therefore, the roles of kinship and the network of fellow villagers are more important factors for Mexican and Chinese immigrants when deciding where to migrate and to settle than the mere availability of better-paying jobs. These nonmonetary factors are probably the most influential factors in explaining migration flows, choice of settlement, and overseas community building.

HUMAN SMUGGLING—A GLOBAL TRAVEL SERVICE FOR IRREGULAR MIGRANTS

Human smuggling has become a global enterprise, raising concerns among most industrialized countries. Although illegal immigration is nothing new, the provision of transportation services in systematic and organized fashions that cater to people wanting to enter other countries in search of better lives is a recent development. Viewed as a criminal activity by governments, but not necessarily so by those who use their services, human smugglers are increasingly controlling the flow of migrants across borders. Increased restrictions in immigration policies in most Western countries and improved technology to monitor border crossings have only made the matter worse. Illegal migrants have come to depend on smuggling organizations, or the "professionals," to arrange the journey.

Governments are often dismayed at their inability to control the criminal organizations that fuel the growing global migration. Despite the often-times inhumane transportation conditions, frequent accidents, and risk of death, large numbers of migrants seem perfectly willing to pay exorbitant prices to be smuggled across borders. Human smuggling organizations benefit from weak collaborations among governments and police agencies, huge profits, and the relatively low risk of detection and prosecution compared with other activities of transnational organized crime. Excelling in adapting their strategies, human smugglers have been able to respond to law enforcement activities in most countries. The routes used by human smugglers may be simple and direct as well as circuitous and hazardous. The journey may last one or two days, months, or even years. Some illegal immigrants are even abandoned by smugglers and left to fend for themselves in transit countries.

Most current human smuggling activities originate in countries in Asia, Africa, South America, and eastern Europe and move to western Europe, Australia, and North America. There are four main smuggling routes. The first is from North Africa through Spain and Portugal to western Europe.

During summer months, Spain faces the arrival of thousands of illegal immigrants from sub-Saharan Africa. With only twenty-one kilometers of water space separating Europe from Africa (across the Strait of Gibraltar), the journey is a short one. Many migrants drown while attempting to reach Europe aboard small and overcrowded boats.

The second frequently traveled route extends from Asia through Kazakhstan, Kyrgyzstan, Uzbekistan, Tajikistan, and Turkmenistan to Russia, and from there, via Ukraine, Slovakia, and the Czech Republic, to western Europe and even onward to North America. The Balkan route in particular, with transit points in central Asian countries such as Iran and Turkey, has become a popular route for illegal migrants to use to reach western Europe. The smuggling route is used not just for human smuggling but also for the smuggling of other kinds of contraband such as drugs and firearms. For instance, in October 2005 the British police arrested eight suspects from a human smuggling organization thought to have smuggled up to 100,000 Turkish people into Britain over the past few years. The illegal migrants paid between £3,000 and £5,000 each to be brought into Britain via elaborate schemes that involved safe houses, trucks with secret compartments, and, in some cases, clandestine flights to airfields in Cambridgeshire and Kent.[57]

Most of the migrants vanished into North London's Turkish community, working in low-paid jobs. Many of them will likely save money to sponsor other family members to make the trip. The eight smugglers charged in the case were all Turkish asylum seekers who had been permitted to remain in Britain earlier. They supposedly had made tens of millions of pounds from the smuggling racket. Turkish smugglers are not the only ones in the business. Chinese and Indian smugglers are also active in the business, transporting their countrymen into Britain. Jing Ping Chen (also known as Little Sister Ping, who was jailed in 2003) was thought to have been responsible for smuggling between 150,000 and 175,000 people. She supposedly made more than £12 million from her human smuggling business.[58] In another case in 2003, a joint British and French operation, code named "Gular," broke up a smuggling network that specialized in transporting Indians into England. Immigrants from India reportedly sold their land and meager belongings to raise the £11,000 needed for each to be smuggled into Britain through ferry ports before being dropped at their chosen destinations as part of a "door-to-door" service.[59]

The third route frequently used for human smuggling is from the Middle East and Asia to Oceania, with Australia as the number one destination. Illegal migrants often enter Malaysia first and then Indonesia, where they can travel on land to the southern Indonesian islands of Bali, Flores, or Lombok; from there they can embark for Australia. The fourth and final route of global human smuggling is to North America, which is often considered the most desirable destination. Despite the relative geographical isolation of this destination, bordering on only one less-developed nation, migrants are smuggled into Canada and the United States quite easily. Smugglers have developed a combination of transportation strategies that use land, sea, and air to move their clients. During the 1990s ships with migrants on board were landing and unloading on the west coast of the United States. Such daring smuggling activities have become infrequent in recent years.

Migrants holding fraudulent or legal travel documents are on the rise at U.S. airports. If they are caught, they immediately petition for political asylum. If not, they will find ways to adjust their legal status or simply overstay their visas. Most illegal immigrants, however, enter the United States by crossing the two-thousand-mile U.S.-Mexican border. Smuggling networks are increasingly using Central and South American countries for transit purposes, allowing Mexican smugglers to forge international collaborations.

HUMAN SMUGGLING IN THE UNITED STATES

Human smuggling has long been an enabling factor in the history of illegal immigration in the United States. Two types of illegal migrants appear to make regular use of smuggling services. The first group of migrants consists mostly of indigenous farmers from interior Mexico, mainly from such central-western states as Michoacan, Guanajuato, and Jalisco, and of migrants from other Latin American countries farther south. These indigenous migrants typically hitchhike their way toward the U.S.-Mexican border on the top of freight trains and trucks or by some other means. Upon arrival at the border regions, they will find a smuggler to arrange for illegal border crossing. The second group consists of illegal migrants from other parts of the world, such as Asia and eastern Europe. Migrants from these places tend to be financially better off and have traversed vast distances through various transit countries. They, too, rely on a network of smugglers to move across the border and enter the United States.

No one knows the true number of illegal immigrants entering the United States overland. Estimates vary wildly depending on what points the authors are attempting to make. According to one U.S. government interagency report, 500,000 illegal migrants are brought into the United States annually by organized human smuggling networks, and another estimated half-million enter without the assistance of human smugglers.[60] Chinese human smugglers, known as snakeheads, have received much attention from both the news media and law enforcement agencies. Chinese human smugglers have reportedly moved immigrants into the United States by maritime vessels, including offshore transfers of migrants, but also by transit through South and Central America, Mexico, and Canada.

The U.S. government estimates that 30,000 to 40,000 Chinese are smuggled into the United States each year.[61] Researchers in the news media and academics have also provided other estimates, such as the estimates that more than half a million Chinese have been smuggled into the United States since 1984[62] or that anywhere from 50,000 to 100,000 Chinese nationals enter the United States illegally each year.[63] A senior intelligence officer from the former U.S. Immigration and Naturalization Service (USINS) estimated that more than 100,000 Chinese nationals are stashed away in countries around the world each year, waiting to complete their journeys to the United States or other Western countries.[64]

Needless to say, many efforts have been made to gauge the magnitude of this problem. A few consensuses have been developed over the years on the patterns of human smuggling and illegal immigration. Most illegal migrants enter the United States overland from Mexico or Canada. The majority of illegal immigrants tend to congregate in a few states in the United States, including California, Texas, New York, Florida, and Illinois. If the number of undocumented farm laborers is any indication, one should take notice that more than half of the U.S. agricultural workforce is made up of illegal immigrants. According to the National Agricultural Workers Survey (NAWS), conducted annually by the U.S. Department of Labor to capture the demographic and employment characteristics of the U.S. agricultural labor force, the percentage of illegal farm workers increased continuously in recent decades. In 2002, 53 percent of farm workers were unauthorized to work in the United States, compared to 28 percent a decade ago. The demand for smuggling services fluctuates with the government's efforts to restrict immigrants from entering the country. The number of apprehensions of illegal immigrants at the nation's borders in the past decade offers a glimpse of the magnitude of the problem, as shown in Table 1.2.

As shown in Table 1.2, for the past decade (more than ten years in fact—further data omitted for brevity), the total apprehensions of illegal immigrants at the U.S. borders numbered more than 1 million per year. Most of these arrests took place along the southern border, where illegal Mexican immigrants made up the majority of the border crossers. Although the arrest figures decreased in 2001 and 2002, presumably as a reprieve after the September 11 events, border crossings by illegal immigrants have returned to their historic levels.

It should be noted that, following years of gradual but steady increases, the apprehensions of illegal immigrants from countries other than Mexico shot up precipitously in most recent years. As usual, most of these non-Mexican immigrants entered the United States by crossing the southern border. It appears that smugglers and illegal immigrants alike are learning to trek the routes developed by Mexican migrants. Mexico has become a back door to the United States for growing numbers of the world's

Table 1.2 Apprehensions at U.S. Borders from 1996 to 2005

U.S. Border Patrol Arrests of Mexicans

Sector	1996	1997	1998	1999	2000	2001	2002	2003	2004	2005
Southern	1,490,712	1,353,252	1,493,860	1,504,555	1,615,081	1,205,389	901,761	865,850	1,073,468	1,016,305
Northern	6,651	10,012	7,485	6,478	7,362	7,444	6,095	5,947	5,495	4,083
Coastal	25,774	24,386	21,571	23,477	14,440	11,213	10,137	10,215	6,040	3,414
Nationwide	1,523,137	1,387,650	1,522,916	1,534,510	1,636,883	1,224,046	917,993	882,012	1,085,003	1,023,802

U.S. Border Patrol Arrests of Non-Mexican Nationals

Sector	1996	1997	1998	1999	2000	2001	2002	2003	2004	2005
Southern	16,308	15,455	22,820	32,445	28,598	30,328	28,048	39,215	65,814	155,000
Northern	5,095	5,332	4,661	5,191	4,746	4,894	4,392	4,210	4,464	3,259
Coastal	5,336	4,516	5,379	6,864	6,211	6,945	4,877	6,120	5,111	6,916
Nationwide	26,739	25,303	32,860	44,500	39,555	42,167	37,317	49,545	75,389	165,175
Combined Total	1,549,876	1,412,953	1,555,776	1,579,010	1,676,438	1,266,213	955,310	931,557	1,160,392	1,188,977

Source: U.S. Border Patrol.

immigrants. Mexico, struggling to cope with its own massive population movement toward its northern neighbor, now has to take on "freeloaders" from other foreign nations. It is reported that Mexico spends more than $9 million per year to apprehend, house, feed, and deport illegal immigrants.[65] Mexican authorities also recognize that these smuggling activities are increasingly orchestrated by powerful gangs, well connected in the underworld and offering services not just to Mexicans but also to businessmen from Asia and the Middle East.[66]

These border apprehension statistics are some indication of the level of human smuggling activities along the border. One study in central Mexico found that one-third of those who attempted illegal entry into the United States were never detected. The same study estimated that more than 80 percent of illegal immigrants entered the United States with the help of human smugglers.[67] The majority of illegal immigrants in the United States entered the country through clandestine channels rather than by overstaying their visas. According to one U.S. government estimate, 59 percent of illegal immigrants entered the country through clandestine channels. In 2004 the General Accounting Office put the figure at 73 percent.[68] All these figures point to an obvious fact: human smuggling is very much an integral part of transnational population migration.

This is not to say that the U.S. government is powerless. Recent efforts at beefing up the U.S. Border Patrol and installing hardware along the U.S.-Mexican border have indeed produced a measurable impact on human smuggling activities. For instance, Operation Gatekeeper in San Diego was successful in shutting down many smuggling routes frequently used by Mexican coyotes. As a response, human smugglers had to move their activities farther east into the desert in Arizona. The rise in smuggling fees in recent years and the number of migrant deaths in remote areas were also indicative of increased challenges that human smugglers and their clients must face during their journey to the north. In the 1990s Mexican smugglers typically charged $200 per person to transport migrants into the United States. It costs $1,000 these days for the same trip.[69] If illegal migrants want to be transported farther into the United States rather than just being dropped off north of the border, additional fees could bring the total smuggling cost up to $2,000 or more. In a recent investigation, federal agents arrested two U.S. Navy petty officers who were allegedly smuggling illegal Mexican immigrants, charging $3,000 apiece, through an old port of entry building at San Ysidro in San Diego.[70]

By most accounts, smuggling fees for unskilled farm workers from Mexico or other Latin American countries are considered inexpensive. The same cannot be said about smuggling fees for unskilled farm workers from Asia, mainly China and Korea. Based on news media reports and research studies, prices paid by immigrants from Asian countries are substantially higher, reflecting the economic backgrounds of these illegal immigrants. Chinese smugglers reportedly pay the highest price to have their clients smuggled across the border, often up to $5,000 per person.

Although personal circumstances and experiences may vary, transnational migration occurs more or less for the same reasons. Global migration, legal and illegal, has accelerated in recent decades amid expanding socioeconomic as well as political changes in developing countries, which have brought about disruptions to traditional livelihood and resulted in massive emigration of populations in search of jobs and better living conditions. Under the pressure for outward migration, coupled with the inadequacy of legal immigration procedures in most destination countries, the enterprise of human smuggling has emerged to meet the need of these migrants for transportation arrangements. The business of human smuggling would not have been possible without a market teeming with prospective migrants who seek such services. Nor would it be possible without the lure of ample opportunities in the destination country. Border reinforcement efforts after the September 11 events have only bolstered the smuggling business because more migrants now are in need of professional assistance to cross the border or to acquire counterfeit documents to slip into the United States.

Conversely, human smuggling has also become a major enabling factor that accelerates the momentum of illegal migration. In regard to legal and regulated immigration, the United States and most other Western countries have adopted administrative measures to import both skilled and unskilled workers to meet the labor market demand. Whereas this regular and planned immigration follows the expansion or contraction of economic cycles of the host countries, illegal immigration follows its own set of barometers outside the mainstream economy, and the flow of illegal migrants responds to a far more complex set of conditions than mere economic conditions.

Parasitic to this context, human smuggling activities are actually encouraged by the pent-up demand for illegal immigration and the very restrictions the government attempts to impose to curtail the influx of illegal migrants. In fact, government efforts in the control of illegal immigration have inadvertently created a market where enterprising agents with appropriate social connections and resources have built a profitable business. The demand for their services continues to rise with governments' efforts to restrict illegal immigration.

Chapter 2

Human Smuggling through Legal Channels

News media stories and government reports often conjure up images of undocumented or fraudulently documented foreign nationals being transported in cramped, unhealthy, and often dangerous conditions to the United States by smuggling gangs or criminal organizations. Such was the story in October 2002 at a Union Pacific Railroad depot, where eleven illegal immigrants were found dead in a locked grain car.[1] Subsequent investigations revealed that the human smugglers, after loading these illegal migrants into the railcar to cross into the United States, simply lost track of the train. Although such a wanton disregard for human lives does occur from time to time, the reality is far more complex. For one thing, human cargoes are not always transported in poor and dangerous conditions. Depending on the connections of the smuggling organization and financial resources of the clients, many illegal immigrants actually arrive in the United States in style and comfort.

In a sense, human smuggling is essentially peddling services for financial gain in exchange for the illegal entry into a country of someone who either does not qualify for or is not willing to go through legal channels. However, human smuggling is not a homogeneous criminal activity. The means of transportation, the use of way-stations and safe houses, the price of a trip, the conditions of travel, and the immigration status upon arrival can vary significantly from one smuggler to another. Long gone are the days when all immigrants needed was enough money to afford a ticket on a steamboat that sailed for weeks to reach New York's Ellis Island or San Francisco's Angel Island and be herded through immigration inspections. Smuggling strategies these days can be grouped into two large categories: (1) going through immigration checkpoints with fraudulently obtained legal or forged documents, and (2) crossing borders into the country or landing illegally on U.S. shores. The line between legal and illegal means of entry often becomes blurred as human smugglers employ multiple routes to transport their clients. The ability to orchestrate smuggling operations with fraudulently obtained legal paperwork separates the resourceful (or the white-collar) smugglers who cater to the well-off clients from the less capable ones whose clients come from rural areas.

ENTERING THE UNITED STATES AS IMMIGRANTS[2]

There are two broad categories under which foreigners may enter the United States—immigrants and nonimmigrants. An immigrant is simply a foreign national who has been authorized to live and work permanently in the United States. With a few exceptions, such as voting rights and employment in security-sensitive occupations, immigrants enjoy very much the same rights and benefits granted to U.S. citizens. The United States welcomes, to some extent, all nationalities to visit and even settle if they can meet certain criteria. The fundamental rationale for admitting foreigners is, in most cases, an economic one.[3] Tourists, businesspeople, and other bona fide legitimate individuals are expected to spend money while they travel the country, which contributes to the U.S. economy. For those who wish to settle in the United States permanently, they mostly have something valuable to offer, be it skills or wealth.

Because legal immigration has many advantages, the venue is a prime target for exploitation by human smugglers. Whichever method one chooses to enter the United States legally (e.g., holding legal identification and travel documents), one must meet certain criteria. For human smugglers, meeting official criteria merely means acquiring proper paperwork to circumvent these legal obstacles. As will be discussed in greater detail in the next chapter, the business of counterfeit documents is thriving these days. The following provides a brief description of how legal immigration works, because these same venues are also exploited by human smugglers.

Foreign nationals who enter the United States as immigrants are often called green card holders. They usually fall under two broad categories—family-based or employment-based.[4] Family-based immigration can be further divided into two categories—immediate family members and others. Immediate family members of U.S. citizens qualify for immediate immigration, and they are not restricted by the quota system. The term *immediate members* means spouses of U.S. citizens (including a widow or widower of a U.S. citizen who was married to the U.S. citizen for at least two years and who is applying for a green card within two years of the U.S. citizen's death), minors (unmarried and under the age of twenty-one) who have at least one U.S. citizen parent, and parents of U.S. citizens (if the U.S. citizen child is over the age of twenty-one).

For all other family-based applications, a quota system is in place. Congress has established a tiered system (officially called "preferences") in which some categories of family members are given a higher priority than others. There are four preferences (ranked numerically according to their perceived importance):

- First: Unmarried sons and daughters of U.S. citizens
- Second: Spouses and children under twenty-one years old of green card holders, and adult children of green card holders
- Third: Married sons and daughters of U.S. citizens
- Fourth: Sisters and brothers of adult U.S. citizens

In all cases, there are statutory limits (or quotas) on how many of these immigrant visas are granted each year. The current quotas for all four categories are set at 226,000 an year. The process of acquiring a visa is rather complex and often requires applicants and their sponsored relatives to seek professional legal assistance. In a nutshell, sponsors must submit applications on behalf of their relatives—in other words, they must get in line. When quotas become available (or their numbers are up), these applicants appear in U.S. consular offices overseas to complete more paperwork. Although overseas consulates handle the immigration paperwork and report back to the Department of State for all qualified applicants, the Bureau of Citizenship and Immigration Services (CIS) in the Department of Homeland Security (a function formerly performed by the Immigration and Naturalization Service, or INS, in the Department of Justice) actually processes the applications inside the United States for the adjustment of immigration status.

The quotas allocated to each category are often reshuffled, depending on the demand in other categories. Unused quotas (or undersubscribed categories) are absorbed by other categories short on quotas. This system of preferential treatment for prospective immigrants based on family relationship reflects the nation's emphasis on family unity. Therefore, depending on the category under which foreign applicants are qualified and the country in which they reside, the wait can be as short as a few years or as long as decades, as illustrated in Table 2.1. For many, the wait has become a trial of patience and often sparks angry words whenever politicians in Washington consider granting legal status to millions of illegal immigrants already residing in the country.

Employment-based immigration refers to foreign applicants who possess skills or knowledge that is either hard to find or in high demand in the U.S. labor market. In the 1990s, rapid expansion in high-tech industries and in other economic sectors in the United States helped to usher in many policy changes favorable to the importation of people with advanced skills and technology or those with money to invest. In the United States, industry-lobbying activities were particularly successful in

Table 2.1 Approximate Wait Time for Family-Based Immigration

Priority	Mainland China	India	Mexico	Philippines	All other countries
1st	4 years 9 months	4 years 9 months	11 years 5 months	14 years 5 months	4 years 9 months
2nd A	4 years	4 years	6 years 9 months	4 years	4 years
2nd B	9 years 6 months	9 years 6 months	14 years	9 years 6 months	9 years 6 months
3rd	7 years 6 months	7 years 6 months	11 years	15 years	7 years 6 months
4th	11 years 5 months	12 years	13 years	22 years 3 months	11 years 5 months

Source: U.S. State Department Immigration Visa Bulletins.

the passing of the Immigration Act of 1990, which nearly tripled the number of employment-based visas issued each year worldwide, from 54,000 to 140,000.[5]

The employment-based immigration process involves more steps than does family-based immigration. Applicants and employers must demonstrate the labor demand and corresponding job qualifications. This process usually requires the employer to initiate the petition. If the foreign applicant is already in the country, as is often the case, an adjustment of immigration status is needed. There are five categories for granting permanent residence to foreign nationals based on employment skills:

- Foreign nationals of extraordinary ability in sciences, arts, education, business, or athletics, such as outstanding professors or researchers, managers, and executives. Extensive documentation is required to substantiate one's uniqueness in his or her claimed discipline.
- Foreign professionals with advanced degrees or exceptional ability who will substantially benefit the national economy, cultural or educational interests, or welfare of the United States.
- Foreign nationals who are experienced and skilled workers or who are unskilled but can perform labor for which qualified workers are not available in the United States. The less-stringent requirements in this category have created a long backlog.
- Special immigrants—such as ministers or priests of a religious denomination that has a nonprofit religious organization in the United States, or employees and former employees of U.S. government agencies abroad (such as embassy staff).
- Foreign nationals who can invest in the United States to create jobs, especially in certain rural or high-unemployment areas.

Although there are unscrupulous employers, human smugglers using the employment-based immigration method are relatively rare because of the complexity of the procedures involved. Client recruitment for human smugglers interested in this method is also problematic because migrants eligible or willing to participate in this type of smuggling scheme are most likely well educated and probably already employed in their home countries. The idea of illegal immigration, particularly at a high price, is not likely to attract many such candidates. For the vast majority of eager migrants who do not possess any special skills or knowledge that the U.S. labor market needs, employment-based migration strategies are simply too complicated and intimidating to even try.

MARRIAGE FRAUD—ASSURED PASSAGE TO AMERICA

Marriage to a U.S. citizen offers a fast lane to enter the United States. Each year, hundreds of thousands of U.S. citizens marry foreign-born nationals and file petitions for their immigration and permanent residency. The spouses of U.S. citizens are considered "immediate relatives" under the immigration laws and therefore are exempt from quota limitations. The United States is not alone in granting special treatment to foreign nationals who marry its citizens. Most countries do. Marriage fraud therefore has acquired a global appeal to human smugglers who devise schemes to bring together native citizens and foreign nationals to circumvent immigration regulations. The practice has expanded to so many corners of the world that even countries such as South Africa have experienced an upsurge in fraudulent marriages in recent years. As the most affluent and prosperous country in the African continent, South Africa has become a magnet to migrant workers from many poorer countries around the world.[6] According to a recent investigation, thousands of South African women who thought they were single had unknowingly been married to some foreigners on paper. The investigation found that corrupt officials took bribes, averaging $750 apiece, to register these "marriages," which entitled the foreign nationals to immediate permanent residency in the country and a work permit. In one case, a corrupt government employee was discovered to have single-handedly registered five hundred false marriages, and the husbands came from all over the world: Nigeria, Egypt, Pakistan, China, India, Bangladesh, and Brazil.[7] A law was subsequently passed in August 2004 requiring foreign nationals who marry South Africans to wait for five years before they are eligible for permanent residency.

All marriage-based applicants must file an affidavit attesting their eligibility for marriage, as well as divulging information on their previous marriages. However, such records are typically kept by local jurisdictions in the United States and are rarely shared with other governments for verification purposes. The fragmented record-keeping systems in governments make it easy for people to file multiple applications at the same time. It will be some time before marital records are linked at the state level, and creating a national database will take even longer. Even then, the system would catch only polygamous applicants. As long as the preferential treatment policy remains, and as long as a U.S. citizen marries a foreigner, he or she is entitled to bring the foreign spouse into the United States.

Marriage fraud is a rather simple scheme, but it can involve many steps and tedious paperwork that can test the patience of all parties. Here are the basics of how U.S. citizens bring their foreign spouses into the country. If the marriage takes place inside the country, the U.S. citizen submits a visa petition to the regional CIS to prove that the marriage is bona fide and was entered in love rather than simply for the foreigner to obtain a green card. Numerous documents are needed to substantiate the union, such as proof of the citizenship, a copy of the marriage certificate, love letters, and photos. At the same time, the foreign spouse submits an application for a green card. An interview will then be scheduled and conducted by immigration officials, usually within a year. Prior to the interview, the foreign spouse usually receives authorization to work and can travel outside the United States.

If the marriage occurs outside the United States, the foreign spouse has two choices—either to remain in his or her country until a green card is obtained (which takes one or two years) or to enter the United States on a temporary nonimmigrant visa (i.e., a "K1" visa) and process the paperwork in the United States (which is much faster for entry purposes). When the foreign spouse comes to the United States on a temporary nonimmigrant visa, the process described above applies. However, because of the clear intent to immigrate, foreign-born spouses can be denied admission at the port of entry when U.S. immigration officials become suspicious of the temporary visa holder. It is, therefore, a rather uncommon strategy for human smugglers to employ. The one-to-two-year wait is usually not a problem for would-be migrants, and it is well worth the eventual outcome from a completed marriage fraud.

If the foreign spouse remains outside the country, the U.S. citizen submits a visa petition either to the regional CIS office or to the U.S. embassy or consulate. Once the visa petition is approved, the foreign spouse receives a packet from the National Visa Center (NVC) located in Portsmouth, New Hampshire, which contains forms to complete and instructions on the various documents to bring (such as passport, police clearance, medical examinations, etc.) for an immigrant visa interview at the embassy or consulate.

For human smugglers who exploit legal channels, nothing surpasses the advantages of marriage fraud. In an era of serial monogamy, when divorce and remarriage are common in American society, the humanitarian-based immigration policy that offers a fast pass to foreign nationals wedded to U.S. citizens has become an easy setup for abuses. Human smugglers have indeed devised many strategies to exploit this legal venue, which takes little more than saying two words—"I do." As long as two adults appear consenting to wed each other, a city clerk will certify the union. Because local governments typically handle marriage registrations in the United States, as well as in most other parts of the world, there is no systematic way to cross-check the veracity of individual marriage claims. However, for immigration purposes, the registration of a marriage has profound implications. The marriage certificate is worth tens of thousands of dollars on some black markets (such as for the Chinese snakeheads), and it expedites a "legal" entry into the United States.

A thriving cottage industry of matchmaking and immigration petitioning has thus emerged, in which career brides and grooms trade in their bachelorhood again and again for handsome fees. In one such case, the Manhattan district attorney charged one woman who applied for a total of twenty-seven marriage licenses from 1984 to 2002, and three other women for marrying more than a dozen men.[8] These women allegedly offered to marry illegal immigrants for about $1,000 apiece. Sometimes they went through with marriage ceremonies, whereas other times they did not. The men who paid for these marriages came from countries including Pakistan, India, Peru, Ecuador, Nigeria, and the Dominican Republic. These cases came to light because the people involved became careless. Many did not even bother to file for divorce before they applied for new marriage licenses.[9]

Official corruption is a contributor to some of these extreme cases, where a simple change in names will allow such fraudulent marriages to take place. In the Manhattan case, one employee in the city clerk's office was accused of receiving a bribe to change a bride's name in the computer system. In that case, the woman, originally scheduled to marry a foreigner, failed to show up, and the "groom" wanted her name removed from the record so that another woman could be substituted and the wedding could go on that day.[10] It was apparent that these schemes were widely known in the social circles of the involved individuals. Although officials did not find ringleaders or organized entities in these fraud cases, it is interesting to note that the "groom" could find a substitute on such short notice. There were apparently multiple U.S. citizen "bachelors" available for a price.

COMMON STRATEGIES IN MARRIAGE FRAUD

Most human smuggling activities involving marriage frauds are successful, except for the most egregious ones. Marriage frauds typically involve one-time accomplices and thus are almost impossible to stop. The marrying parties will go through with the wedding ceremonies, produce records of joint residence and bank accounts, and show up together for immigration interviews.

There are several versions of marriage frauds. The fastest or most convenient is the K-visa version, in which the scheme is carried only far enough to convince the U.S. consulate to issue a K1 visa allowing the foreign fiancée to enter the United States to complete the marriage. The K-visa scheme is expedient because all parties involved do not have to be entangled for years. Once the foreign fiancée enters the United States, the smuggling operation is consider completed. All smuggling fees are settled. In one such case, two brothers (David and Michael Cheng) in Virginia were found guilty of such a smuggling scheme in July 2003 that transported Chinese nationals into the United States as fiancés of American citizens.[11] These two brothers recruited young Chinese-Americans and offered them $10,000 each to participate in the charade. They flew to China, meeting their "fiancées/fiancés" and posing for romantic photographs at engagement parties. Letters of undying love would then be exchanged. These "love" letters would be used as supporting documents in a petition for a visa that would allow the fiancés/fiancées to travel to the United States to consummate the marriage. The families of the illegal immigrants in China in return paid the Cheng brothers $40,000 for each successful case. Both brothers faced a maximum prison sentence of five years and a fine of $250,000.

Although the K-visa method is expedient, with limited involvement of all parties, it has gained much notoriety in the U.S. diplomatic corps. Visa officers in the U.S. embassies overseas are usually skeptical of such arrangements, and they often reject such visa applications. In response, many human smugglers actually go all the way to fabricate an entire marriage and family. Marriages, at least on paper, actually take place to substantiate the application for an immigration visa and eventual settlement in the United States. This often requires a longer period of time, as well as a careful accumulation of other documents, to prove that an intimate relationship has been in existence for a few years.

In one such case, a native of Cambodia pleaded guilty on a marriage fraud charge in a federal court in Connecticut in February 2004. Chan Champa and his accomplice in California recruited U.S. citizens who were paid to travel to Cambodia and marry Cambodian nationals so that the Cambodians could obtain immigrant visas, permitting them to enter and live in the United States.[12] For $7,000 each, the recruited U.S. citizens traveled to Cambodia to meet with their prospective "spouses," who were total strangers, and participate in marriage ceremonies. The U.S. citizens usually received half of the $7,000 at the beginning, and the remainder would be paid once their "spouses" immigrated to the United States.

In a similar case, Remigijus Adomaitis, a twenty-eight-year-old green card holder originally from Lithuania, recruited and paid a U.S. citizen to travel to Lithuania in November 2004 to marry a Lithuanian woman he had never met. The marriage took place, and the smuggling handler accompanied the U.S. citizen to the U.S. embassy in Warsaw, Poland, to file immigration paperwork for his "newlywed" to come to the United States. The Lithuanian spouse was instructed to write letters to her fiancé pretending there had been an ongoing love affair. The U.S. citizen was paid $1,000 as a down payment and an additional $250 a month for two to three years until his Lithuanian wife received her green card.[13] Meanwhile, another Lithuanian smuggler negotiated a marriage agreement with a U.S. citizen at a Denny's in Mundelein, Illinois, for $8,000. The smuggler and the U.S. citizen traveled to a Rockford residence to discuss the terms of the marriage. At that time, the U.S. citizen met his Lithuanian "fiancée" for the first time. After both parties reached an agreement, they took photographs in which they pretended to be an intimate couple. That same day, the U.S. citizen obtained a marriage license at the Boone County Courthouse.

Despite its many advantages, marriage fraud has several restrictions. After decades of abuses, Congress passed the Immigration Marriage Fraud Amendments of 1986, in an effort to crack down on fraudulent marriages. Foreign spouses are now admitted only as "conditional" resident aliens. The condition carries a two-year term. In other words, once immigration officials believe the marriage is bona fide, a foreign national will be issued a green card valid for only two years. Both the alien spouse and the U.S. citizen are required to file a joint petition to remove the condition within ninety days immediately before the two-year period expires.[14] If the petition is granted, the foreign spouse becomes a regular permanent resident.

The granting of a permanent green card after two years is not automatic. Immigration officials must still be convinced, through face-to-face interviews and documentations, that the marriage remains valid and was not for immigration purposes. If immigration officials find that the marriage is a sham or that the marriage has been judicially annulled or terminated, the conditional status will be revoked, and the foreign spouse is subject to deportation proceedings. Even when a permanent green card is obtained, the foreign national is still not home free. A divorce shortly after the granting of a permanent resident status can still cause suspicions among immigration officials. Although the green card is permanent and cannot be easily taken away, should the American citizen wish to marry another foreign national inside or outside the United States, it will be viewed with increased suspicion by immigration officials.

The two-year conditional residency status is a rather arbitrary decision. There have been no empirical studies to substantiate just how effective the wait period is in deterring marriage frauds. Human smugglers can work out reasonable payment installments to satisfy the participants. In one such case, a Chinese snakehead, who specialized in marriage fraud in the Los Angeles area, claimed that long-term arrangements are indeed the norm in the Chinese smuggling community.[15] This smuggler came to the United States by way of a fraudulent marriage herself in 1997. Her "husband" was a habitual gambler who was desperately in need of cash. She paid a total of $51,000 for herself and her two children, which, according to her, was a bargain at the time. Most of her clients (both the U.S. citizens and their Chinese "spouses") entered the scheme with a clear understanding that all are expected to "remain" in the relationship for years. According to her, it is not enough just to have verbal agreements. Payment plans must also be structured to encourage the U.S. citizen to stay in the arrangement. Except for a sizable down payment (usually around $3,000 to $5,000), the U.S. spouse typically receives no monthly installments or just a few sporadic payments before the permanent green card is obtained, at which time another $5,000 to $10,000 will be paid out. Sometimes arrangements are made to carry the scheme to the ultimate goal—U.S. citizenship, which usually takes five years or longer. Once citizenship is obtained, the foreign national can petition for other family members to immigrate to the United States. Furthermore, he or she can get a divorce and become eligible to make more money in another marriage fraud. Prices for fraudulent marriages vary tremendously from one source country to another. The highest is in Fujian Province, where prospective migrants expect to pay $70,000 or more for the entire package, from entering the United States to acquiring the green card.

Although the two-year condition has some limiting effects on marriage fraud, because many of these marriages tend not to last, this policy also has unintended consequences. Some critics charge that this two-year provision potentially traps victims of domestic violence.[16] The two-year wait provision was later expanded to allow exceptions under certain circumstances. If the marriage is terminated by reason of divorce, death of the citizen spouse, or spousal abuse, the foreign-born spouse may apply for a waiver of the joint petition requirement. These administrative changes make it possible for the foreign national to file an application to obtain permanent status, if he or she is divorced or the U.S. spouse refuses to cooperate. But this is not an easy process either. The foreign spouse must prove that

- the original marriage was entered in good faith and was not a sham;
- a deportation will cause extreme hardship (for instance, for women with young children); or
- the U.S. spouse was abusive.

Of all human smuggling strategies, none offer as many advantages and assurances as marriage fraud. The humanitarian provision of the U.S.

immigration laws is intended to prevent the separation of its citizens from their family members or loved ones. By law, those who marry only for immigration purposes are barred from gaining entry into the country. Such marriages, even though they may be legal on paper, are considered shams and punishable by fines, deportations, or jail terms. The challenge is for visa consuls in overseas posts and immigration officials at home to sift through all applications and uncover those based on fraudulent claims. According to the CIS and the State Department, more than half of all the marriage applications they process are based on shams. It is not surprising, then, that the CIS is especially careful about investigating marriage cases.

In sum, marriage frauds for immigration purposes are fairly easy to arrange and carry out. Human smugglers are scouting casinos, people on welfare, and other less fortunate segments of the society for eligible candidates. For those who are in no hurry to engage in any committed relationship, their bachelorhood can be put up for sale and garner thousands and sometimes tens of thousands of dollars. The beauty of this scheme is that nothing is permanent: two to three years after the illegal immigrant obtains his or her permanent legal status, a divorce can be filed and the U.S. citizen is free to do it again.

ENTERING THE UNITED STATES AS NONIMMIGRANTS

Although "legal" immigration based on marriage fraud offers many advantages, not all human smugglers can find willing participants. Furthermore, involved parties, particularly the U.S. citizens, must continue the charade and periodically supply supporting documents and face grueling interviews by suspecting immigration examiners. In contrast, nonimmigrant visas have few strings attached, and the enormous underground economy in the United States does not care about work authorization.

There are several categories of nonimmigrant visas for foreign nationals who seek to enter the United States. These nonimmigrant visas are often turned into admission slips for migrants to gain entry into the United States. The following is a list of nonimmigrant visas commonly exploited by human smugglers:

B1: temporary visitor for business
B2: temporary visitor for pleasure
F1: foreign student (academic)
H1: special occupation
H3: trainee
J1: exchange scholar
L1: intracompany transferee (management personnel and specialists)

The most common travel documents issued to foreign nationals are B1/B2 visas. B1 visas are mostly for people to engage in business activities in the United States, such as contract negotiations, business visits, inspections at manufacturing facilities, and participation in research projects.[17] B2 visas are for tourists. B1/B2 visas vary in their lengths of validity. At the port of entry, immigration inspectors usually inquire about the purpose of the visit and determine the length of stay in the United States, which can vary from a few days to six months. The length of stay is recorded on the I-94 card, which is typically stapled with the visitor's passport and must be surrendered when leaving the country. Although the immigration inspectors inspect the I-94 cards, no one is in charge of collecting them when the visitors leave the country. Commercial airlines collect them at check-in counters, but no one gathers them at any land border exit points. Each year millions of foreign nationals enter the United States under various temporary visas, but the nation does not have a way of telling how many of them leave.

Human smugglers have developed many strategies to procure temporary visas, such as through arranging official visits by "business delegations." It should be noted that although the U.S. overseas posts are charged with reviewing applications and issuing visas, it is the responsibility of the Bureau of Citizenship and Immigration Services in the Department of Homeland Security to inspect and admit visitors into the United States at ports of entry. Therefore, it is possible that a foreign national holding a valid visa can be denied entry into the United States. Because all visa applicants are suspected of seeking employment in the United States, foreign nationals must prove that their visit is temporary and that they are gainfully employed in their home countries where they hold a permanent residence. Furthermore, visa applicants must show evidence that they have specific plans to return to their home countries and that they have sufficient funds to cover their expenses while in the United States. Visa applicants must also divulge if they have submitted a petition to immigrate to the United States. In other words, visa applicants must convince the visa consuls that they have every reason to return to their home countries.

Therefore, in addition to obtaining a B1/B2 visa, human smugglers must also prepare their clients to pass immigration inspection at the port of entry. Interestingly enough, what legitimate B visa holders are advised to do to ensure a smooth passage through U.S. immigration inspection has provided a training menu for the smuggling business. These guidelines include the following:

• Always have a round-trip ticket, with a specific return date (usually well within the period that the visa is valid).
• Always have business cards that identify one's employment affiliations.

- Always have a detailed story to explain what the trip is about—for instance, negotiating a contract, inspecting a piece of machinery, or signing a contract.
- Have a copy of the invitation letter and other business communication from a business in the United States.
- Have a story about how many tasks are waiting for you at home and how you wish you could stay a few more days just to relax and sightsee.
- For tourists, have a vacation plan and an itinerary with hotel bookings as well as continuous airline tickets.
- Carry enough cash to demonstrate that you are financially well-off, plus a few credit cards in your wallet.
- Have a copy of hotel reservations indicating where you will be staying.

Some human smugglers go to a greater length in preparing their clients to cover additional grounds beyond those listed above, such as bringing along financial statements from banks showing business transactions or carrying pay stubs or savings books to show their financial situation. All of the paperwork can be acquired through a counterfeit document vendor. For a small fee, a few travel agencies can produce genuine-looking airline tickets and travel itineraries. Smugglees need to memorize the information and make sure their stories sound reasonable. Few immigration inspectors will ever have time to verify any of the documents. Even if any inspectors become suspicious and conduct additional interrogations at secondary inspections, the most they can do is contact the U.S. businesses listed in the invitation letters. There are many answering services in the United States that are willing to provide business support and take messages for a fee.

In addition to B1/B2 visas, other temporary nonimmigrant visas are abused by human smugglers. Foreign students who are attending schools in the United States can apply for F1 visas. Visa applicants need to prove that they have been accepted by bona fide schools in the United States and that they have sufficient financial means to pay the tuition and the living expenses for the duration of the study. They must also demonstrate sufficient knowledge of the English language. Because these documents can be readily obtained through fraudulent channels, counsels at U.S. diplomatic posts routinely reject student visa applications even when legitimate I-20s (formal school admission documents) and financial documents are presented. Many counsels suspect that the applicants are using the student visa only to gain entry into the United States to work.

Foreign scholars or educators as well as students can use the J visas to participate in official exchange programs in science and education or to present papers at professional conferences. Foreign companies with branches in the United States can use the L-1 visas to relocate their management staff. As is the case for all nonimmigrant visas, foreign nationals must provide evidence of a permanent residence outside of the United States and binding ties that will compel the applicants to leave the United States after the studies are finished. They must also prove that they have sufficient funds to cover all expenses and sufficient knowledge of the English language.

Although some of the nonimmigrant visas are more exploited than others in the human smuggling business, one main element remains consistent—producing sufficient documents. The key is to construct one's work histories and identity paperwork and assemble financial records in ways that satisfy the U.S. officials at the consulate. As will be discussed in greater detail in the next chapter, counterfeit document production is a booming business. With the help of corrupt officials and shady businesses, human smugglers have little difficulty acquiring the needed documents. In some cases, owners of legitimate businesses directly use their companies to transport illegal immigrants.

A few less-exploited nonimmigrant visas include the O visa, for outstanding people of national or international acclaim in the sciences, arts, education, business, or athletics; the P visa, for artists, entertainers, and athletes recognized at an international level; and the Q visa, for participants in cultural exchange programs to introduce the history, culture, and traditions of their home countries. In addition, there are D visas, which allow foreign crews to join their ships or aircraft, and C1 visas for international transfer. Some of the nonimmigrant visas allow the holders to work (e.g., H, O, and P visas), whereas most do not permit gainful employment while the holders are in the United States. However, because of the small volume of foreign nationals who qualify for these visa categories and their rather unique requirements for approval, they are not commonly used by human smugglers.

EXPLOITING THE LEGAL CHANNEL—THE STORY OF AN ILLEGAL CHINESE IMMIGRANT

Not all illegal immigrants hire smugglers to acquire U.S. travel documents. Here is a story by an illegal Chinese immigrant, who began his sojourn in 2000 with a job in a joint Sino-Mexican project. Mr. Sun (not his real name) was a graduate of a reputable university in China, where he majored in international business. Upon graduation, he landed a job in a private furniture-manufacturing company owned by an overseas Chinese from Chicago. This businessman took advantage of the North American Free Trade Agreement and set up a facility in Sonora. Mr. Sun soon came to Mexico to work on a two-year contract. During the contract period, he was able to obtain a tourist visa to visit the United States a few times and explored his other options. When his contract expired in Mexico, he decided to head to the United States:[18]

It was really easy to obtain a U.S. visa from Mexico, particularly if you can speak Spanish. I had to learn Spanish because we were doing business there. All technical and business employees at the manufacturing facility were from China, but the labor was hired locally in Mexico. We were able to sell our products in the United States with "Made in Mexico" labels. I spoke Spanish when I was interviewed at the U.S. consulate. My multilingual skills easily got me a tourist visa. After two years, my contract was over, and I was supposed to return to China to the same position I had before. I didn't like that. I wanted to make more money. So I just headed to the United States. I had no problem entering the country, as I had previously been there several times.

I found this job through an employment agency. There are many of these agencies in L.A., and jobs are all over the country. I came by bus, and the owner went to pick me up at the bus station. Some come to make money, whereas others come for their children to have a better future. They always apply for political asylum, and when they get their approval they will petition to get their families over immediately. If their petitions are rejected, they will disappear and make as much money as possible to send home.

Back in China, even if you want to work hard, there is no place for you to do so, because there are so many people looking for jobs. In the United States, even waiting tables or doing dishes can make $1,500 to $2,000 a month. One year in the United States equals almost ten years in China. That is the difference we are talking about. I think the main problem in China is that there is no sense of security. When there is no safety net, people are afraid of spending. Once you are out of money, you are out of luck. The government is not going to save you when you are out of money. But in the United States, there is a safety net and people spend a lot of money. This is an important factor. In China, no one knows what's going to happen when they get old. If I work here for a few years, and even if my political asylum is not successful, I can return to China with enough money to last the rest of my life. Because I now work in a restaurant, and the owner provides food and lodging, I have practically no expenses of my own, so I can save all my income.

As soon as I arrived in the United States, I spent $4,000 to hire an attorney to file a political asylum petition on my behalf. The attorney told me it would take about three to five years for the whole thing to run its course. If my case is rejected at first, I have opportunities to appeal, which will cost more money. But at least I have up to five years to work here. I came to the United States for free, unlike most other illegal immigrants. These days, it costs 200,000 yuan (about $26,000) for companies in my province to arrange a smugglee into a business delegation. There are many of these snakeheads in northern China now. Many northerners come by way of business delegations. The United States has increased its enforcement. They are scrutinizing these delegations carefully now. The U.S. consulates in China are closely examining the company entities and the business they are doing. It is not easy to get business visas anymore. There are increasingly more northerners now. They usually come in their forties and fifties, quite older than most illegal Chinese.

According to an investigation by Congress, one-third of all illegal immigrants currently in the United States are foreigners who have overstayed their visas.[19] The preceding story illustrates just how easy it is to exploit the legal venues.

Chapter 3

The Game of Counterfeit Documents

One crucial aspect of the human smuggling business is the acquisition of identification documents that enable migrants to travel, to gain employment, and hopefully to apply for adjustment to a permanent status in the United States. To remain viable, any smuggling organization needs to develop a well-thought-out channel to acquire these documents. Manufacturing and circulating counterfeit documents has long been a staple of the underground economy, allowing members of criminal organizations and other fringe elements to conceal identities or develop multiple identities. The growing demand from human smugglers has further spurred the expansion of this black market across the world, where a wide range of counterfeit documents can be obtained—from birth certificates to clean police records, and from academic diplomas from any home countries to employment paperwork.

In one such case, federal agents uncovered a $240,000-per-year counterfeit document operation at Chicago's Mega Mall. Undercover agents purchased counterfeit identity documents including green cards and Social Security cards. These identity documents typically came in sets, each containing a fake Social Security card and green card, and they were sold for about $80 per set. The thirty-six-year-old shop owner, himself an illegal alien, received $50 for each set of documents made and sold. It was estimated that three to five sets of these documents were sold at the shop each day. The documents were produced in various print shops in the Chicago area and then shipped to the Mega Mall and sold to illegal immigrants.[1]

All human smuggling activities, other than crossing the borders or landing on U.S. shores illegally, require some documents, forged or genuine, that allow migrants to travel. Depending on transportation strategies and the transit countries involved, smugglers may use genuine passports and visas or fraudulent ones, or a combination of both. For those who have entered the United States on temporary visas with the intention to stay permanently, other documents are needed to adjust the status. For those who have spent money to adjust for permanent status through marriage fraud, still more documents are needed.

Document fraud in human smuggling falls into two basic categories: (1) forged or altered documents and (2) genuine documents under false identities. Because passports and visas are the most important travel documents in transnational smuggling activities, a significant part of the following discussion will focus on passport fraud.

PRODUCING COUNTERFEIT DOCUMENTS

The ability to acquire official-looking documents has always been keenly pursued by criminal organizations of all kinds. Passport fraud largely falls into four basic categories: (1) portions of genuine passports are physically altered (usually by substituting the photo or inserting a visa page or biographical information) to match desired travel requirements; (2) entire passports or visa pages are fabricated; (3) genuine passports are obtained through the use of stolen or illegally obtained identity paperwork; and (4) genuine passports, stolen or purchased from the black market, are used by illegal immigrants assuming the identities printed in the documents (i.e., acting as imposters).

The quality of counterfeit documents varies tremendously, depending on their intended uses. If a photo-substituted passport is to be used to pass immigration, where inspectors are trained to look for flaws under special lighting and with the aid of magnifying glasses, great craftsmanship is required. If the phony document is to be used to gain employment or to lease an apartment, the quality requirement is less stringent. In fact, some of the counterfeit documents for day-to-day uses are downright shoddy—for instance, car window tinting films are sometimes used to mimic magnetic strips on ID cards.[2] The business of counterfeit documents covers a wide range of operators. Some have mastered holographic designs and use high-end laminating equipment to produce an entire passport, whereas others focus on less challenging tasks such as transferring a photo to a legitimate passport.

With easy access to high-quality paper and high-end printers, sophisticated graphic design computers and software, and laminating machines, counterfeit artists can produce remarkable look-alike passports. For instance, in November 2003, federal and local law enforcement agencies broke up a sophisticated counterfeiting laboratory in Lynnwood, Washington, and arrested four Mexican nationals. A variety of counterfeit identity documents were found in the lab, in addition to cash, loaded weapons, and ammunition.

The two-month investigation began on a tip from an arrested drug trafficker. Undercover agents and police officers were able to purchase Washington State driver's licenses, green cards, Social Security cards, and Mexican consular cards from the counterfeiters. At the apartment where the lab was located, investigators found computers and printers, scanners, color copiers, cropping boards, cameras, magnetic strips, and a laminator. Among the array of documents in various stages of production were laminates, some with holographic images of federal emblems and seals.[3]

It is surprisingly easy to acquire counterfeit documents in the United States. According to one report, "for about $150 on street corners in just about any immigrant neighborhood in California," one can acquire a set of counterfeit documents, which contains a green card and a Social Security card.[4] Because employers are liable only if they *knowingly* hire illegal immigrants, few bother to authenticate the documents presented by foreign nationals. The Immigration Reform and Control Act of 1986, which was supposed to tighten employment authorization enforcement, neglected to hold employers responsible for authenticating identification documents. This oversight has become a major loophole that allows employers to turn a blind eye to counterfeit documents. Many employers simply claim that they have neither the staff nor the resources to verify whether the Social Security cards presented to them are real. As long as job applicants present IDs that appear authentic, employers, eager to fill their vacancies, will ask no questions. Even military contractors were found lax in their employment authentication efforts.[5]

The most common form of passport fraud is photo-substitution, especially for passports lacking security features (such as lamination). Although many developing countries continue to issue passports that are easy to alter, most Western countries have adopted printing technologies such as watermarks, lamination, holography, and biometrics to make official documents difficult to counterfeit. These tamper-resistant technologies have certainly driven some amateurs out of the business. In one such case, a Chinese human smuggler, who once was also a counterfeit artist, decided that the cost of keeping up with the counterfeit technology was simply too high in comparison to other ways of making money. Although a few of his friends managed to stay in the business, he quit the counterfeit business and focused instead on acquiring genuine documents:

I used to mostly specialize in getting authentic passports and replaced the pictures. At the beginning I was doing the photo-replacement business with a friend. He bought the original equipment and chemicals. We had to be very careful when peeling off the lamination. The temperature had to be right. I ruined a couple of passports at first. But I became very good at it. I mostly changed Chinese passports. Some foreign passports were not easy to alter and had to be sent out to our contacts in Guangdong. I think those passports were actually altered in Macao or Hong Kong. Passports are more difficult to alter now, and I don't do them anymore. It is a lot of work. These days I simply buy real ones from people who come back from the United States, Taiwan, Japan, or Korea. Instead of *Shatou* (changing the mug shot), we simply *Diaobao* (switch the luggage)—taking on someone else's identity as an imposter. *Diaobao* is much easier.

EXPLOITING GENUINE TRAVEL DOCUMENTS

A recent report by the Government Accountability Office (GAO; formerly General Accounting Office) found that the United States faces serious challenges to its passport fraud detection efforts. Major deficiencies include a lack of centralized databases, a lack of a common platform for information sharing, inadequate training, and understaffed investigations. In one GAO audit, in which sixty-seven federal and state fugitives were checked against the State Department's Consular Lookout and Support System (CLASS) database for passports, more than half of them did not exist.[6] One of the fugitives was on the FBI's Ten Most Wanted list. In other words, half of these fugitives could have applied and obtained U.S. passports. There have been numerous examples of foreign nationals as well as U.S. citizens obtaining passports using false identities. In fiscal year 2004, of the five hundred individuals arrested for passport fraud, 69 percent had fraudulently and successfully used other people's identities to obtain U.S. passports.[7] The State Department issues millions of passports each year (8.8 million in fiscal year 2004). Tens of thousands of applications are rejected each year, based on suspicious identities and those are referred to local fraud prevention offices.[8]

Assuming the identity of a valid passport holder or the owner of other identification papers has long been used by human smugglers to circumvent border control. More than a century ago, the "paper son" racket was devised by Chinese immigrants in San Francisco in response to the exclusionary laws passed by Congress. Under this scheme, Chinese nationals bought legitimate citizen papers and then posed as the sons of U.S. citizens by native birth. In an era of no photo identification or fingerprint cards, assuming someone else's identity was easy to accomplish. One needed only to memorize the information on the purchased paper upon arrival at the port of entry. These documents soon became a hot commodity, and they were sold and resold to those who wanted to come to America.[9]

The same practice continues today. Human smugglers pay high prices to acquire genuine travel documents. In some countries, even legitimate blank passports can be obtained because of corruption, theft, or misplacement.[10] Obtaining genuine passports through identity theft has also become common in recent years because the documents required for passport applications are often kept by different local government agencies that can be easily manipulated.

There are several common methods in passport fraud. One is to obtain a passport by posing as someone else, with a photo ID and the legitimate birth certificate. It has been demonstrated that with some planning, one can obtain a U.S. passport with a birth certificate acquired through assuming the identity of a dead person. Birth certificates are kept by local governments, and anyone can retrieve a copy of his or her own upon presenting a photo ID (which can also be purchased on the black market). Local governments do not always reconcile birth certificates with death certificates. The federal passport agency has no way of verifying whether an applicant is indeed the owner of the birth certificate.

Another method is to acquire expired passports from the black market and renew them with photographs of individuals who resemble the original passport holders. Child substitution and counterfeit citizenship documents are other strategies. The child substitution scheme is relatively easy. The counterfeit artist needs to find collaborating U.S. citizens who are willing to sell the identities of their children. In one such story, a woman was convicted for organizing and leading a large-scale passport fraud ring that involved recruiting American women to sell their children's identities so that foreign nationals could fraudulently obtain passports and enter the United States illegally.[11] The woman targeted drug-dependent women and their children, paying them about $300 for each identity and then using the identities to apply for passports. The woman then sold the passports to illegal aliens for as much as $6,000 each.[12]

There are other means to acquire genuine passports. One common strategy is to purchase the passports from traveling U.S. citizens, who then report that their passports were lost or stolen. U.S. passports receive far less scrutiny at immigration checkpoints than do foreign passports. U.S. citizens can also travel visa-free to many countries in the world. These obvious benefits have made U.S. passports a highly prized commodity on the black market, fetching $10,000 to $15,000 apiece. The demand for U.S. passports is so high that each year thousands upon thousands of passports as well as green cards are stolen or simply sold on the black market. According to the Department of State's Bureau of Diplomatic Security, false claims of lost, stolen, or damaged passports and other documents accounted for about a third of all detected passport fraud in 2004.[13]

U.S. passports are not the only ones sought by human smugglers. In one recent case, the U.S. Border Patrol noticed an upsurge in the number of people caught using South African passports to try to enter the United States through Mexico.[14] Many of these illegal immigrants appeared to be holding genuine South African passports and were looking for ways to sneak into the United States. They were later found to be from Congo, Namibia, and Nigeria. Because South Africans can visit Mexico without a visa, human smugglers are purchasing South African passports, either on the black market or through corrupt South African government officials, and sending their clients to Mexico.[15]

Passports from Japan and other countries that enjoy visa-waiver agreements with the United States command high prices on the black market.[16] Passports from countries that enjoy regional visa-waiver or visa-free arrangements are also sought after. For instance, when Slovenia, Latvia, and a few other eastern European countries became members of the European Union, the value of their passports increased immediately on the black market. These low-security passports allow their holders to enjoy the same freedom as those tamper-resistant ones, but they afford expanded venues to criminal organizations. The pressure of globalization has only added to the complexity of passport and visa controls at border checkpoints, because the flow of goods and services depends on expedient travel arrangements. Just how many fraudulent passports are currently in circulation in major immigration destination countries is anybody's guess.

Passport fraud may be straightforward in concept, but its actual use in human smuggling often requires careful planning and execution. For instance, the Chinese snakeheads are known for their penchant for acquiring passports from the United States and other Western countries whose bearers are of Asian descent. There is a widely held belief in the Chinese smuggling business that "all Asians look alike to Westerners." Chinese human smugglers do not randomly solicit foreign visitors outside souvenir shops or tourist attractions. The process of acquiring a passport is elaborate and cautious, involving scouting, approaching, persuading, negotiating, and purchasing. It is an ongoing process, with snakeheads constantly searching for prospective sellers as well as buyers. It generally works this way: Snakeheads send out inquiries continuously to their referral sources (or purchasing agents) in the community to gather information regarding which families in the villages or townships have relatives returning home for a visit from the United States, Japan, or other countries, whose passports are worth buying. As soon as a prospective candidate appears, the local contact approaches the family to inquire whether the travel document is up for sale. Such inquiries are mostly carried out in social conversations. Oftentimes families or relatives have made arrangements well before the actual passport bearer comes home.

Prices for these foreign travel documents are set as much by the black market as by the sellers and their families. The acquisition sequence usually works in this way: first, a foreign passport is obtained; then prospective clients are screened until one is found to resemble the biographical information in the passport. One snakehead in China described how she conducted her screening when looking for a suitable client:

> I have to screen my clients myself. They don't always match perfectly. But there are two types of clients I don't want: those who look like a peasant and those who are very handsome. Both types attract attention from border checkpoint inspectors. I prefer the plain-looking ones. They don't attract attention. I want immigration inspectors to ask as few questions as possible. I usually ask my possible candidates to come to Fuzhou, and my recruiter will come with them. I will then talk to these clients and ask them questions. I don't want anyone who can't answer questions quickly or come up with the right answers to my inquiries. The slow ones will be rejected. It doesn't happen often because my recruiter must screen clients first, and he knows who I want.

According to this snakehead, once a client passes through the matching and screening process, departure and entry training begins. The client must memorize all the biographical information in the passport and acquire basic geographical knowledge of the U.S. city in which he or she supposedly "lives," as well as the name of the restaurant at which he or she supposedly "works." This training usually requires close assistance from the family or relatives of the passport holder. Well-prepared clients usually have already learned enough English to pass basic questioning at the airport. Learning to speak English is not only trendy but also expected these days in smuggling-active communities in China. Pasted on walls throughout many of these townships are flyers advertising various schools that teach conversational English; many of these schools specialize in restaurant vocabularies.

The actual use of a fraudulently obtained passport is a carefully orchestrated event. The imposter must leave the country first before the "loss" can be reported to the local authorities. Oftentimes it is arranged for the passport bearer to travel to a different city or popular tourist location where the passport is "stolen," and a police report is filed.[17] Depending on the actual smuggling methods and transportation routes, sometimes the report of a "lost" or "stolen" passport can be made to a local police agency ahead of time to make the subsequent application for a replacement appear "legitimate." Because local police agencies usually do not have a direct way of sharing information with border control agencies or the U.S. consulates in China, by the time the U.S. consulate receives information regarding the lost passport and communicates it to the U.S. border control agencies, the client has already arrived.

Not all passport frauds are carried out in such a neatly organized fashion as described above. Human smugglers are as varied as their clients. Some are careful in their planning, whereas others are not. In cases where the stolen passports do not match their clients well or where travel documents have changed hands several times, human smugglers must resort to risky measures. One strategy in Chinese human smuggling is called *chuang-guan* (which literarily translates to "dashing through an immigration checkpoint"). In this strategy, neither the clients nor the smugglers are confident of whether the fraudulently acquired documents have been used before or are already in the U.S. border control system. They leave the country with additional paperwork prepared for possible asylum application. As usual, there are always a lucky few who can get through immigration inspections. Those who end up being detained at the port of entry will promptly apply for political asylum and hope to be released on bail during the court proceedings.

Another strategy is called *taitou* operations, which translates to "lifting one's head." As soon as the airplane takes off from an international airport, the smuggling operation is considered complete, and the smuggling fee must be paid. These are high-risk operations, and they usually involve insiders at border checkpoints in China. A snakehead in China described how the scheme works:

> In *taitou* operations, both the smugglers and their clients know that they are holding altered passports or visas that will most likely be caught by the U.S. immigration inspectors. They always surrender to authorities as soon as they reach U.S. soil and apply for political asylum. These clients don't even bother to *chuang-guan*. They have already made up good stories for political asylum, and they hope to be bailed out during court proceedings, for about $5,000 per person. Some of these *taitou* clients are repatriated immediately. That's when the trouble starts, because the Chinese government will track down the border inspectors on duty when the illegal migrants left. The officers on duty would always claim innocence by saying they did check the travel documents and were probably not paying enough attention to the details. Because these inspectors are part of the Chinese Armed Police, they are soldiers. The worst thing that can happen to a soldier is to be discharged from his military service. That's why border control officers who agree to collaborate with smugglers often charge the maximum bribe, about 100,000 to 120,000 yuan a person, with the idea that they may be caught and sent home after one deal. Keep in mind, the money is not made by one officer; it has to be distributed among up to seven people in one inspection unit, from the line officers sitting in inspection booths to the supervisors and the plainclothes officers roaming the international terminals. They work in packs.

According to this snakehead, *taitou* smuggling operations tend to cost less, but they pose the greatest risk for clients. There are only two major expenses in this smuggling method—the costs of bribing the checkpoint inspectors and of purchasing the fraudulent passport. Any altered passport will do as long as the smuggler has secured the border control inspector. But the drawbacks are also significant in the *taitou* business. Illegal migrants must often spend months in jail in the United States, and they are sometimes repatriated. Unlike other types of smuggling methods, in which snakeheads often provide a money-back guarantee should the operation fail, clients in *taitou* operations know that the money they spend will not be refunded. The snakehead in Fuzhou explained that some clients still chose *taitou* operations regardless:

> It is fast and usually does not involve other transit countries. These clients enter the United States knowing they will be detained, and the political asylum petition will be filed. Many live in INS detention centers for months before they can be bailed out. On the other hand, I am doing some *taitou* cases through Canada. The Canadian authorities don't lock up illegal immigrants for long, probably one month at most. If they can't find evidence to prove you intentionally entered the country illegally, they will give you a refugee status. Once you are released, there will be people waiting outside the jail to pick you up and arrange for your transfer to the United States. The main difference here is the length of incarceration. Many of my clients like to go to Canada for transit purposes.

THE GLOBAL CHALLENGE OF COUNTERFEIT DOCUMENTS

Passport fraud is by no means the exclusive purview of human smugglers, but the smugglers are certainly among the most eager customers in this counterfeit black market. The recent surge in forged passports and other official documents has received much of its impetus from the demand created by global human smuggling activities.

Countries big and small, developed and developing, are confronted with the growing challenge of controlling lost and stolen passports and tightening border controls to detect fraudulent travel documents. In Africa, transnational criminal organizations are known to obtain genuine passports through illegitimate means (i.e., bribery and corruption) or to alter passports that have relatively weak security features to facilitate the transportation of illegal migrants.[18] In Sri Lanka, human smuggling has become so serious that airline clerks at check-in counters routinely call foreign embassies to verify travel documents, and those caught carrying fraudulent paperwork are handed over to the police.[19]

Passport fraud does not always originate from criminal organizations. A few rogue nations, especially those in financial trouble, are also known for selling their nation's identification documents to whoever can pay the fee. The tiny nation of Nauru in the Pacific is such an example. With just eight square miles of territory and phosphate, its only prized resource, depleted, Nauru has been living on foreign aid for a few years. Its current government is largely sustained by Australia. In the 1990s Nauru set up "economic citizenship" for wealthy foreigners with money to invest in the country; more than a thousand passports were processed for $15,000 and up, and anyone with $25,000 could open a bank account in the country without even being physically present.[20]

The U.S. government also alleges that Suriname has become a major transit country for cross-national human smuggling. The Surinamese government issues tens of thousands of work visas to foreign nationals each year, more than there are actual jobs available in the country. It does not matter whether the Surinamese economy can absorb these "foreign workers" because most only want to use the country as a transit for their journey toward North America.[21]

In November 2004 police across Europe were alerted after a raid on a few underground printing houses in the Lithuanian city of Kaunas led to the seizure of 8 million highly crafted counterfeit notes in €100 denominations, as well as passports and other financial documents that even experts found difficult to distinguish from the real thing. Police officials admitted that they had no idea how many counterfeit notes were already in circulation in Europe.[22] Many of the best forgers reportedly had worked as printers under the old Soviet regime. When Lithuania became independent, they set up their own print shops.[23] Because Lithuania is a member of the European Union, its citizens can move freely in member states and use forged passports to settle in different countries. According to the National Criminal Intelligence Service in England, Lithuanian gangs were buying expensive cars with forged bank drafts from unsuspecting owners who had placed ads in automobile magazines. In another racket, a Lithuanian forger used a college in Hampshire as a cover for smuggling in illegal immigrants posing as students. His customers were given fake passports with bogus British immigration stamps.[24]

New Zealand has long been plagued by passport fraud. Its passports are highly prized in the transnational criminal world because they attract little attention from other countries. A New Zealand passport can command $60,000 on the international black market. About 12,000 are lost or stolen each year.[25] Information about lost passports is usually sent between different foreign affairs departments by a third-party note, a process that can take weeks or months, by which time a stolen New Zealand passport has probably been used several times. In an effort to correct this situation, New Zealand is spearheading a cooperative effort among thirty Pacific Rim nations, including Australia and Japan, to expedite information sharing to deal with people-smuggling and cross-border crimes involving the use of stolen and forged passports. The proposed system will allow details of stolen passports and other travel documents to be sent between countries quickly by computer, cutting the time required to alert authorities from weeks to hours. At present New Zealand authorities are able to share passport details "in real time" with only Australia.

The most active black market for passport fraud is probably Thailand. Known not only for its knockoff Armani suits and Rolexes, Thailand's vibrant underground economy attracts customers from around the world, including human smugglers, drug traffickers, fugitives, and at least one Al-Qaeda-linked terrorist, Hambali, who was the mastermind of the 2002 Bali attacks and alleged leader of the Al-Qaeda-linked Southeast Asian terror group Jemaah Islamiyah. Hambali, posing as a businessman, was carrying a forged Spanish passport when he was arrested in the central Thai city of Ayutthaya in August 2003.[26] Belgian, French, Portuguese, and Spanish passports are the most popular forgeries because of their weak security features. In a sting operation, Thai police posed as prospective buyers and seized 353 passports from a Greek courier en route to London in March 2004, and 100 from a Spaniard and a Dutchman.[27] Another 452 passports were taken from an Algerian-born Briton on his way to London in August 2004. Most counterfeit passports produced in Thailand are headed for London, and they are used mainly to open bank accounts or rent apartments. These passports can be bought for $25 to $50 apiece.

In another sting operation, Thai police captured a counterfeit artist from Sri Lanka and seized 255 passports from thirty-three different countries, mostly from Europe and Asia. Police also discovered seventy-three fake visa and immigration stamps from around the world, including Thai and Indonesian consular stamps from Munich, Madras, Paris, and Vientiane. During the subsequent examination, the forged passports were found to be impeccable; however, the work was thought to have been crafted with simple tools such as a laminator, a blow-dryer, a hole puncher, a paper cutter, and a desktop computer, all in a modest studio apartment workspace.[28] The altered passports were mostly shipped via FedEx in a hidden compartment cut inside a children's book.

The more expensive passports are the lost or stolen ones, which can be used to pass immigration controls. Some 10 million foreign tourists visit Thailand each year. Some of their passports are sold to counterfeit artists who then alter the biographical data or substitute the photos, whereas others are used by imposters. Passports with visas to the United States or the United Kingdom, which are difficult to produce, can sell for $2,400 each. A U.S. passport with a changed photo can fetch $2,900. Because of the rampant counterfeit activities, law enforcement agencies from a long list of countries, including Canada, France, Spain, Italy, Germany, Japan, Australia, and the United States, have set up intelligence and liaison offices, and they meet with their Thai counterparts regularly.[29]

BEYOND PASSPORT FRAUD

Counterfeit travel documents are useful for gaining entry into the country. However, illegal immigrants are interested in more than just getting into the United States. They also want to work, move around, and settle permanently if possible. To satisfy these needs, other types of documents are also needed once an illegal immigrant arrives. An illegal immigrant in Sacramento described her situation:

> My brother and sister filed for political asylum immediately because they were both detained at the port of entry. They had to apply for political asylum. I did not get arrested. I came by way of Canada using a fake passport, and someone drove me through Vancouver into the United States. I first went to New York. But I also filed for political asylum because I need to obtain a legal status. Unfortunately my application was rejected, and I have also lost my appeal. I am nervous these days. I have no idea what is going to happen to me. I don't drive, and I can't have a regular job. I am here to help out my friend in this restaurant, and I have worked for him for many years. There is no other way. I am waiting for some miracles to happen. Maybe an amnesty.[30]

Many illegal immigrants are eager to obtain other legal identification papers once inside the United States. There are three main areas where the business of counterfeit documents has converged with the business of human smuggling: (1) documents that allow illegal immigrants to work (the case of Social Security numbers for rent); (2) documents that are used in filing for adjustment of immigration status (the case of Operation Watermark); and (3) documents that allow illegal immigrants to move freely (the case of the Tennessee Driving Certificate Experiment).

Social Security Numbers for Rent

Many identification papers are easy to obtain from the black market as long as they are not examined too closely. A Social Security card with a number that can withstand an employer's background check is difficult to obtain. How does an illegal immigrant acquire a valid Social Security number? He or she rents one. It has been reported that many green card holders are returning to their home countries to live. However, to accrue enough Social Security savings for retirement purposes, one needs to work for at least a total of ten years (or accumulate forty points). These homebound green card holders instead offer to rent out their Social Security numbers to illegal immigrants, who then can work "legally" in the United States. This illicit trade emerged years ago but attracted little attention from U.S. authorities.[31]

It is impossible to estimate just how many people participate in this trade. The practice of lending out one's Social Security number is common in immigrant communities because it makes good economic sense for all parties involved. For the green card holders who spend more time in their native countries than in the United States, renting out one's Social Security number results in contributions to their otherwise idle Social Security account. Sometimes a Social Security number is rented for free through referrals by friends and relatives; other times there is a small charge.[32] And there are many takers, as hundreds of thousands of illegal immigrants arrive in the United States each year from Mexico and other countries. Demand for Social Security numbers among the illegal immigrant population has only grown in recent years as the federal agencies have increased their crackdowns on employers that hire undocumented labor.

Renting out one's Social Security number is particularly attractive to green card holders who do not want to live in the United States permanently. Because green card holders will be questioned by immigration officials and even barred from reentry into the United States if they stay outside the country for extended periods of time (usually longer than one year) without legitimate reasons, having someone contributing to their Social Security accounts becomes an attractive option not only for maintaining their "presence" in the United States but also for accruing the extra benefits. Although many illegal immigrants turn to the black market for fraudulent documents, fraudulent Social Security cards tend to cause payroll problems when employers submit payroll taxes. For instance, the Social Security Administration sends hundreds of thousands of letters each year to employers requesting corrections on their earnings statements on mismatched individuals.[33] A genuine Social Security number, rented or borrowed, allows illegal immigrants to work with little fear. With the addition of a fake driver's license or green card, the illegal immigrant can even pick and choose where to work.

Operation Watermark

The thriving business of human smuggling increases demands on fraudulent documents of all sorts. Identification papers are only part of the game. Many other documents are needed for various purposes. These documents include school transcripts, company invitation letters, payroll documents, and company brochures. The following case describes an investigation by Immigration and Customs Enforcement (ICE) agents who broke up a counterfeit document print shop in Los Angeles that had been in operation for years and had supplied a wide range of official-looking documents to illegal and legal immigrants for their immigration application needs. Operation Watermark was an investigation into the production and sale of counterfeit documents to illegal immigrants from the People's Republic of China for the purposes of filing for asylum and other immigration benefits.

In early 2001 the Organized Crime and Vice Division of the Los Angeles Police Department (LAPD) was tipped off by an informant about a print shop in the Los Angeles area that was allegedly producing and selling documents to people from China to permit them to file for immigration benefits. After a brief investigation, the LAPD notified the Counterfeit Document Unit of the Immigration and Naturalization Service (INS) in Los Angeles. Soon a formal investigative operation was launched, code-named Operation Watermark. Federal agents began monitoring the shop's telephone calls, stalking out the storefront, and conducting undercover operations to purchase some counterfeit documents.

Working with the informant and their LAPD counterparts, federal agents quickly found that the owner of the print shop had also come to the United States under dubious circumstances. Soon after he entered the country in New York in 1997 on an L-1 visa (designated for intracompany transferees), he filed for political asylum, which was granted in 1998. His coconspirator, a female immigrant, possessed no documentation whatsoever that would allow the law enforcement agency to verify her country of origin or immigration status, a technique often employed by illegal Chinese immigrants from China to thwart deportation efforts. Without proper identification or other collaborative evidence, China cannot simply accept deportees claimed by the U.S. government to have come from mainland China.

During the yearlong investigation, federal agents learned that the shop was producing official documents from various provinces in China, including birth certificates, police clearances (i.e., clean criminal record), and adoption certificates. Prospective customers came to the shop and examined samples before they ordered the actual documents. The business even claimed that the documents provided by the shop could be used in applications for green cards, adjustments to H-1 visa status (temporary work visas), and petitions for family members.

With the help of several informants and authorized wiretaps, federal agents probed the shop's capability of producing counterfeit documents. During one undercover operation, an informant, cash in hand, was wearing a listening device and a hidden video camera as he walked into the shop. He was greeted by a female Asian storekeeper who claimed to represent the owner and agreed to assist in acquiring the needed documents. She even allowed the informant to use the store phone to call the owner, who pleasantly offered discounts to encourage the transaction. In this case, the informant wanted to purchase a Chinese birth certificate, a clean criminal record report, and a Chinese diploma. The informant claimed that he had no formal education in China. This was not a problem.

The female storekeeper presented samples of diplomas and other documents that are commonly found in China and assured the informant that the diplomas produced in the shop were good enough to apply for jobs in the United States or even for immigration to Canada. The female storekeeper added that she personally notarized all the documents and that people believed that the notarizations performed by the shop were genuine and valid. The informant filled out a form with his biographical information, including name, place of origin in China, and a contact telephone number in the United States, and gave the storekeeper his picture.

Prices for these documents were reasonable. The birth certificate and criminal record report cost $290 each. The diploma cost $580. A $50 deposit was required for each document. The total production time would be eight days. The storekeeper even issued a receipt for the deposit.

A few days later the female assistant called the number left by the informant and left a message asking for a callback because she needed another picture. Within three days the informant went to the shop and delivered two pictures. A week later the documents were ready for pickup. The informant asked how much money he should bring to pay off the balance. He was told to bring $920, an amount less than what was originally agreed to. It took a few more days for the informant to obtain the money from his federal handler. The end products were delivered in a yellow envelope—a Chinese birth certificate, a Chinese police clearance report, and a university diploma with the English translation and a notary seal and certification from China.

Over the next few months, federal agents conducted additional undercover operations with the help of other informants. The same investigative tactics were repeated (i.e., wiretapping and videotaping of the transactions). Throughout the investigation, the print shop owner and his female assistant appeared oblivious to the illegitimacy of their business and rarely grew suspicious of the inquiries about their business.

In each of the undercover operations, the informants openly admitted their illegal status and disclosed that the documents were to be used to circumvent government regulations and gain immigration benefits. In each case, informants were assured that they would encounter no problems when producing the documents and that the quality of their products was high enough to pass the scrutiny of immigration examiners. They would give out business cards with their phone numbers and ask for the clients' contact information. It was all business. This one-stop shop was able to provide all the documents commonly required by mainland Chinese when applying for immigration benefits or other governmental functions.

The store could produce not only documents commonly sought by immigrants applying for benefits but also authentic-looking university diplomas, official transcripts, and other academic documents. For university transcripts, the store was able to provide standard as well as customized courses and grades to satisfy whatever the clients deemed necessary in their immigration or job applications. The store would ask clients to examine transcript or diploma proofs to make changes in the wording and titles before the final production.

According to one federal agent involved in this case, the produced documents were of high quality and difficult to distinguish from the genuine ones. The watermark on the documents and the official seals bearing the issuing agencies' names all appeared to be genuine when compared to the real ones. It was later discovered that official-looking seals were reproduced, and special chemical agents were used to paint the watermark on the paper. In order to distinguish whether the watermark was painted on the surface of a document or embedded within the paper's fabric, special lighting and magnifying glasses are needed.

What was truly amazing was the audacity of the counterfeit artists in this case. They claimed the business to be the sole agent authorized by the Chinese government to provide notarized documents for all provinces in China. They placed ads in multiple Chinese-language newspapers in the greater Los Angeles area frequently read by Chinese immigrants. The ads even proclaimed that "official samples" from different provinces were available for examination and that an exclusive FedEx account was established to secure timely shipment of official documents to and from different parts of China. The store's sign, which hung over its entrance in the mall and featured big Mandarin characters, translated roughly to "Mainland Notary Service" (even though the business license issued by the city was for translation services only).

Few in the Chinese community ever suspected that the business was a complete fraud. To be sure, federal agents even contacted the Chinese consulate general in Los Angeles and interviewed the consul in charge of the visa section regarding the proper authorization procedure to produce these official documents. The Chinese government prohibits such documents as birth certificates and clean criminal records to be produced overseas or by any foreign entities. Such documents must be obtained from the local government office inside China with jurisdiction over the area in which the concerned person lives.

Although the consulate general has the authority to issue birth certificates and other Chinese identity documents, such authority is rarely exercised because of the difficulty and complexity involved in verifying one's birthplace or police records outside China. For a Chinese national residing the United States who has legitimate reasons to obtain such documents, a power of attorney must be obtained through a Chinese consulate (or embassy), which allows a relative or a friend in China to act on behalf of the applicant.

The Tennessee Driving Certificate Experiment

It is no secret that many illegal immigrants drive in the United States without a license or insurance. In an effort to correct this problem,

Tennessee started issuing driver's licenses to illegal immigrants in early 2001. More than 180,000 obtained driver's licenses before the September 11 events put a stop to the practice. In 2004 driving certificates were created as a compromise to satisfy Homeland Security's concerns while allowing illegal immigrants to drive with certified proficiency.[34] Tens of thousands of these certificates (51,000 in the eighteen months following July 2004) were issued, but not all went to people living in the state.[35]

The driving certificate, a purple card that resembles a driver's license, is clearly marked under the state flag with the words "For driving purposes only—not valid for identification." Unlike the driver's license, which is widely used in the United States for legal identification purposes, the driving certificate only allows one to drive a car and be insured. To obtain a driving certificate, applicants must provide two types of documents, such as utility bills or bank statements, to prove residency in Tennessee, as well as a Social Security number—or a sworn affidavit if there is none. The rest is the same as regular license procedures—an eye exam, a written test, and a road test. Most certificates are valid for one year. If the applicant has immigration paperwork that is valid for more than one year, the certificate will last the length of the immigration documentation, up to a maximum of five years.[36]

Much confusion has been engendered by this neither-here-nor-there document. Few people know what to make of these driving certificates. In June 2004 Tennessee Department of Safety officials said that they would advise state and local law enforcement agencies to reject the driving certificates as identification, but later in the same month an official announcement instructed law enforcement agencies to accept the wallet-sized laminated cards as valid ID when issuing misdemeanor tickets.[37] With regular driver's licenses, people can board airplanes, buy guns, cash checks, rent cars, open bank accounts, and even visit border towns in Mexico and Canada. It is not clear what kind of impact these driving certificates will have on Tennessee's highway safety. Advocates for immigrants argue that the certificates will single out the holders' legal status and make them inferior in the eyes of the state. Anti-immigration activists argue that driving certificates give illegal immigrants legitimacy they should not have.

While the debate continues, immigrants are paying hundreds of dollars on the black market and traveling hundreds of miles to get these certificates. Many believe that illegal immigrants from Latin American countries are taking advantage of this document. Two major federal investigations led to multiple arrests of members of a New Jersey-based group in July 2005 and of a Georgia-based group in December 2005, who were accused of operating an underground express, transporting illegal immigrants willing to pay $950 to $1,500 apiece to come to state licensing centers in Knoxville.[38] Most were South and Central American immigrants who applied for the driving certificates using fake residency papers.

State license examiners in Murfreesboro, outside Nashville, were also accused of accepting bribes to provide illegal immigrants with driver's licenses and certificates without testing. A woman was accused of bringing as many as one hundred immigrants from New Jersey to Knoxville to obtain the certificates. In one case, Knox County sheriff's deputies discovered that fifty-eight illegal immigrants had used the same Knoxville address to get certificates.[39]

Tennessee's experiment has been closely followed by many other states in the nation. In California, for instance, after rejecting proposals for years, former governor Gray Davis in 2003 signed a bill to allow undocumented immigrants to receive California driver's licenses. This move quickly became a liability in the recall campaign, in which Arnold Schwarzenegger defeated Davis. As soon as Schwarzenegger came to office, he lobbied the state legislature to repeal the bill.

Tennessee's experiment with the Certificate of Driving was suspended in 2006, but it serves as an example of how a well-intended legislative attempt can be quickly exploited by human smugglers. It should not come as a surprise that this or any other quasi-official identification document enables smugglers to transport illegal immigrants across the country on open roads. These driving certificates can also become stepping-stones to other forms of official paperwork, such as banking documents, school registrations, and utility bills, all of which can be used to acquire still other forms of identification for accessing social services and employment.

Chapter 4

Smuggling through Illegal Channels

With the exception of Mexican nationals who typically cross the border overland, human smugglers often make use of a combination of legal and illegal strategies to transport their clients from place to place. The following sections describe three major smuggling strategies: (1) overland; (2) maritime; and (3) by air.

HUMAN SMUGGLING OVERLAND

Resourceful and well-connected smugglers charge a premium to acquire proper travel documents to smooth the transportation process. For most illegal migrants, however, trekking across unguarded terrains remains the most viable option. The scheme is simple. The vast majority of illegal immigrants, more than 1 million each year, enter the United States simply by crossing the borders illegally. The number of illegal immigrants who arrive by going through immigration control pales against the masses from interior Mexico and other Latin American countries that rely on enterprising agents (i.e., *coyotes* or *polleros*) to cross overland into the United States.

The United States shares about five thousand miles of border with Canada and close to two thousand miles with Mexico. There are an additional 93,000 miles of shoreline. As of 2005, there were a total of 11,300 Border Patrol agents.[1] Assuming all were on active patrol duties and all were on the southern border, the average number of agents per mile would still be fewer than two per day per shift.

To stop and apprehend migrants scattering to evade detection would obviously take more than two agents on any occasion. While one group of migrants might be apprehended, the rest of the mile would be left open to other groups of migrants waiting to dart through. Human smugglers and drug traffickers alike routinely employ distraction strategies, such as setting off sensors or sending scouts, to draw Border Patrol agents away from intended crossing points. Although there are hundreds of video cameras and close to 12,000 ground censors monitoring illegal border crossing activities, they are only as effective as the number of agents available to respond.

Instead of subjecting themselves to long lines and security checks that legitimate travelers must go through at airports (e.g., presenting identity papers, removing shoes, taking off belts and emptying pockets), thousands upon thousands of illegal immigrants simply walk across the border from Mexico and Canada, not having to show anything.[2] Once inside the United States, these illegal immigrants often acquire counterfeit documents to mask their true identifies, and live and work in the country comforted by the fact that millions of others are just like them.

The United States has historically paid little attention to people crossing into the country from Mexico and Canada. Neither does the United States care how many of its own citizens cross into the neighboring two countries. Cross-border smuggling activities (including drugs, alcohol, and illegal migrants) have been going on for centuries, ebbing and flowing with time. The September 11 events have brought the border situation to the forefront of the nation's awareness. Illegal border crossings are now viewed as a national security issue.

Human smugglers of diverse nationalities have discovered ways to work with their Mexican counterparts in moving their clients into the United States. The number of illegal immigrants from countries other than Mexico (i.e., OTMs) has increased steadily over the years. From 2004 to 2005, the number of OTMs more than doubled, from 75,000 to 165,000.

Human smuggling activities have spread far beyond the border areas into the heartland of America. Near Des Moines, Iowa, on May 6, 2005, a twenty-two-year-old Mexican male was caught driving a Chevy Tahoe on Interstate Highway 80 in Jasper County, Iowa. When he was pulled over by a deputy sheriff for license plate violations, there were nine people inside the vehicle. Suspecting their illegal status, the deputy contacted local ICE agents, who determined that the driver and his eight passengers were all illegal immigrants.[3]

Not far from where this incident took place, a twenty-seven-year-old Mexican female driving a Ford Expedition on Interstate Highway 80 near Des Moines was pulled over for speeding by an Iowa State Trooper. The trooper discovered eleven people crammed inside. An ICE agent responded to the scene and determined that all were illegal immigrants. Such sightings have become commonplace across America. In half of fiscal year 2005, the ICE office in Des Moines apprehended 281 illegal migrants in twenty-five smuggling vehicles, already 45 percent more than during the entire previous fiscal year.[4]

Overland Smuggling Tactics

Human smuggling, as an entrepreneurial effort, seems to attract individuals who are persistent in their efforts and ingenious in their strategies. The following are a few examples of the strategies devised by human smugglers in recent years.

Posing as U.S. Citizens

In December 2004 federal agents broke up a smuggling organization that flew eastern Europeans out of Warsaw, Poland, and other cities in Europe, to Mexico City, and then on to Tijuana, where they would pose as U.S. citizens in order to cross the border.[5] The smuggling group, which was believed to have been active since the mid-1990s, transported illegal migrants, including women and children, from Russia, Lithuania, Ukraine, and Poland. Believing that these illegal immigrants would pass as White Americans, the smugglers drove them into the United States as if they had just been in Tijuana on a day trip. On one occasion, a smuggler was caught driving an illegal immigrant in a Mercedes-Benz at the border checkpoint. Federal investigators found that some of the illegal immigrants smuggled by this group had in their possession counterfeit passports as well as authentic passports issued in other people's names. These illegal migrants have paid from $5,000 to $9,000 apiece for the entire journey.[6]

Recruiting U.S. Drivers to Shuttle Illegal Immigrants

There is a chronic shortage of drivers to shuttle illegal immigrants who just cross into the United States and need to continue the journey to such major hubs as Phoenix and Los Angeles, from where they can be transshipped elsewhere. Even before the events of September 11, 2001, major border crossings in Southern California had been fortified with additional fences, floodlights, and ground censors. The increased surveillance and interceptions have pushed illegal crossings into remote areas that Border Patrol agents cannot easily access. It is at these ever-changing points of illegal entry that the driver scarcity is most felt by smugglers.

Because human smugglers are often illegal immigrants themselves, their lack of valid drivers licenses often poses obstacles in transporting clients around the border region. Therefore U.S. citizens are recruited to provide transportation services. In San Diego one favorite recruiting place is outside casinos, where habitual gamblers are easy targets.[7] Open around the clock and close to the border area, these casinos become a staging point for human smugglers to receive and transfer clients, and to launder money. Smugglers stake out parking lots and approach gamblers who appear to be down on their luck with the promise of quick cash for a short drive to the border.

According to one news report, prospective drivers are offered up to $1,600 to drive two illegal immigrants across the border from Mexico.[8] The diverse crowds that frequent casinos and busy parking lots provide an ideal cover for human smugglers to carry out their activities without drawing attention from the authorities. In one case, a U.S. citizen was offered $50 per person to drive ten undocumented immigrants crammed in a utility truck. After he was stopped at a Border Patrol checkpoint on Interstate Highway 8, he admitted that a man at a local casino had offered him cash to make the delivery. The fifty-seven-year-old handyman from a nearby town had been stopped a month earlier by Border Patrol agents for running similar smuggling operations with his utility truck. On both occasions he claimed that he had been recruited by strangers in a parking lot outside a local casino, offering cash to pick up some people.[9]

In recent years human smugglers have focused their efforts on recruiting willing U.S. citizens to provide transportation services in the border area. Because the penalty for U.S. citizens caught in transporting illegal immigrants is relatively minor, mostly involving fines, human smugglers can greatly reduce the risk and cost of doing business by hiring local help. According to U.S. Customs and Border Protection, about half of those caught smuggling migrants across the border at the two major ports of entry in San Diego (i.e., San Ysidro and Otay Mesa) before September 11, 2001, were U.S. citizens. The figure has since reached 80 percent.[10] Aside from gamblers, high school students and even homeless people are hired to drive smuggling vehicles.

Using U.S. Government Vehicles to Transport Illegal Migrants

To conceal smuggling activities and evade law enforcement detection, two human smugglers in Laredo, Texas, decided to use U.S. government vehicles assigned to their official duties as Marine recruiters to transport illegal immigrants. The two U.S. Marines stationed in Laredo were caught in uniform driving a government vehicle loaded with illegal immigrants.[11] The disguise was almost unimaginable under normal circumstances for any law enforcement agency.

Acting on tips provided by an informant, federal agents and Texas troopers began tailing U.S. government vehicles driven by military personnel, suspecting that some of them were involved in human smuggling activities. On July 22, 2005, at around 5 p.m., twenty-seven-year-old Marine Victor Domingo Ramirez was in uniform driving a U.S. government minivan when he was pulled over by a Texas state trooper north of Laredo on Interstate Highway 35. Another Marine was also riding in the vehicle, together with three women.

Not knowing that the feds had been tracking their movement all along, both soldiers claimed that the female passengers were U.S. citizens. The ICE agents who responded to the scene determined that all three women were illegal immigrants. The three women had earlier entered the United States illegally and been picked up by Ramirez. He subsequently passed through a Border Patrol checkpoint on I-35 and told checkpoint inspectors the women were U.S. citizens. Unsuspectingly, Ramirez had been under surveillance by ICE agents who tape-recorded his dealings with the informant as he assured the informant he would have no problem transporting the illegal immigrants by driving a government van and wearing his military uniform.[12]

Crossing the Sonoran Desert

The journey to the U.S.-Mexican border is treacherous and dangerous. Illegal travelers from Central and South American countries must first cross into Mexico over its loosely guarded border between Guatemala and Mexico. The smuggling of contraband and humans is common along Mexico's border with Guatemala. Authorities from either side rarely intervene. Migrants of limited resources often hitchhike or hop on freight trains heading north. Many fall prey to corrupt police and gangsters. Freight trains are often controlled by gangsters in different regions. Extortions, beatings, and rapes frequently occur.

Female migrants are especially at risk. They must not only endure the same horrendous transportation and living conditions as their male counterparts, but they also face frequent sexual assaults by their smugglers or fellow migrants. One news story reported that rape has become so prevalent that many women take birth control pills or shots before the journey so they do not become pregnant.[13] It is considered part of the price for crossing the border.

Although the search for economic opportunities remains the primary motive, factors contributing to recent increases in female border crossers are complex. Some women have husbands and children in the United States, whereas others leave their families behind in Mexico to search for better-paying jobs. Of these women, those from Central America face even greater risks of being accosted and raped because they have a much longer journey to make before they reach the border.

Once at the border, illegal migrants must find *polleros* to help them navigate the vast desert. Because of increased border enforcement efforts in Texas and California, migrants are now converging on a few remote and isolated stretches of the U.S. Mexico border. Small, dusty border towns in Mexico (such as Altar and Sasabe) have become popular staging points for migrants and have developed an economy dependent upon the steady flow of the transient population.[14] Ranchers have stopped raising cattle or growing crops and instead set up guesthouses and eateries. Street vendors briskly sell jugs of water, first-aid kits, garbage bags, and other items that a border crosser may need.

Thousands of migrants pass through these border towns each day, congregating in flophouses and preparing for the crossing. Those traveling on the cheap can rent a bed in a flophouse for $3 a night, while those with more money can pay $30–40 to stay in an air-conditioned motel.[15] In recent years, cell phones have also become hot items for border crossers. Because of the many deaths reported by the media and warnings posted by the U.S. and Mexican authorities of the dangers of the desert, a growing number of migrants purchase emergency-call-only cell phones before they set off on the journey. In one case, a group of twenty three illegal immigrants were lost in the desert where temperatures exceeded 100 degrees.[16] Exposed without shelter and out of water, the group used a cell phone to call 911. They were rescued.

Migrants typically hike for days in the desert to prearranged rendezvous points to be picked up by smugglers waiting on remote stretches of highways, whereas others are spotted and apprehended by the Border Patrol and sent back to Mexico. Still others, often ill-prepared or already sick, succumb to extreme temperatures. Nevertheless, they still try, again and again, to get inside the United States to find jobs so they can send the money home to support those left behind.

Border Control Initiatives as Impetus to Human Smuggling Business

Human smuggling is a growth industry, with well-established networks of facilitators making job and housing arrangements, drop-house keepers providing shelter to migrants in transit, and transporters crisscrossing the country in cars crammed with illegal migrants. Many critics have dismissed the border-hardening measures in recent decades as more for symbolic and political motives than for any real solutions.[17] Most would agree that illegal border crossing is no longer as easy as it used to be. These border control reinforcement measures have produced two clear outcomes on which most would agree: (1) more illegal migrants rely on human smugglers to cross the border, and (2) human smuggling as a business has become more organized. Increased difficulties in crossing into the United States have greatly rewarded smuggling organizations with more prospective migrants and higher smuggling fees.

Earnest efforts to harden the nation's border began during the Clinton administration. A major shift in border enforcement policy took place, from apprehension, to deterrence and prevention. A key component of this policy shift was to use technology (including night-vision scopes, motion sensors, and integrated computer systems) and to erect physical barriers to stop unauthorized entrants from Mexico. A series of campaigns were launched in the early and mid-1990s as politicians competed to get tough on illegal immigration. The following is a list of well-publicized border control initiatives.

Operation Hold the Line

Begun in September 1993 in El Paso, Texas, the operation was first launched as Operation Blockade and later changed to Operation Hold the Line. Agents were deployed to forward positions along the border with an emphasis on stopping migrants from entering the country illegally instead of apprehending them after they had scattered into the urban alleyways. Agents were positioned within close proximity to one another along a twenty-mile stretch of the border around the clock. Broken border fences were repaired in the downtown El Paso area. The effect was immediate. There was a drastic reduction in attempted illegal border crossings and apprehensions at the border area as well as inland.[18] In 1997 the operation was expanded into southern New Mexico.

Operation Gatekeeper

Modeled after the El Paso experiment and launched in October 1994, with extensive media fanfare, the U.S. Border Patrol deployed agents to the front line and installed numerous stadium-type lights, extensive fencing, new roads along the fences, infrared goggles, and motion sensors in an effort to deter illegal migrants from sneaking in, as well as to make immediate arrests of those who managed to breach the line. A computerized system called IDENT was installed to help Border Patrol agents identify repeat offenders. IDENT is essentially a centralized fingerprint verification system designed to allow federal authorities to quickly identify repeat border crossers and criminal aliens. A prototype was in operation in October 1994, and several modifications have been made since to improve its record-matching ability and data accuracy. Despite its many technical glitches and uneven use across the country, the system has improved over the years as more and more agencies sign on to use the system in their border patrol and immigration enforcement operations.[19]

The San Diego sector is relatively short compared to other sectors along the southern border. However, the sixty-six miles of border projecting inland from the Pacific Ocean historically has been the busiest Border Patrol sector because of the two major urban centers—San Diego and Tijuana. For instance, in fiscal year 1993, the Sector tallied 531,689 apprehensions out of a total of 1,263,490 Border Patrol apprehensions nationwide.[20] Unlike

El Paso, with the Rio Grande as a clear border demarcation, large portions of the San Diego region feature rough terrains with deep canyons and cliffs where motorized patrol is impossible. A study found significant reductions in illegal crossings in places where fences were constructed and motorized patrol was possible.[21] However, the effect was not as clear in isolated and remote stretches of the border. In recent years, Operation Gatekeeper has been extended eastward to Yuma, Arizona.

Operation Safeguard

Nogales, Arizona, historically draws large crowds of illegal migrants from Nogales, Mexico, a town right across the border. The twelve-foot fence that has separated the two cities for decades is easy to scale. Once on U.S. ground, illegal immigrants can easily blend into local neighborhoods. In 1994, around the same time that Operation Gatekeeper was initiated, Operation Safeguard was launched as part of the same federal funding package to achieve the same goals as its predecessors in Texas and California, that is, to make illegal border crossings more difficult in Arizona's expansive and hilly deserts.[22] Operation Safeguard increased the presence of uniformed agents by improving the visibility of their posts and by reinforcing border fences, making them difficult to scale. Mobile units were deployed at strategic locations for fast response to any attempted entries. Sensors and stadium lighting (powered by mobile generators) were also installed to improve the sightings of illegal crossings at night time. In 1999, as illegal entrants moved from California into Arizona deserts, Operation Safeguard was reinforced with additional Border Patrol agents from the San Diego and Tucson sectors.[23]

Operation Rio Grande

Launched in August 1997 in Brownsville, Texas, this new phase of border enforcement was designed to expand border control along the remainder of the Texas border, starting east from Brownsville, and covering different areas of the border throughout Texas and New Mexico. Areas with high illegal traffic were targeted by a combination of additional patrol agents and new technology (including low-light television monitors, night vision equipment, night scopes, and encrypted radios).[24] This multi-year operation deployed special response teams to crossing sites. IDENT (the automated biometrics identification system) was installed for rapidly checking the criminal records of detained migrants at ports of entry. There was also an increased emphasis on integrating various parts of the immigration enforcement system, including agents on patrol, inspectors at ports-of-entry, investigators, intelligence analysts, and detention and deportation officers.

Since the September 11 events, additional and similar operations have been launched under various names, all with the same goals: to reduce the flow of illegal immigrants and to disrupt human smuggling activities. The enforcement initiatives include Operation ICE Storm (2003), a targeted, intelligence-based operation that aims at breaking up violent smuggling organizations in the Phoenix area. As a result of ICE Storm, more than 340 human smugglers have been prosecuted for a variety of crimes, including money laundering, kidnapping, narcotics smuggling, and weapons charges.[25] A critical aspect of the operation targets smugglers' financial assets as a strategy to cripple the networks' operations.[26]

The Arizona Border Control Initiatives (2004), currently in its second phase, uses permanent and tactical checkpoints to increase apprehension of illegal migrants and disrupt human smuggling operations. This operation also pursues joint investigations and aggressive prosecution against human smugglers.

It is difficult to gauge the success of these border enforcement efforts. Although the number of apprehensions is a questionable measure of the effectiveness of border hardening initiatives, there are other corroborative indicators. One indicator is the number of illegal migrants who rely on smugglers to cross into the United States, and the other reflects changes in pricing for smuggling services.[27] There is a greater reliance on human smugglers to assist in illegal entry, and the prices have gone up for most smuggling services. On both measures, the trend has moved upward significantly as U.S. border control measures have been implemented. The rate of migrants using smugglers to cross into the United States was most pronounced, and it had already reached about 95 percent around 1996.[28]

Deaths in the Desert

The significant buildup at the targeted sectors of the U.S. southern border since the early 1990s also proved to be deadly to many migrants. A displacement effect has occurred. Like an unyielding river, the influx of illegal migrants has simply found other paths to continue the flow across the border. First illegal migrants moved to the east, just far enough away from the busy San Diego crossings to cross at the Otay Mountains. As the border reinforcement intensified in late 1990s, illegal migrants moved even farther east to cross the mountains of Tecate. By the end of 1990s, as more border sections were reinforced by Operation Gatekeeper in California and Operation Hold the Line in Texas, the flow of illegal migrants was diverted toward the Arizona desert.

Thousands have perished since the early 1990s as a result of exposure to extreme temperatures while trying to cross into the United States, particularly during the blistering summer. In 2005, more than four hundred illegal migrants died, mostly from heat-related causes. More than half of the bodies were found in the deserts of southern Arizona.[29] Since the Border Patrol started keeping records of migrant deaths in 1998, deaths due to exposure have averaged in the hundreds each year. As of May 2006, the U.S. Border Patrol had recorded a total of 2,881 migrant deaths.[30]

Another report estimates that as many as 3,500 people have died crossing the Southwest border illegally since January 1995.[31] This figure represents the body count from the U.S. side alone, because Mexican authorities do not keep a record of migrant deaths along the border. In the summer of 2005, the situation became so bad in Pima, Arizona, that the county coroner had to rent a refrigerated truck to store the bodies found in the desert because its facility had run out of space.[32] The corpses were waiting to be identified, autopsied, and returned to Mexico. Although U.S. authorities share information about the unidentified bodies found in the desert, such as personal items, fingerprints, and DNA samples, with their Mexican counterparts in the hope of locating family members, about 30 percent of the victims are never identified.[33]

In the face of increasing deaths of illegal migrants in the desert, the U.S. government initiated the Border Safety Initiative Program in 1998, in cooperation with the Mexican government, to provide emergency medical training for agents and initiate rescue patrols in remote areas, particularly during summer. Public announcements and advertisements were posted in Mexico and Central America warning migrants of the dire consequences of crossing the desert. These efforts were intensified in 2003, as the number of deaths rose sharply and condemnations by migrant rights organizations mounted.[34]

Operation Desert Safeguard was launched to deploy tactical units to search and rescue migrants along the "West Desert Corridor"—the stretch of Sonoran Desert that extends from Mexico's State of Sonora into the State of Arizona.[35] As part of the operation, 150 more agents were assigned to patrol duties in the desert corridor. To strengthen mobile tactical units for search and rescue activities, all-terrain Hummer vehicles were retrofitted specifically for desert operations, and a new horse patrol unit was added. Aerial surveillance was also increased in the region. A total of twenty search and rescue beacons were placed in high-risk areas that would alert Border Patrol Communication Center when activated by stranded migrants.

Migrant rights groups also put up rescue stations to provide water, food, and other emergency services to stranded migrants. Hundreds of thousands of water jugs are left at places likely to be crossed by migrants. These efforts prompted ridicule from critics, who declared that these about-face measures would do nothing to curtail the flow of illegal immigrants. Conservative writer Michelle Malkin even suggested, sarcastically, that in addition to water and food, pillows with mints be handed out to illegal immigrants at the border.[36] The much-traveled Sonoran Desert, much of it supposedly protected as natural reserve, is now littered with plastic water jugs, food wrappings, soiled clothing, feces, and other garbage discarded by illegal immigrants.

Critics of border enforcement measures, however, argue that the primary result of these order measures has been increased danger and higher expense for border-crossing. The increased difficulties in crossing into the United States have forced migrants to turn to smugglers and other criminal organizations. Threats to personal safety have increased. As a result, illegal immigrants are more likely to stay in the United States, contributing to the rapid growth of an illegal population in the country.[37]

On the other hand, some researchers have questioned the actual impact of these border initiatives on migrant deaths. After extensive data collection and interviews with Border Patrol agents, medical examiners, funeral directors, law enforcement agents, undocumented migrants, and human rights advocates, researchers from the University of Houston could establish only a partial link between increases in transient deaths and the redirection of migrant flows to the Sonoran Deserts of Arizona and southeastern California and to the ranchlands of South Texas.[38]

Deaths due to exposure to extreme weather had been reported for years before these operations were initiated. In examining death records from both sides of the border, these researchers found that motor vehicle accidents and drowning were the leading causes of migrant deaths, neither of which was related to border enforcement activities. In fact, migrant deaths from drowning were more closely related to the water levels in the Rio Grande than to border enforcement activities. The protracted draught in the Rio Grande basin through most of the 1990s actually kept the number of drowning deaths low.[39] Migrant deaths caused by auto-pedestrian accidents and homicides along the border actually declined as the congested crossing points in San Diego were sealed.

HUMAN SMUGGLING BY SEA

Although the United States has much longer coastlines than land borders, human smuggling by maritime means is far less prevalent than border crossings overland. There are similarities as well as differences between these two methods of transportation in the smuggling business. Similar to illegal border crossing, migrants participating in maritime operations appear to do little preparation. When migrants decide to work with a particular smuggler, they typically wait to be notified of the time and location to meet. No travel documents are needed because most maritime smuggling involves illegal landings in Canada, Mexico, various South American countries, and peripheral U.S. territories where border authorities are sparsely situated or nonexistent.

Maritime smuggling, though popular from the late 1980s to mid-1990s and favored by the Chinese smuggling organizations, has many limitations because of the inherent logistical challenges. In comparison to other methods of transportation, maritime smugglers often require large numbers of clients to fill the space to make it worth their while. Multiple networks of smugglers and recruiters may have to work together to gather enough clients to make the investment worthwhile.

Unlike climbing over border fences or trekking across the desert in Arizona, maritime smuggling requires greater organizational skills and financial resources. Securing vessels and preparing for extended journeys on open seas often requires months of planning, coordinating, and financing that few entrepreneurs have the means or organizational structure to undertake individually. Maritime smugglers maximize their profits by filling a boat to its capacity, and they do not always have the time to carefully screen their clients before letting them get onboard. Therefore some immigrants without adequate financial means have managed to stow away. Stories of torture and beatings have been widely reported by illegal immigrants who could not make payment upon arrival.

Maritime smuggling also poses many technical challenges. Unless human smugglers themselves are sailors, engineers, navigators, or captains, they must have enough money to hire the necessary professionals. Therefore, to make an operation financially worthwhile, a smuggling organization must find enough fee-paying clients to more than pay for the cost. That is no easy task, as recruiters most often rely on personal networks. As recruitment activities increase, so does the possible exposure of the clandestine operation to law enforcement agencies. In comparison, land-based smuggling activities require minimal investment and are much easier to carry out.

Still, maritime smuggling remains a lucrative enterprise. With more than 90,000 miles in total shoreline, the commercial and recreational activities inside and around the U.S. marine territories are almost impossible to monitor. Because of geographical proximity, human smuggling through seafaring takes place frequently between Cuba and the southern tip of Florida. In early April 2006, three smugglers were fired upon by the Cuban coast guard while navigating their forty-foot U.S.-registered speedboat near the coastal province of Pinar del Rio.[40] There were thirty-nine Cuban migrants onboard the smuggling vessel. The smugglers reportedly refused to heed orders and rammed the Cuban coast guard boat. One smuggler was killed and another injured. Cuban government officials claimed that the speedboat had been used numerous times in past smuggling trips. Because the water between Cuba and Miami is heavily patrolled, Cuban migrants often opt for a much longer journey by entering Mexico first and then crossing overland into the United States.[41] The preferential refugee policy toward Cubans who land on U.S. soil also encourages such a transportation method. If Cubans are caught on waterways by the U.S. Coast Guard, they are usually returned to Cuba immediately.

The majority of maritime smuggling operations that caught the attention of authorities have involved barely seaworthy vessels carrying migrants hidden under the deck in deplorable conditions. However, a few smugglers, working under the assumption that the rich and wealthy are rarely bothered by the U.S. Coast Guard, have used expensive yachts to transport their clients. Like car rental companies, yacht rental businesses do not verify the intended use of their patrons. Human smugglers can easily cloak their activities with an aura of wealth and leisure. In one such case, two men leased a luxury forty-four-foot sailboat in late August 2004 in Los Angeles Harbor and headed to Ensenada, a port city in Baja California, Mexico, for a daylong trip. The boat rental agency had no idea that these two men, one from Florida and one from Southern California, were going to use the yacht for a smuggling operation.

Private yachts operated by U.S. citizens are rarely boarded and searched by the Coast Guard. However, as the French-built luxury yacht approached the Angels Gate entrance to the Los Angeles Harbor under the cover of the night, three Coast Guard boats appeared. Homeland Security officers boarded the vessel and discovered fifty Mexican nationals, including women and children, crammed into the vessel's small cabin designed to sleep eight people.[42] The yacht was escorted away to the nearby Coast Guard station where the sailors and the illegal migrants were detained. Authorities later learned that the illegal migrants paid $3,000 each for the trip. The main conspirator, forty-two-year-old Craig Lightner from San Pedro (south of Los Angeles), had previously been caught smuggling migrants as well as protected tropical fish from Mexico.[43]

Maritime Smuggling by Chinese Snakeheads

Of all human smugglers who engage in maritime smuggling operations, none rival the scale and sophistication of Chinese snakeheads that have attracted worldwide attention with their daring operations. Illegal Chinese immigration to the United States through maritime routes began 150 years ago. Trans-Pacific steamships brought loads of cheap laborers from southern China to the U.S. West Coast to work in such diverse sectors of the fledging economy as railroad construction, cooking, laundering, farming, tide-land draining, and mining. Chinese "coolies" soon drew hostility from European immigrants and were blamed for a host of social problems from decreased wages to unemployment. The anti-Chinese sentiment spread quickly and ultimately led to the passage of the Chinese Exclusion Act in 1882 by Congress, the first American immigration law targeted at a particular group of people based on their race.[44]

The legislation barring Chinese immigrants from entering the country also brought about the enterprise of human smuggling. Except for a few exempt classes (e.g., merchants, diplomats, or children of U.S. citizens), ordinary Chinese nationals must rely on illegal channels to enter the United States. By exploiting legal loopholes and official corruption, Chinese smugglers were able to devise strategies to circumvent regulatory restrictions imposed by the exclusion laws, and they effectively became the first entrepreneurs in transnational human smuggling. It should be noted that, although the Chinese may have been the first to devise maritime smuggling operations, by the early 1900s, many more immigrants from other countries chose land borders as an alternative to immigration inspections at American seaports.[45] Syrians, Greeks, Hungarians, Russian Jews, Italians, and some "maidens" from France, Belgium, and Spain were the main groups entering through Canada and Mexico.

Of the many schemes that enabled early Chinese migrants to board the trans-Pacific steamships, the most well-known was the "slot racket" or "paper son" scheme.[46] In this scheme, Chinese migrants posed as the sons of U.S. citizens by native birth. Because early Chinese settlers often returned to China to get married or sent their American-born children back to home villages to be raised, these so-called "derivative citizens" were allowed to return to the United States. Their citizenship papers became a hot commodity. The "paper son" scheme hit an all-time high in 1906 when the earthquake and ensuing fire in San Francisco destroyed most government buildings along with birth certificates and citizenship papers. The loss of official records gave thousands the opportunity to launch successful claims to citizenship or declare they had sons or wives in China eligible to immigrate. Thousands were granted citizenship, which generated more immigration papers for sale on the black market.

Modern-day human smuggling from China to the United States started in the early 1980s shortly after the two countries resumed diplomatic relations. Nearly all smuggling activities were through sea routes. Many of the illegal immigrants came to America, either as stowaways or as crews working on ocean freighters. By the early 1990s, idle fishing trawlers and cargo freighters in Taiwan were recruited to transport illegal immigrants with hundreds crammed beneath the deck. Criminal organizations from Taiwan have been implicated in many of these maritime smuggling operations.[47] Stories began to appear in newspapers in the early 1990s about suspicious boats unloading people on the shoreline along the Pacific coast. It was reported that at the height of maritime smuggling activities in the early 1990s, as many as twenty-five ships with thousands of illegal immigrants sailed to the United States in one month.[48]

Maritime smuggling proceeds through several stages. First, recruiters need to find clients, typically through friends and relatives, whereas other smugglers need to hire small boats for ferrying clients to the mother ship. Then the mother ship, often a fishing trawler or a freight boat, must be leased and stocked with supplies. Still other snakeheads work to coordinate the overland transportation needed to get their clients to the loading points at the shoreline. One maritime smuggler in Fuzhou, China, said that there are many things to consider when transporting clients on boats. He claimed to have undertaken many tasks in maritime operations, including leasing boats, hiring crew, and stocking supplies:

> When looking for a boat to lease, I have to consider such issues as how much space there is, the fuel capacity, and where to find a captain experienced enough to navigate to the U.S. I have to find engineers and other experienced and responsible crew. Even the musclemen on board must be able to control the crowd and prevent riots from breaking out. There are many headaches during a trip, such as mechanical problems or shortages of water or food onboard. I can get supplies from other countries or get a different boat. My biggest worry is when the ship loses communication with people on the mainland.

In most cases, maritime smugglers pick up multiple groups of clients in several locations along the coast. Recruiters working in different locations typically know little about who else is contributing to the boatload. They know only that their clients are heading for the United States, and that they are responsible for bringing them to a seaport. One advantage of smuggling by boat is that no documents of any sort are needed.

U.S. authorities believe that Chinatown gangs and other criminal organizations are playing a major role in transnational human smuggling. Although researchers are still debating the extent of involvement by traditional Chinese criminal organizations, it is generally agreed that gangsters are frequently hired to maintain order on smuggling vessels. Occasionally human smugglers may give discounts to a few migrants to act as musclemen. Order maintenance during playtime and mealtime becomes a vital role in carrying out maritime smuggling operations. This is particularly the case when the journey is prolonged for unanticipated reasons (e.g., mechanical problems and bad weather), and water and food must be rationed.

The involvement of gangsters also solves another headache for human smugglers—payment collections. It is particularly a problem for maritime smugglers because of the large number of migrants. Many migrants either lie about their financial resources or make only partial payments to get on board. In some cases, because snakeheads are in a hurry to fill the boat, many board with nothing more than a promise to pay upon arrival. As clients default on their payments, snakeheads turn to street gangs in Chinatown for help. Hostage taking and torture ensue, as snakeheads are eager to collect their fees. It has become a standard practice in the smuggling business that all illegal migrants are held in safe houses upon arrival until all payments are made. As a result, stories of migrants being assaulted, tortured, and even killed have appeared frequently in the news media.

The most well-known smuggling incident was that of the *Golden Venture*. In early June 1993, a rickety smuggling vessel was deliberately beached in the Rockaways off Queens after the transfer boat failed to show up to ferry the illegal migrants to the shore. Gangsters onboard this Panama-registered freighter urged the 286 illegal immigrants to jump and swim to "freedom." Many did. Ten of them drowned. The *Golden Venture* incident in 1993 shocked the nation with televised images of undocumented Chinese immigrants wrapped in blankets walking in long lines under the watchful eyes of U.S. law enforcement officers. The nation was besieged by fears of massive waves of illegal immigrants from the world's most populous nation.

Changing Strategies by Chinese Maritime Smugglers

Maritime smuggling activities by Chinese snakeheads peaked around the mid-1990s and have declined since. By the early 2000s direct landings of illegal Chinese immigrants on U.S. mainland shores had become rare. Increased surveillance and interception on the open seas appear to have significantly reduced the success rates of sea-based operations. The U.S. government has learned, albeit slowly, to improve intelligence gathering in overseas posts and to deploy patrols strategically over targeted waters. Some even suggest that the U.S. government has enlisted high-tech underwater listening devices that were designed during the Cold War to track Soviet submarines to monitor the movements of all suspicious ships heading towards the United States.[49]

The hardship on the smuggling ship and the perils of the rough seas have also dampened enthusiasm among prospective clients. Even in villages where throngs of individuals eagerly await a chance to leave, few express a desire to get on a boat and live underneath the deck for weeks. Those who have been smuggled by boat to the United States often tell their bitter experiences that discourage others from following in their footsteps. One low-level smuggling operative in China relayed some of the horror stories he heard:[50]

> A friend of mine told me that his son was deceived by a snakehead. Before the trip, the snakehead told him that there would only be a dozen or so clients on the boat and that the boat was well-equipped and stocked with lots of supplies. In reality, more than one hundred people were crammed into the boat, and they had little to eat or drink. The crewmen were physically abusive to the clients.

Nonetheless, the sea route has not been abandoned entirely by human smugglers, but the seafaring strategies have changed. Human smugglers now drop their clients at peripheral locations such as U.S. territories in the

Pacific or Mexico or Canada, hoping to gain entrance through a series of land-and-ocean relays. Toward the end of the 1990s and the early 2000s, scores of smuggling ships were intercepted off the waters of Guam and the U.S. Virgin Islands, where hundreds of illegal Chinese migrants were detained and repatriated. In August 1999, about 130 illegal Chinese immigrants landed at the southern tip of the Queen Charlotte Islands, located on an isolated section of Canada's Pacific coast.[51] In the summer of 1999, Mexican authorities detained more than two hundred Chinese nationals in Ensenada, Baja California, after their safe house was reported to authorities by suspicious neighbors. Mexican immigration authorities admitted that Chinese smugglers often used Latin American countries to move clients overland through Mexico's southern border.[52]

Besides landing at neighboring countries or distant U.S. territories, Chinese snakeheads have found cargo containers to be an effective method of infiltrating U.S. border defenses. Cargo containers outfitted by snakeheads to transport illegal migrants began to attract attention at the beginning of 2000, when in a span of weeks hundreds of illegal immigrants were found at major ports along the West Coast, including Los Angeles and Long Beach, California, Seattle, Washington, and Vancouver, British Columbia.[53] This tactic was exemplified during the New Year's weekend of 2000 when twenty-five Chinese immigrants were found inside a container on a freighter docked at the Port of Vancouver, British Columbia.[54] The ship had left Hong Kong on December 20 and was heading for Seattle when it was diverted to Vancouver because of a port backlog in the United States.

Acting on a tip from U.S. authorities, Canadian Customs and Immigration agents searched the freighter and heard voices coming from one of hundreds of containers onboard. One day earlier, eighteen people had been found inside a container in Long Beach, California. On Christmas Day 1999, twenty-one illegal Chinese immigrants were detained at the Port of Long Beach after arriving on board a Danish cargo ship. Nine others at neighboring Los Angeles Harbor were also detained after arriving on Christmas Eve on board the MS Sine Maersk.[55] Later it was learned that the U.S.-based smugglers had failed to show up on time to pick up the container, and the illegal immigrants were tired of waiting and had decided to climb out on their own.

More recently, in early April 2006, twenty-two illegal Chinese immigrants were detained at the Port of Seattle after enduring a fifteen-day journey in a forty-foot container aboard the freighter Rotterdam from Shanghai.[56] The eighteen men and four women, all in their twenties and thirties, were crawling out of the container when they caught the attention of a security guard on patrol, who immediately notified the authorities.

These human cargo containers are typically equipped with car batteries to power lights, portable toilets, bottled water, canned food, cell phones, and mattresses. Because only a small percentage of containers are equipped with soft tops, which are typically stacked on the top, smugglers often have no control where their containers may be loaded in the cargo hold. Poor air circulation often causes the smuggled people to suffocate to death. In January 2000, three of eighteen illegal Chinese migrants were found dead inside a container on a freighter that arrived in Seattle from Hong Kong.[57]

Each year millions of containers arrive at U.S. ports on both sides of the continent. Fewer than 5 percent of the containers are inspected. Homeland Security officials admitted that without intelligence or operational mistakes by smugglers, chances are slim for any illegal immigrants arriving in containers to be caught.[58] Nearly all human smuggling cases involving cargo containers have thus far been instigated by Chinese snakeheads. Most customs and immigration officials in the United States and Canada do not believe the shipping companies were knowingly involved in the smuggling operations.

SMUGGLING BY AIR

In August 2004 a Cuban woman shipped herself by hiding in a wooden crate in a DHL cargo plane that flew from the Bahamas to Miami International Airport.[59] In March 2004 a man arrived in Miami from the Dominican Republic by hiding in the wheel well of an American Airlines jet.[60] Daring smuggling-by-air feats such as these are rare in the business of transnational human smuggling. The vast majority of migrants who travel by air typically use some form of documents that either allow them to enter the United States directly, such as on temporary visas, or permit them to make transfers in other countries.

Far less hazardous and arduous than riding fishing trawlers for weeks or trekking the desert for days, smuggling by air is the preferred choice of transportation for prospective migrants who have the connections and the money. It is by far the most sought-after method among prospective Chinese migrants. Smuggling by air can be viewed as a Siamese twin of the counterfeit document enterprise, a subject that is discussed in greater detail in Chapter 3. The following sections present some of the unique strategies that are found only in by-air smuggling activities.

Business Delegations

A common strategy to obtain legitimate travel documents is to create bone fide purposes for traveling to the United States or to a transit country. These travel purposes may be commercial, cultural, or for some other reasons. Such business or otherwise official delegations are typically initiated by legitimate corporations or public entities, but the identities of the delegates do not always match the real individuals. In the hands of low-level government bureaucrats and business managers, prospective migrants can be transformed into various official positions on the company roster and become formal members of the delegation. In some cases, companies with legitimate businesses in the United States knowingly place would-be migrants into their delegations, either to make money, to help pay their own expenses, or both.

In one such case, a twelve-year-old Chinese girl, who was supposedly attending a youth camp in Alabama, disappeared soon after she arrived at the San Francisco International Airport. A massive search ensued. The California state law enforcement agency even issued an Amber alert on illuminated highway signs, notifying all motorists of a possible kidnapping. The girl was later found at her relatives' residence on the East Coast.[61] According to the summer camp organizers, as a precaution against possible defections, participants in this program all signed an affidavit proclaiming that they had neither relatives nor intention to defect in the United States. The smuggler in this case was able to work through the organizing agency in Beijing to get the girl on the roster while planning and coordinating transfer details with her relatives in the United States.

In comparison to maritime or land-based smuggling activities, the air route involves elaborate preparations and training procedures to ensure that migrants can interact properly with immigration officials. Migrants who use either forged or fraudulently obtained travel documents must be prepared to answer questions pertaining to their identity and occupation. Almost all smugglers who use air routes must prepare their clients before departure. Predeparture training can be as elaborate and complicated as learning about a company (for which the delegation is formed) or as simple as memorizing the basic biographical information printed on the passport. In many cases, clients must also learn a few English words to appear educated. Some even involve mock interviews and rehearsals. One female snakehead in China sent her clients to Chengdu (the capital city of Sichuan Province), where they would be included in legitimate business delegations. Predeparture training was mandatory, as she explained:[62]

> Before departure, all my clients must learn about the companies that organize the delegations and their "official" positions. For instance, one client was assigned to an accounting position in a delegation. He had to learn about the company's profit and loss profiles and staffing and payroll structures. All my clients must also learn the provincial vital statistics such as the leaders of the province, the population, major geographical locations, and agricultural products. There is a lot to learn. That is why I screen my clients carefully and make sure they can learn these things and be able to respond to questions at the airport.

Transactions at the Airport

By-air smuggling often involves complex and well-timed sequences of events and transactions in which different players (e.g., smugglers, corrupt officials, and their clients) come together to complete the intended journey. Unlike smuggling overland or by sea, the air route is the most risky method in terms of being caught because of the tight security at most international airports. Although inspections at some airports are tighter than at others, human smugglers must work with their existing resources and determine where their clients can depart. As a result, a few strategies have been devised to move clients through the airport checkpoints.

Takeoff-Only Smuggling Operations

Of all assets a smuggler has, few can beat the value of a corrupt official at an international airport checkpoint. Corrupt officials are particularly useful when illegal migrants travel with forged documents that cannot pass any careful examination. In the context of Chinese human smuggling, a practice called "takeoff-only operations," has emerged as a strategy to protect both the corrupt security official and the snakehead. In these cases, the snakeheads make it clear to their clients that their forged documents will most likely be caught at the U.S. port of entry. During the flight, the illegal migrants will destroy all their identification papers and flush them down the toilet. Upon arrival at a U.S. airport, the smugglees promptly demand political asylum, citing religious persecution, forced abortion, or some other causes. Depending on how they tell their stories, many illegal Chinese migrants detained at the U.S. port of entry are afforded an opportunity to appear in front of a federal judge, at which time they often become eligible for bail while waiting for the outcome of their asylum applications. Meanwhile, they can work and send money home, or simply disappear into the vast underground economy. One Chinese snakehead explained how he did his "takeoff-only operations":[63]

> I know who is on duty on the day my client leaves and at which inspection booth. I will stand in the back and watch my client approach the specified counter. The officer in the inspection booth sometimes knows the names of the clients, while at other times he will see me standing in the distance. All parties in this scheme know what to do, and no instructions are needed. The inspector will take a cursory look at the travel document and let my client pass. As soon as the airplane takes off, the entire smuggling fee will also be settled immediately. In this scheme, all parties involved are fully aware that the travel document will likely be

caught at the U.S. immigration control. My clients often destroy their passports and flush them down the toilet, then surrender to U.S. officials upon arrival and request political asylum. Some clients may try their luck with falsified passports and see if they get through U.S. immigration.

Boarding Pass Swapping

Switching boarding passes and passports has been a major smuggling strategy for decades. For most of civil aviation history, once passengers pass the security and enter the waiting area, they need only a boarding pass to board the plane. It is in the waiting area that travel documents and boarding passes are switched to allow the would-be migrants to head to their intended destinations.

Although there are variations in this scheme, the basics are the same. For example, two smuggling escorts with legitimate travel documents arrive in Hong Kong from Taipei on their way to the United States. In the meantime, their two clients from mainland China also arrive in Hong Kong on their way to Vietnam. While waiting for their connecting flights, these two pairs swap their documents and assume each other's identity. The two clients heading to the United States have already been prepared to assume the identities and will mail the passports back to their facilitators.

In response to increased human smuggling activities, and particularly after the September 11 events, most U.S.-bound airlines now double-check passports against boarding passes at the gate before boarding. However, one can still find many flights heading to the United States that do not require passengers to undergo a careful verification process. Even with a second passport inspection at the gate, smugglees can still use the photo substitution scheme to pass untrained eyes. When passengers line up to board the plane, most airline staff have neither the time nor the proper training to thoroughly inspect travel documents or interrogate possible imposters.

In summary, there are three basic strategies to transport illegal migrants into the United States. One is to travel to Mexico or Canada by some means and then illegally cross the border into the United States. A second strategy is to transport migrants as stowaways in fishing trawlers, freighters, luxury yachts, or cargo containers to reach a U.S. port or unguarded shoreline. A third strategy is to fly into the United States, either directly or through transit countries.

Human smugglers often employ a combination of these methods. Of the three methods, smuggling by air remains the most desirable because of its expedience. Migrants smuggled by air typically have fraudulent documents to allow them to board commercial airliners. In the world of transnational human smuggling, brokers who specialize in by-air transportation methods are considered the elite. Relying on well-established social networks and corrupt officials in different transit countries, these smugglers charge premium prices to blend their clients into the stream of commercial travelers and reach destination countries through official checkpoints. The sea route and illegal border crossing are for the masses, but most human smugglers employ a combination of methods to deliver their clients into the United States.

Chapter 5

Sister Ping—The Snakehead Queen[1]

Few human smugglers, male or female, have ever ascended to the height and notoriety in this business enjoyed by Cheng Chui Ping, known to most in the Chinese smuggling community as Sister Ping. Stories are mixed about what kind of person Sister Ping was. To U.S. law enforcement agencies, she was a ruthless, underworld mafia-type boss in New York's Chinatown, the "Mother of all snakeheads," and a cut-throat underground banker. But to her clients and many Chinese human smugglers who claimed to know her, she was thought of as almost a goddess who helped her fellow villagers in and around her hometown seek a better life in America, looked after her clients' welfare, charged fair prices, and loaned money to her clients with generous terms. She was affectionately called *Yi-Ping-Jie* (or Big Sister Ping) both in her hometown in Fujian Province, southeast China, and in New York's Chinese community.

For more than a decade, Cheng ran a variety of successful rackets, eluded law enforcement agencies, and beat the U.S. justice system. Her many exploits became legendary. Her reputation loomed so big in the Chinese smuggling community that many snakeheads in the United States or China claimed to be her associates or to work in her network. These claims, most of which were simply bogus, were nothing more than a scheme to boost the snakeheads' otherwise obscure statuses in order to attract clients or to charge higher fees. Sister Ping's saga finally came to an end when a multinational manhunt ended in her arrest in Hong Kong in 2000. On March 16, 2006, she was sentenced in a federal court in New York to thirty-five years on charges of conspiring to commit alien smuggling, hostage taking, money laundering, and laundering ransom money.[2]

HER ENTRY INTO THE SMUGGLING BUSINESS

The exact circumstance of how Sister Ping entered the United States have remained a myth. According to snakeheads who claimed to know her, she was at one time an illegal alien herself, entering the United States with the help of fraudulent documents. According to a *Time* magazine investigative report, she first entered Hong Kong from mainland China and then the United States in 1981, and she somehow obtained naturalization papers.[3] Perhaps as a result of her own experience, she realized the enormous potential in developing a business of assisting others to come to the United States. She was well ahead of most other Chinese human smugglers in this business. Sister Ping began smuggling Chinese immigrants in the early 1980s, among the first few people who knew how to organize smuggling operations. Her reputation was established long before the U.S. government became aware of such activities. Her early clients were mostly relatives and villagers from her hometown in Shengmei in coastal Fujian Province.

During the early days, she would personally travel back to her hometown, recruiting and coordinating smuggling operations. She used a combination of by-air and by-land routes to transport her clients first to Canada by using fraudulent documents and then across the border into the United States. Hong Kong was often used as a transit point. With the help of corrupt officials in China, she was able to obtain entry and exit permits for her clients. As her business grew, she established additional smuggling routes through Mexico, Belize, and other Central American nations.

After she had a few successful operations, stories of her clients made their way back to Shengmei and nearby townships. Villagers came looking for her. What Sister Ping and other early snakeheads started in the early 1980s has become a unique transnational migration phenomenon. For more than a decade before the mid-1990s, the vast majority of illegal Chinese immigrants came from a highly concentrated geographical region surrounding Sister Ping's hometown. This region comprises Fuzhou (the capital city of Fujian Province) and its adjacent three coastal counties—Changle, Lianjiang, and Fuqing. People of this region share the same dialect and customs. A few pioneers, such as Sister Ping and those before her, settled in New York's Chinatown. That was all that was needed to turn the flow of transnational migration from a trickle into a flood. Tens of thousands of illegal immigrants crowded onto rickety fishing trawlers and freight boats, hid inside shipping containers, and boarded commercial airliners with fraudulent travel documents to join the stream of trans-Pacific migration.

As illegal immigrants settled in New York's Chinatown and elsewhere, they pooled their resources and sent for other members of their families. The crackdown on the student-led democracy movement in Tiananmen Square in 1989, which cast a long shadow over China's political landscape, further spurred outward migration. President Bush senior, issued an executive order in April 1990, providing temporary refuge status to all Chinese nationals then living in the United States legally or illegally. The intent was to protect the tens of thousands of students enrolled in various American universities on temporary student and scholar visas. At the sponsorship and advocacy of U.S. representative Nancy Pelosi, Congress passed the Chinese Student Protection Act of 1992, which made the temporary status permanent. The amnesty became a godsend to all illegal Chinese immigrants who had used false papers to become students or who claimed to have participated in antigovernment or prodemocracy activities. The human smuggling business boomed, as thousands more tried to get into the country to take advantage of the amnesty.

By now Sister Ping's business had moved beyond just transporting small groups of aliens into the United States from Canada. Her network had expanded into specializing in maritime operations. Estimates vary as to how big her operation had become at the pinnacle of her smuggling career. Some claimed that she was transporting hundreds in each operation by boats. Sister Ping also gained the reputation of being a generous and fair-minded business person. Because maritime operations typically moved large numbers of migrants, many migrants could not find enough money for the journey. Sister Ping would charge a small down payment, allowing her clients to pay her back in installments, a rare practice by most other snakeheads. She even helped her clients to find jobs in Chinese restaurants and garment factories.

During the early years, she and other smugglers typically charged $18,000 to smuggle a person to America, a figure that had become so widely known in the sending communities of Fujian that it became a prefix to people who made the journey. At the peak of smuggling activities in the early to mid-1990s, the term *wan-ba-sao* (which literarily translates "wives *of the $18,000ers*") was coined in the region where Sister Ping was from to describe a class of women whose husbands had been smuggled out of the country for a fee of $18,000. These women stayed behind looking after the old and rearing the young, living off the remittances sent by their husbands. There were so many of these women in the region that a male-prostitute industry emerged to cater to them. The term is still used today in reference to married women with overseas husbands who are on the lookout for sexual adventures.

At the height of her operations, Sister Ping owned restaurants, a clothing store, and real estate in Chinatown, as well as apartments in Hong Kong, and a farm in South Africa.[4] The U.S. government estimated that, for more than a decade, Sister Ping smuggled as many as three thousand illegal immigrants from her native China into the United States, amassing more than $40 million from her smuggling business.[5] In the Fujianese community, Sister Ping was reportedly generous to her fellow countrymen in need of help and even offered to pay compensation and smuggle free of charge next of kin in the family should any of her clients die during the journey to the United States.[6] Despite the enormous profits Sister Ping supposedly had made, she was often seen driving an old American car, wearing plain clothes, and appearing humble in her demeanor. People who visited her variety store across the street from the Bank of China in New York's Chinatown saw her tending to her customers with smiles and kindness.

THE BANK OF SISTER PING

For years she was atop the list of big snakeheads tracked by the U.S. immigration agents, but her trouble with the U.S. government was not limited to human smuggling. She was also running a large money laundering business. Although often overshadowed by her reputation as the "Mother of all snakeheads," people close to her claimed that Sister Ping was far more successful at underground banking than at any of her other business ventures. Several snakeheads in China even questioned her actual capability. One snakehead in Fuzhou said the following:

> Sister Ping got in the smuggling business early and her reputation was greater than her actual ability. She was successful for a while in the early 1990s, but her days are long gone. I know people in Fuzhou who are far more successful than Sister Ping. She is probably better known for her underground banking business than for human smuggling.

She may have made some money from a few successful smuggling operations, but her underground banking business provided her a steady stream of income that grew steadily as the illegal immigrant population grew in New York. Her entry into the underground banking business, though fortuitous, was perfect in timing. As soon as illegal immigrants settle into a job, their immediate concern is to find a way to send money home. The remittance is first used to repay the smuggling debt and then to support other family members left behind. This is no easy task because illegal immigrants cannot access mainstream banking institutions. Even for legal immigrants, conventional banks are slow and expensive for the many small amounts of money they send home. In the late 1980s the demand for underground banking services exploded as the newly arrived immigrants settled in and wanted to send money home to pay smuggling debts and sponsor other family members for the journey.

According to her associates, Sister Ping largely pulled out of human smuggling activities after having a few run-ins with the law in the early 1990s. She had served prison sentences and even agreed to work with federal investigators as an informant. Instead she directed most of her attention to underground banking, using connections already established from her previous smuggling ventures to send money home for her clients. Her reliable and timely money transferring operation quickly won her more clients. The underground banking also proved to be a much more stable source of income for her because sending money home was the most common service that undocumented migrants wanted.

Much of the transmitting was done in so-called "mirror" transfers, in which she took in the money in the United States and placed a call to instruct her partner in China to deliver the money, either in U.S. dollars or Chinese yuan to her clients' families. When individuals and even legitimate businesses wanted to send money to the United States, the process was reversed. No money was physically transmitted. This practice continues today in many overseas Chinese communities. With so much money remitted to China each year, it has become commonplace for families in migrant-sending communities in China to hold large sums of foreign currency, which in turn serves as the backbone of this underground banking system.

By most accounts Sister Ping was regarded as an efficient and reliable underground banker. People who used her service had nothing but praise for her. As her reputation grew in the Fujianese community, she needed no advertisement. Both smugglers and illegal immigrants used her banking service to send money home or to finance smuggling operations. Her fees and exchange terms were always superior to those offered by legitimate banks. Unlike the Bank of China in the early years, which forced customers to convert their U.S. dollars into Chinese currency at official rates, Sister Ping's clients had a choice of receiving their remittances either in dollars or in Chinese yuan with a much more favorable exchange rate. For many years she was said to have drained business from Bank of China's branch located in New York's Chinatown.

Although "mirror" transfers usually balance themselves out on both sides of the Pacific, there are times when couriers have to be used to carry large sums of cash (mostly dollars) in person. These carriers are mostly underground bankers themselves. In the early 1990s, while visiting her hometown, Sister Ping was once caught carrying more than $100,000 in cash. She was able to bribe her way out of police detention and subsequently disappeared.

Although Sister Ping was officially charged with engaging in and financing maritime smuggling operations, many snakeheads and people who claimed to know her suspected that she was likely involved in lending money to would-be migrants to finance their journeys. As she gained status in the immigrant community, snakeheads and clients alike turned to her for payment assurance. Would-be migrants or their families in China would borrow money from her, whereas smugglers would count on her to vouch for her clients. She in turn collected smuggling fees from clients and their families. In an environment where business transactions are neither legally recognized nor protected, her banking business served a vital role in facilitating the transactions of all parties involved. She also made untold millions along the way.

SISTER PING AND CHINATOWN GANGS

The U.S. government suspected that Sister Ping continued to smuggle Chinese immigrants while she purported to be cooperating with the FBI.[7] She used her illegal proceeds to finance the purchase of smuggling vessels and used gang members to transport and guard her clients. The involvement of gangsters ensured that she would have no payment problems. She was believed to have joined hands with the Fuk Ching gang in New York's Chinatown to hold illegal immigrants hostage and to extort smuggling fees from delinquent clients. The gang, headed by Gu Liang-chi (a.k.a. Ah Kay), was made up mostly of youths from Fujian Province. Their shared cultural identity and linguistic heritage supposedly forged a cozy working relationship between the snakehead queen and her musclemen. Sister Ping's relationship with Fuk Ching culminated in their collective involvement in the smuggling operation of the ill-fated rust bucket, the *Golden Venture*. The freighter was deliberately beached in the Rockaways off Queens in June 1993 after the transfer boat failed to show up to ferry the illegal immigrants ashore. Gangsters onboard urged some three hundred illegal immigrants to jump off the ship and swim to "freedom." Many did. Ten of them drowned. It was a watershed event that awakened the United States to the horrors of the human trade.

Although Chinese snakeheads have been known to use gangsters to extort payments, many still believe Sister Ping's affiliation with street gangs was tenuous at best. In the world of human smuggling, payment problems are generally rare and most illegal migrants pay their fees promptly. Violence is used only as a last resort to extract payment, and the job is usually contracted out to gangsters. By and large, the Chinese snakeheads avoid entanglement with criminal organizations and street gangs. It does not help their business or reputation if they are known to be affiliated with gangsters in the Chinese community. Sister Ping claimed to be a victim herself, trying hard to appease gangsters by paying them protection fees. According to many sources in the smuggling community, Sister Ping was known for her concerns over her clients' safety and travel conditions. She demanded that her underlings and affiliated street gangsters not mistreat her clients because they were her customers just as those who ate at her restaurant. A male snakehead in New York gave his impression of Sister Ping:

> People in the community don't consider Sister Ping a criminal. In fact she is highly regarded, because she has never used force to collect smuggling fees. Some of her clients who could not come up with the balance, were set free to work. She allowed these people to work first and pay her later. Not only that, she's known for her humbleness and generosity. Whenever she invited people to dinner or lunch, she would make sure everybody ate well. She would rarely eat herself, but busy herself with serving her guests.

Contrary to these claims from New York's Chinese community, testimonies from members of the Fuk Ching gang detained by the authorities led federal investigators to Sister Ping and confirmed her role in the *Golden Venture* incident.

THE FALL OF THE SNAKEHEAD QUEEN

Sister Ping was no stranger to the U.S. justice system. Both she and her husband had been arrested before for human smuggling activities. She was on regular surveillance lists in Canada, the United States, and Hong Kong.[8] Although indicted after the *Golden Venture* incident on smuggling and money-laundering charges, Sister Ping had been able to evade authorities for years by hiding in her native Shengmei village. Although U.S. law enforcement agencies believed that Sister Ping continued to run her smuggling operations from her village house, many in the smuggling community believed it was probably her previous associates who were running their own smuggling businesses under her name.

Like so many other well-known fugitives, such as Pablo Escobar, the drug kingpin of Medellin's Cali Cartel, who gave out his location by talking to his son for a few seconds too long, Sister Ping finally made the same mistake of exposing her own Achilles's Heel. While she was in hiding in her home village, her son and husband continued to live in the United States and traveled to China on occasions. In April 2000 Sister Ping ventured out to see her son off at the Hong Kong's Chek Lap Kok airport as he was returning to the United States. She did not realize that her son was being watched. With the help of Hong Kong's drug enforcement police, with which the U.S. Drug Enforcement Agency maintains a close relationship, Sister Ping was detained at the airport. At the time of her arrest she was holding three different passports: one from Hong Kong, one from the United States, and one from Belize. Authorities later determined that Sister Ping had managed to make several visits back to the United States under different identities.

She fought extradition for three years while being held by the Hong Kong authorities, hoping her wealth and official connections would somehow save her. In the end, none panned out. Hong Kong Chief Executive Tung Chee-hwa signed her extradition orders to the United States. For such a high profile case, many believed that the extradition received tacit approval from Beijing. Although her lavish spending and donations to local charities had fended off law enforcement inquiries in China, none of her official contacts could save her from the extradition order. In July 2003 she was handed over to U.S. authorities for trial.

The case of Sister Ping is a complex one. Some revered her while others considered her a monster. By all official accounts, she single-handedly built a smuggling empire stretching to different parts of the world. However, empirical research has consistently shown that smuggling operations are mostly run by loosely affiliated entrepreneurs who pool resources and form temporary alliances. It is unlikely that Sister Ping, a woman who had received little formal education and who spoke few words of English, was capable of building a global smuggling network. However, her ascent to prominence in the smuggling business had its own unique set of reasons.

Female snakeheads are not uncommon in Chinese human smuggling activities. Some of these women have come to personify the audacity and scope of illegal Chinese migration to the United States and other Western countries. Most highly regarded snakeheads in North America and Europe, so far as the law enforcement agencies and the news media are concerned, have turned out to be female. Research has shown that gendered cultural expectations have afforded female snakeheads unique opportunities in the human smuggling business. Because female snakeheads are generally considered more reliable and trustworthy, they are often preferred by would-be migrants. This preference for female snakeheads is more than a simple reflection of the general Chinese expectations of gendered roles and responsibilities in social interactions. It is also the product of the collective knowledge of many illegal immigrants who have experienced the differences in the ways male and female snakeheads handle their clients. In a business full of uncertainties and hazards, gendered cultural expectations and a few fortuitous successful operations seemed to have catapulted Sister Ping into a venerable position in the Chinese smuggling community.

Chapter 6

The Enterprise and Organization of Human Smuggling

Human smuggling is essentially an underground travel business that involves arranging and coordinating logistics to transport fee-paying customers to their destinations. The mindset of a human smuggler is not much different from that of those who sell knock-off Rolex watches or Louis Vuitton handbags. Their goal is to make money. Although their activities are often portrayed as clandestine, most of their services are often provided in the open.

Thanks to increased efforts by the U.S. government to shore up its borders, human smuggling has become a booming business. The vast wilderness beyond the fences that separate the United States and Mexico has provided abundant money-making opportunities for those who know how to dodge motion sensors, cameras, bandits, and the *verdes* (i.e., Border Patrol agents who wear green uniforms) with night vision goggles. While some smugglers have formed well-established networks in Mexico and the United States that can deliver clients deep into urban centers, others are border residents or illegal immigrants themselves who have crossed the border and been caught a few times.

Despite being politically trendy as a subject for study, human smuggling has not been a topic with much empirical research. For instance, although Mexican nationals account for the vast majority of illegal migrants entering the United States each year, there has been practically no systematic research on how Mexican smugglers organize their activities in the border region or the interior of Mexico. Our knowledge about how *coyotes* (or *polleros*) operate is still limited to stories provided by news media and government reports. The same paucity exists in our knowledge on human smugglers of people of other nationalities, such as the Lebanese, the Korean, the Russian mafia, and those from Eastern European countries. The only exception is research on Chinese human smugglers. Several empirical studies have examined the organizational profiles and operational patterns of the Chinese snakeheads. Borrowing from the studies on Chinese snakeheads, the following analysis attempts to describe some general patterns about the individuals involved in this business and their organizational and operational attributes. The following analysis is built upon the assumption that most human smugglers are enterprising agents who form groups with loose memberships and limited command structure.

PEOPLE WHO PARTICIPATE IN HUMAN SMUGGLING ACTIVITIES

The Characteristics of Human Smugglers

People of diverse backgrounds participate in this business. They include government officials, law enforcement representatives, taxi drivers, waiters and waitresses, legitimate travel agencies, immigration lawyers, street vendors, and even habitual gamblers. Because human smuggling as a business does not require any special skill or training, anyone can participate as long as he or she has the right connections and resources that can help circumvent immigration regulations.

Although most human smugglers are private citizens, there are some rather unusual participants, such as Navy sailors, Marine Corps recruiters, government officials in charge of immigration affairs, and customs inspectors. Many human smugglers were once illegal immigrants themselves or are still illegally residing in the United States. By and large, most human smugglers do not engage in smuggling activities full-time. They hold other jobs. Unlike any other racketeering activities, such as prostitution and loan sharking, human smuggling does not carry the same social stigma because for most it is not considered predatory. For years the U.S. government has accused traditional criminal organizations as the main players in transnational human smuggling activities. Many news reports still link human smuggling to traditional organized rime. In reality, transnational human smuggling has remained an enterprise largely dominated by entrepreneurs.

Entry into the Smuggling Business

Entry into the business follows a similar path for most human smugglers: People with fortuitous social contacts converge to offer services to one another, and together they contribute to a business that rakes in profits in the billions by sending people to wherever they desire to go. Although specific circumstances can vary from one smuggler to the next, money remains the main motive for people to participate in the business, and there is a lot of money in this business. The penalty, if one is caught smuggling illegal immigrants, is far less severe than if one is caught trafficking drugs. However, human smuggling can be as profitable in some instances as trafficking drugs. For example, "mules" hired to drive a load of marijuana over the border can earn up to $1,000 per trip. A Mexican human smuggler who guides illegal immigrants across the border can earn as much as $400 per person. If migrants want to be delivered to Los Angeles or Phoenix from the border region, the cost goes up to $3,000 a person for the 150-mile journey. Illegal immigrants from some ethnic groups, such as Chinese and Korean, pay even more to be smuggled into the United States. Migrants from China's southern province Fujian typically pay $65,000 or even $70,000 each to be smuggled into the United States.

Not only is the money good in this business, but the business also enjoys a rather benign reputation in the migrant community. Few migrants, if any, view their smuggling handlers as criminal. Studies have found that illegal immigrants often consider their handlers to be either philanthropists who want to help others or ordinary people who just want to make some money.[1] In Mexico, *coyotes* are heroes to tens of thousands of prospective migrants who are saving money and looking for opportunities to make the journey to the north. Mexican migrants trust their *coyotes* to evade U.S. Border Patrol agents and ground sensors. Similarly, most illegal migrants from China are grateful to their snakeheads for helping them enter the United States.

These images of human smugglers and the smuggling business are a far cry from the heartless and unscrupulous thugs that news media and government officials often portray. Furthermore, entrepreneurs in the smuggling business openly discuss their services and prices with their prospective customers. Yet, in smuggling, as in all businesses, there are dishonest smugglers who either exaggerate their capabilities or take the money but fail to deliver promised services. There are also reports of violent outbursts among rival smuggling gangs competing for clients and turfs where migrants are caught in the crossfire. At a news conference in the Phoenix area in November 2003, federal officials displayed several assault rifles seized from smugglers and asked the public to report immigrant-smuggling suspects.[2] The U.S. government even provides immigration incentives to people who tip off the government about smuggling organizations. There have been few takers. Most criminal cases against human smugglers as reported in the media or included in government reports did not originate from undocumented immigrants.

Human smugglers do not view themselves as criminals either, and they do not view their activities as predatory. Some even think of their business as a legitimate alternative to those who would otherwise have no opportunities to advance in life. The fact that neither illegal migrants nor their handlers consider human smuggling a crime may explain why so many otherwise law-abiding people, including reputable business owners and community leaders, are affiliated with this trade. Another important reason is, of course, the seduction of the tremendous profits one can make from an "occupation" that requires neither fixed working hours nor special skills. Nonetheless, most smugglers and their clients are aware of the illegal nature of their business and monitor law enforcement activities closely so they can adjust their strategies accordingly.

THE BUSINESS ENVIRONMENT OF TRANSNATIONAL HUMAN SMUGGLING

To understand how human smugglers operate, one needs to learn about the market environment within which these enterprising agents and clients interact. Transnational human smuggling is different from traditional racketeering activities (e.g., prostitution, loan sharking, and fencing) in many aspects. Their patterns of operation as well as strategies are largely determined by or in response to the market conditions unique to the business. Most of their activities revolve around assessing and mitigating perceived risks in the marketplace, such as border enforcement activities.

Fear of Arrest and Asset Forfeiture

Pervasive in the minds of all smugglers is the fear of arrest and possible forfeiture of their assets. The U.S. Congress has in recent years passed legislation that has significantly increased the penalties for human smuggling. Whereas previously human smugglers served six to eighteen months in prison, the Violent Crime Control and Law Enforcement Act of 1994 stipulates that persons who knowingly bring illegal migrants into the United States are subject to possible imprisonment of ten years and/or fines of up to $250,000 per smuggled person. If bodily injuries occur, the maximum penalty can go up to twenty years per migrant. Life imprisonment and even the death penalty can be imposed, should death result from the smuggling offense. Federal prosecution guidelines also clarify circumstances of when to press serious felony charges against smugglers, such as willful endangerment of clients during transportation (e.g., concealment in the trunk of a car).

To further raise the financial stakes, the U.S. Senate passed the Foreigners Alien Smuggling Act in 1995 to allow law enforcement agencies to use RICO (Racketeering-Influenced and Corrupt Organizations) legislation to fight human smuggling. That legislation provides tools such as expanded wiretap and asset forfeiture powers that have traditionally been reserved for traditional mafia families in New York and Chicago. The increased attention from law enforcement agencies has forced smugglers farther underground. Smugglers must conduct clandestine transactions and seek as little attention as possible, thus eliminating the possibility of any active and open recruitment of prospective clients.

Unstable and Limited Clientele

Human smuggling is a business without a stable clientele. This argument may appear counterintuitive, because the supply of foreign nationals who want to come to the United States seem endless. The reality is that only a handful of prospective clients can qualify as worthy of being recruited and transported. One must first have the financial wherewithal to even begin looking for a smuggler. Mexican nationals may not have to pay much to cross into the United States, but for migrants from other parts of the world, particularly from China, enormous amount of money must be raised to make the journey. Most smugglers have established procedures to verify whether their prospective clients are capable of paying the smuggling fees. Unless the client can pay cash, elaborate guarantee or "brokering" systems must be established wherein the smugglers involved can get paid upon the completion of each leg of the journey. A common way to prove one's financial capability is to provide proof that one has close relatives in the United States with enough savings to send for him. Otherwise one must find a relative or friend of significant social standing in the community who can vouch for the client and promise to pay upon arrival. Without verifiable evidence of enough finance, few become eligible clients.

Clients' ability to pay is only one of the obstacles. Human smugglers must also find these "worthy" clients because they are not visible. Transnational migration follows unique routes and tends to concentrate in but a few geographical locations. For instance, the vast majority of illegal Chinese immigrants come from Fujian Province in Southern China, whereas the majority of undocumented migrants from Mexico come from central-western states such as Michoacan, Guanajuato, Jalisco, and more recently Oaxaca and Guerrero. In other words the stream of transnational migrants is not dispersed widely or evenly. People's decisions to migrate internationally are closely related to connections with those already residing overseas, thus restricting the business of human smuggling to regions where such populations can be found. Even when prospective clients are found, each family or each social network has only a limited number of members contemplating migration. Once these members migrate, the social networks are depleted of prospective clients, at least in the short term. With the exception of Mexican migrants who make occasional trips to home villages on major holidays, the vast majority of illegal immigrants tend to stay inside the United States for extended periods of time. Therefore, there are also few return customers in this business.

Moreover, transporting human beings over vast distances and through illegal channels is an expensive proposition that requires significant capital outlay, thus limiting the number of people who can organize smuggling operations. The clandestine nature of the business, the need to make careful selections of prospective clients, and the small and concentrated regions where eligible clients may be recruited combine to dictate that this business can accommodate only a small number of enterprising agents who have a rather restricted range of territory to peddle their services.

Sporadic Smuggling Opportunities

A direct consequence of an unstable clientele is sporadic business opportunities. Eligible clients are not always available even when a smuggler has the proper contacts to go into action. It also takes time for prospective clients to gather financial backing. Then the smuggler needs to make arrangements to ensure that he will be paid. Furthermore, the acquisition of travel documents takes time and often depends on the availability of other members of the smuggling organization. Because of the many stages involved, smugglers often wait for long periods between operations for things to happen, and such waiting periods make the business rather protracted in execution as well as unpredictable in outcome. Such a market condition helps to explain why most smugglers hold other jobs or run other businesses. It also explains why most smuggling organizations are temporary alliances oriented toward one operation at a time, and why smugglers usually focus on doing one or one set of tasks at a time.

Operational Complexities

Illegal movement of illegal migrants across borders faces many logistical challenges, from arranging transportation and providing meals and lodging to safeguarding clients and evading attention from authorities. Depending on the smuggling method and its complexity, smugglers must plan the trip, acquire travel documents, and coordinate the schedule with other partners along the smuggling route. This process does not take into account interference by law enforcement activities that can greatly postpone or even disrupt the entire operation. For instance, many would-be migrants from China prefer to pay high prices to fly directly into the United States. However, those who can arrange such operations are extremely few. Most must go through multiple transit countries and use a combination of transportation methods to come to America.

One consistent finding from news stories, government reports, and academic studies is that the greater the smuggling distance (such as from Asia or Africa), the greater the reliance on elaborate transportation schemes arranged by multiple groups of brokers and facilitators. Ethnic enclaves along the smuggling route often provide the most important infrastructure that sustains international migration, legal or illegal. The Chinese communities scattered across the world provide shelter, cultural and culinary comfort, and technical know-how to move their countrymen successively through multiple transit points to their eventual destinations.

Because of their geographic adjacency and relatively lax immigration control, Canada and Mexico rank atop the list of transit countries. In Europe there have been consistent reports that human smugglers are heavily using former eastern block countries as way stations to forward their clients to Western Europe and North America. Major smuggling hubs have also appeared in Milan, Madrid, Frankfurt, and Amsterdam.

Hazardous Business Environment

Transnational human smuggling is an enterprise prone to hazards. Often depicted as ruthless and heartless by news media and law enforcement agencies, smugglers have been accused of abandoning sick and weak clients in the desert.[3] In these unfortunate events, human smugglers must help the largest number of clients reach their destinations so they can get paid. It is often the group's decision as much as the smuggler's. After paying hundreds and even thousands of dollars, migrants do not want to be caught by the *verdes* (i.e., U.S. Border Patrol). As businessmen human smugglers are concerned about their reputations. Prospective migrants also screen for reliable smugglers and rely on word of mouth to find reputable smugglers.

Inherent in all transnational smuggling activities is the danger of accidents and mishaps. In one incident in June 2002, eleven illegal immigrants were loaded into a northbound freight train from the Rio Grande Valley. But the smugglers lost track of the rail car, which sat in a train yard near Oklahoma City for four months, and was then sent to Iowa.[4] The rail car could not be opened from inside, and the bodies of the eleven, mostly Central American illegal immigrants, were later discovered by a cleaning crew. The ring leader of the smugglers, Juan Fernando Licea-Cedillo, was sentenced in Houston in November 2005, to more than twenty four years in prison. The train conductor who sold train schedules to the smuggling group received a forty-one-month prison term.

Compared to illegal migrants who die during transportation, there are many more nonlethal accidents that often bring a smuggling operation to a premature end. A single glitch (e.g., failing to pick up clients at a pre-arranged location, or engine trouble in a smuggling vessel) can disrupt the sequence of the events and cause the entire operation to collapse. For instance, in August 1999, a group of eighty-two Chinese nationals was taken into custody in Ensenada, Mexico after the local police found them wandering near a highway.[5] The group had arrived by boat five days earlier and had been without food for four days. When the local contact person failed to show up, these immigrants had to leave their hideout and venture out on their own.

It would be misleading to suggest that human smugglers in general look after the welfare of their clients. However, they must provide a level of comfort that can be tolerated and agreed upon by their clients. Human smugglers are neither as compassionate as most would like to portray themselves during client recruitment nor as heartless as many news stories and law enforcement reports have portrayed, subjecting clients to inhumane and horrendous travel conditions. Illegal immigrants and their village compatriots are vital to sustaining the smuggling business. A bad reputation ruins a smuggling group's credibility and its chances to stay in the business. Hiding in cargo containers, railroad cars, or underneath crates of vegetables may be the only concealment technique available to the smuggler or the only mode of transportation that the clients can afford. Smugglers, fearing their own detection and the detection of other clients, must leave behind those who cannot keep up while trekking across the desert. When smuggling by sea, smugglers must ration food and water in order to keep all, or at least most, of their clients alive.

An enterprise prone to mishaps tends also to be one with unpredictable results. Unexpected delays and extra expenses often lead to hostilities between migrants and their handlers, which if not resolved quickly can expose the entire smuggling operation. All human smuggling operations consist of sequential activities, any of which is vital to the eventual success. Ironically, because human smugglers are mostly entrepreneurs who guard their own trade secrets, the precautions and measures they take to protect themselves also increase the likelihood of operational disruptions and mishaps.

Absence of Monopoly

As a result of the aforementioned market constraints, the enterprise of transnational human smuggling has remained fragmented and dominated by groups of loosely affiliated entrepreneurs. An alliance will continue as long as there are opportunities to make money and will disband when there are no clients or when a key member whose service is vital to the operation drops out. Although there have been reports of smuggling gangs competing for clients and for the control of various stretches of railroads along Mexico's southern border, there is no evidence to suggest that the business of transnational human smuggling is moving toward any form of monopoly or consolidation. Nor is there evidence of overt competition among smugglers vying for control of specific geographical regions, either along the U.S.-Mexico border or in the interior of Mexico. On the contrary, smugglers in most cases are collaborating with friends, relatives, or other business associates.

ORGANIZATIONAL CHARACTERISTICS OF SMUGGLING GROUPS

Many news stories and government reports have alleged that human smuggling is dominated by criminal organizations or gangs made up of people of particular ethnic groups. In reality, most smugglers form loosely connected groups. Although smugglers tend to work with people of their own kind, this does not preclude them from working with whoever can provide the needed service for a fee.

Different Ways to Study Organized Crime

All criminal organizations share some common attributes, such as secrecy and conspiracy, for the purpose of profiting from illicit goods and services. However, scholars differ in their opinions on how to best explain criminal organizations—whether they resemble formal social organizations with a clear hierarchy, or loosely connected groups of entrepreneurs who gather because of their mutual need to make money. It has been a challenge to explain the essential elements that constitute organized crime and to clarify the difference between organized crime and crime that is organized.

An alternative perspective is to view criminal organizations as a continuum that is shaped by the specific illicit market. Criminal organizations contract and expand in response to varying market demands, thus assuming a variety of organizational structures to achieve optimal results. Some criminal organizations, such as those involved in construction or gambling businesses, may require a clear hierarchy and division of labor, which are necessary organizational prerequisites to remain viable in these illicit businesses. Others, such as those involved in loan sharking and fencing of stolen goods, require little or no formal organizational structure.

Different conceptualizations can lead to different understandings of criminal organizations and bear different policy implications. Therefore the development of a theoretical framework is not a purely academic exercise. It can provide greater insights into the phenomenon under investigation and predict its trajectories and outcomes where effective law enforcement strategies can be devised, implemented, and improved upon.

Hierarchical Structures of Human Smuggling Organizations

With a few exceptions, most human smuggling organizations do not have any identifiable command structure. Although some smugglers are more successful than others and thus become better known in the smuggling community, rarely does anyone have the ability to control the entire transportation process outside his or her own immediate social network. Human smuggling is a process of multiple stages from migrants' hometowns to their eventual destinations (e.g., recruitment, travel preparation, departure, transit, arrival, and payment collection). Even within a smuggling group that controls one particular stage, leadership is negotiable depending on whose tasks are more important at the time of the operation. The more valuable resources one brings forth, the more influence one has over the direction and pace of an operation.

There are multiple layers of operatives involved in the smuggling process who must support one another in order to achieve the eventual goal of delivering clients to their final destinations and collecting their fees. On the other hand, just because smugglers must collaborate with each other does not mean these entrepreneurs share their contacts and resources. By controlling their resources, smugglers can maximize their profits while minimizing exposure to risks. Such a business practice ensures that human smugglers at one stage have no control over those at another stage and are at their partners' mercy for the delivery of promised services. This is, after all, an illicit enterprise with all involved trying to protect themselves from the authorities and from each other. Other than one's own social network, there is no market mechanism for smugglers to shop for partners. Smugglers, therefore, perform their tasks solely for the eventual financial reward rather than out of deference to any hierarchical command structure.

Specialized Roles

Although smuggling groups do not develop a clear hierarchical structure, members of a smuggling group all know their own responsibilities and tasks. The division of labor is never ambiguous among human smugglers. The specialized roles emerge in response to specific tasks involved in smuggling operations, such as those who acquire fraudulent documents, recruit prospective migrants, serve as border crossing guides, drive smuggling vehicles, and operate safe houses. Many smuggling roles tend to evolve over time as smugglers become established in the business. The gradual accumulation of experience and contacts in the business appear to be the main impetus behind the shift in roles. Generally, smugglers evolve from simple and low-level tasks to more profitable ones where their services are more valuable.

Depending on the complexity of the smuggling plan, some operations involve more specialized tasks than others do. Generally, smugglers who employ a combination of by-land, by-air, and even by-sea methods tend to involve greater operational complexity. The following is a list of the key roles in the business of human smuggling.

- *Recruiters*: People who make a nominal fee by referring prospective clients to smugglers. These are often the relatives or close friends of illegal migrants who know the smugglers. They may or may not have any further involvement in a smuggling operation.

- *Coordinators (or brokers)*: People who know the key contacts in some segments of the smuggling process and organize their services. A coordinator plans the operation, pays recruiters for their referrals, and keeps track of the smuggling activities. These people are central to smuggling activities, but they have nothing more than the right connections to acquire the necessary services for a fee. Their survival depends entirely on the maintenance of their service providers.
- *Drivers*: People who provide underground shuttle services to move illegal immigrants across the United States or elsewhere. Transporters come from diverse backgrounds and are scattered along the smuggling route. Many are illegal immigrants themselves who are familiar with smuggling details.
- *Safe house operators*: Individuals who use their properties as rest stops for smuggling operations. There are many networks of private houses, motels, and apartments across the country that smugglers use to hide or hold their clients, either for the next leg of the journey, or for the smuggling fees to be delivered. Together with drivers, these safe house operators form the backbone of the logistical support to the smuggling industry.
- *Local guides*: People, typically local residents, who know the terrain well. Their primary task is to move clients across less-guarded points along the border. Not all guides are local residents. In the case of legal border crossings, guides (or escorts) are often used to assist migrants to complete forms and stand in the lanes and provide last minute instructions on how to respond to immigration inspectors.
- *Document vendors*: People who specialize in acquiring or producing documents to facilitate the transportation of illegal migrants through various checkpoints. Some travel documents are authentic and obtained through official channels, while others are forged or fabricated.
- *Corrupt public officials*: Government officials who hold resources vital to smuggling activities, such as reviewing and issuing travel documents or inspecting passengers at border checkpoints. Smugglers with official connections tend to be more successful and profitable than those without. Official corruption does not occur just in sending countries such as Mexico and China. It also happens in the United States.
- *Enforcers*: People, mostly illegal immigrants, who are hired to work on the smuggling vessels or guard safe houses. They are responsible for maintaining order and for distributing food and water.
- *Debt collectors*: People, often connected with local gangs, responsible for extracting payments from illegal migrants. Debt collectors also harass the families and relatives of smuggled migrants in their hometowns for prompt payment of smuggling fees.

These roles are usually played out in successive stages following the sequence of a smuggling operation, with the recruiter working in the front and the debt collector coming in the end. They are by no means exhaustive. Not all roles are required in every operation, and some smugglers may assume more than one role. In most cases, the smuggling process consists of multiple groups of smugglers in charge of tasks pertinent to the leg of transportation. There are, however, exceptions to this observation.

In one such case, a smuggling organization appeared to have established an extensive network capable of carrying out most smuggling roles. In October 2006 federal and local police officers fanned out across southern Arizona and several other states looking for fifty-five people allegedly involved in a family-run human smuggling ring suspected of bringing in thousands of undocumented migrants across the U.S.-Mexico border in the remote eastern sections of Arizona's desert.[6] Based in the tiny Arizona town of Bowie, the smuggling organization, headed by a husband-wife team in their early thirties, catered primarily to Mexicans and other Central Americans. This smuggling organization established an elaborate network that extended from Arizona to New Mexico, California, Minnesota, and Ohio. Affiliated with the Bowie Group were "enforcers" who guarded illegal proceeds and safe houses, "guides" who walked migrants across the U.S.-Mexican border into the United States, "drivers" who transported migrants to prearranged locations, and "money runners" who collected smugglings fees. Most of the funds were sent through wire transfers, and, to avoid suspicion, "money runners" would pick up the wired funds at the Western Union offices in the area. The recruiters of the Bowie organization worked in Agua Prieta, Mexico (just across the border from Douglas, Arizona), and solicited individuals wanting to be smuggled into the United States. Migrants crossed the border with the help of a guide to a rendezvous point along Highway 80 where drivers would be waiting. The journey from Agua Prieta to Bowie cost about $500 to $800. For destinations outside Arizona, the cost could be as high as $2,000. Once in Bowie, illegal migrants were held until the balance of the smuggling fees was paid by family members or other smuggling "brokers." The Bowie Group would then coordinate their transportation to Phoenix, Arizona, and other destinations throughout the United States.

The organizational features of smuggling groups point to a pattern of mixed attributes. On the one hand, smugglers meet through familial networks and fortuitous social contacts and supply services to move fee-paying clients to their destinations. Smuggling organizations consist of loose associations of individuals with diverse backgrounds, and the relationships among core members are mostly peerlike, without clear leadership. On the other hand, most smuggling operations seem to involve highly specialized tasks with little redundancy. The flow of information is highly restricted, and responsibilities along each successive stage of an operation are clearly defined.

These small groups of enterprising agents appear to have kept the smuggling industry vibrant as a whole by being highly adaptable to market constraints and operational uncertainties. When a few groups break up due to a loss of key members or lack of opportunities, others quickly fill in the void and continue to provide services to meet the market demand.

THE OPERATIONAL PATTERNS OF HUMAN SMUGGLING

The business of transnational human smuggling is irregular in its planning and execution, and uncertain in its outcomes. The manner in which each segment of a smuggling operation is carried out largely reflects the personality and work habits of the individuals involved. The following presents major characteristics of how smugglers conduct their business.

Informal Procedures and Specialized Service

Human smuggling remains an informal business with most transactions, if not all, conducted through verbal agreements among small groups of individuals within close physical proximity. Payment between and among smuggling partners is mostly made in cash or cash equivalent. Prices for agreed-upon services are seldom disputed. Despite the sensational news coverage of botched smuggling operations or tortures of illegal immigrants, smuggling operations, in most cases, and their transactions are mostly uneventful. Although transactions in the smuggling *business* are informal, smuggling *services* are often specialized. Some smugglers specialize in marriage frauds, while others prefer arranging business delegations to the United States.

Temporary Alliances and Sporadic Engagement

Most crime syndicates, in a traditional sense, are interested in building organizational *continuity* in their criminal activities so that the stream of income becomes stable. This is the not the case with human smuggling organizations, which in most cases involve only temporary business alliances. Smuggling partnerships are formed as quickly as they are dissolved once their purpose has come to its end. Each smuggler operates within a limited, albeit well-connected, circle of associates or friends. When there are no suitable opportunities to acquire clients, smugglers simply remain dormant, some for a prolonged period, until another opportunity arises.

Because of the temporary nature of most smuggling operations and the secrecy of most transactions in order to ensure the survival of those involved, smuggling organizations tend to be highly susceptible to changes in membership. Any removal of a link along the smuggling chain

of processes can lead to an overall breakdown. Such breakdowns sometimes lead to disastrous outcomes or even tragedies.

Intergroup Violence

Because transactions in illicit businesses are not legally recognized and
therefore cannot be legally protected, violence is instrumental in protecting one's interests in traditional organized crime.[7] In traditional organized
crime circles, violence can serve two functions: (1) internal, when it is
used to maintain order and to discipline members within the group; and
(2) external, when members of one criminal organization use it to prevent
or settle disputes with either rival organizations or customers and to
silence witnesses or to eliminate competition.

Drug traffickers are well-known for using violence to protect market
shares and safeguard trafficking routes. The Medellin cartels and the subsequent Cali cartel in Columbia, and the Arellano-Felix brothers in Mexico,
have long been known for their use of violence for instrumental purposes
in order to protect their business interests and increase influence on major
social institutions such as elected offices, law enforcement agencies, and
even the military.[8] For years the exploits of drug kingpins, such as Pablo
Escobar, the Ochoa brothers, Jose Gonzalo Rodriguez Gacha, and the
Arellano-Felix brothers in corrupting government officials through
bribery or neutralizing state power through assassinations have created
the image of large multinational corporations made possible by the ruthless efforts of these crime families.

Human smuggling, however, does not fit this traditional model.
Although the use of force has been reported as a method of extracting
payment from delinquent clients, smugglers themselves rarely use violence
against other smugglers. Business conduct in human smuggling appears
to be regulated mainly by a mutual desire to make money and to maintain
a good reputation to attract clients. Perhaps this collective fear of the
negative consequences arising from a breach of obligations keeps most
human smugglers focused on carrying out their part of the deal. The
desire to build and maintain a trustworthy image thus becomes a crucial
benchmark of success in this business. Besides, human smuggling is a
business without a turf. When monopoly is not possible, there are no
territories to occupy, and violence therefore is of little use.

Risk Management as an Overarching Strategy

The best way to understand human smuggling organizations is to
understand how smugglers manage the perceived risks in an uncertain
marketplace. One needs to examine their risk prevention, control, and
absorption strategies to fully appreciate the structural and operational

ingenuity. A criminal organization, whether made of complex command structures or simple peer groups, takes its shape to mitigate risk factors in the market place to achieve successful transactions. Therefore, human smugglers mostly interact with people of the same social circle and mostly engage in one-on-one communication. This interaction pattern is needed for insurance purposes because such an arrangement can provide mechanisms or guarantees to buffer the effects of unanticipated events and to provide contingency plans during the smuggling process.

Risk management thus becomes the defining factor that determines the group structure and operational style. It begins at the very front of an operation with client screening, and it continues until the very end when the smuggling fees are collected. There are several protective strategies used by smugglers to deal with constant safety concerns and to reduce uncertainties inherent in the business, including ethnicity. These strategies include linguistics, familial relationships, underground banking, frequent change of cell phone and pager numbers, and spontaneous meeting locations.

One-on-one interactions are probably the most common relationship maintained by human smugglers. Such transactions, although conducive to protecting individual smugglers, probably have also contributed to a fragmented business environment whereby few smugglers know anyone above or below their direct contacts. Smuggling networks may consist of only a tight inner circle that few are able to penetrate. Although some scholars have questioned the notion of ethnic ties as a key component of organized crime,[9] being a member of a culturally distinct group still provides one of the best assurances and protection among people as to who can be trusted to fulfill their obligations in a cooperative but illicit economic activity. Speaking the same dialect and sharing the same ancestral townships can greatly strengthen the expectations of mutual interests and commitment to the illicit activities; it is also the best way to prevent the intrusion or infiltration of outsiders.

Official Corruption and the Smuggling Business

Official corruption is a vital part of the smuggling business. By acquiring government-controlled services that are otherwise untenable through legal means, human smugglers can significantly improve the efficiency of their transportation. Corrupt officials tend to occupy crucial governmental functions, such as passport inspectors at border checkpoints, clerical staff for passport applications, and officials issuing residential registrations or marriage certificates.

Official corruption is often reported in migrant-sending countries such as Mexico. For instance, in March 2004 police carried out a nationwide sweep against a large migrant smuggling ring. The operation arrested forty-two current and former government employees in twelve of Mexico's thirty-one states who allegedly participated in the smuggling of Cubans, Uruguayans, Brazilians, Asians, and Central Americans from the south. Those arrested included agents and former agents of Mexico's National Migration Institute who allegedly helped foreigners sneak into the United States. Mexican authorities claimed that corrupt officials illegally freed captured migrants, falsified papers, and guaranteed safe passage to the United States. Even top justice officials openly acknowledge that corruption is the main obstacle in cracking down human smuggling.[10]

The United States is not free from corruption. In fact, when U.S. officials guarding the entrance become corrupt, their service can be invaluable. In July 1996 a nineteen-year veteran officer, Jerry Wolf Stuchiner, with the Immigration and Naturalization Service was arrested in Hong Kong. Stuchiner was the Officer in Charge of INS interests in Honduras at the time of his arrest. He arrived in Hong Kong using a U.S. diplomatic passport and was found to be carrying five fraudulent Honduran passports.[11] Also arrested was an El Salvadoran woman traveling with Stuchiner. The arrest was the result of a joint investigation by both U.S. and Hong Kong authorities, who suspected Stuchiner facilitated the sale of fraudulent Honduran passports and visas to Chinese immigrant smugglers. He played a vital role in supplying Chinese snakeheads with Honduran passports and airline tickets to Central America, from where they would then smuggle clients into the United States. Several of his Hong Kong collaborators were also subsequently arrested.

THRIVING ON MARKET CONSTRAINTS

Human smugglers operate in a similar fashion as many other peer-group entrepreneurs. They develop a network of social contacts and pool their resources toward a profit-seeking activity. However, unlike peer groups in legal economic activities, smugglers rarely engage in teamwork (i.e., collective engagement in similar tasks or resource sharing), their relations with each other are usually secretive and involve mostly one-on-one (i.e., dyadic) transactions, and they have minimal organizational structure and a limited hierarchy. Each smuggler may develop and maintain additional circles of contacts and resources that are also clandestine in nature and dyadic in format.

Such an organizational arrangement appears to have many advantages that allow smugglers to thrive in an uncertain and risky market environment. First, in a business environment in which transactions are based on verbal agreements and without a mechanism of legal protection, interactions with one's friends and relatives can increase shared understanding of the tasks that need to be completed. An agreement of what service is needed and for how much money must be reached effectively between two parties or the dyadic transaction will not occur. This one-on-one network thus effectively minimizes interpersonal tension and increases personal accountability. A satisfying trading atmosphere can be sustained because only those individuals who can perform and deliver agreed-upon services are likely to join and stay in the network. Those who cannot will be excluded since there will not be any meaningful roles for them to play. Shared expectations are therefore easily promoted in these small groups. This small group environment reduces uncertainty, increases collective commitment, and produces smooth transactions.

Second, small group interactions reduce the distance of transactions and improve decision-making, particularly when most exchanges are on a dyadic basis. These one-on-one transactions, which are common in most smuggling operations, prevent any large complex smuggling organizations from emerging. Because of their deliberate efforts to evade law enforcement agencies, smuggling can involve complex stages of transportation routes and rendezvous points before migrants can reach the final destination. Small group interactions can reduce sequential complexity in smuggling operations. Each cluster of individuals focuses on completing one or one set of tasks, such as obtaining fraudulent documents, arranging transportation, and securing cooperation from corrupt officials at border checkpoints. Timely adaptation in decision-making is therefore possible when there are only a small number of individuals involved in a limited number of immediate tasks. Maximum efficiency can thus be achieved with minimal redundancy in the number of players, and the exchange of information occurs over the shortest distance—mostly between two individuals.

Third, one-on-one transactions can achieve maximum security with minimal exposure to law enforcement activities or other operational hazards. Because of restricted flow of information and limited contacts with other members along the smuggling chain, individual members of a smuggling ring are insulated from one another. When one human smuggler is arrested, or one stage fails to materialize, the remaining members of the group will not likely face imminent danger. Therefore the survival of the human smuggling business does not hinge upon the success of any specific organization, but rather on the collective entrepreneurial efforts of many groups of individuals participating in the market place.

Additionally the one-on-one network increases transactional security against unscrupulous partners. For any pair of smugglers to engage in a transaction, one expresses what she needs while the other indicates whether he and only he can supply the service. Even for services that one cannot render, a human smuggler can withhold the information about who can. Instead this smuggler will acquire the needed service and turn around to sell it. The smuggler will try to control the source of service for as long as possible. Because services vital to human smuggling activities are exclusively held and carefully guarded by individuals, there are few opportunities to shop around, although over time a smuggler may develop alternative routes or resources. The minimum level of redundancy and one-on-one transactions ensure that maximum profits can be realized for the involved individuals. The protection for one's share of the profit relies on one's ability to keep his or her resources inaccessible to others.

Fourth, in circumstances where smuggling activities are unpredictable in their outcomes and vulnerable to disruptions, an enterprise made up of small groups of entrepreneurs can expand and contract in response to market uncertainties. By being small and nimble, smuggling organizations can take advantage of new opportunities and adjust to different client demands and transportation strategies. Most smugglers participate in other legitimate or illicit businesses and gather only when there is an opportunity. After the completion of one operation, these smugglers will disband and go about their business as usual. Therefore, small exchange relations can better withstand the few opportunities in the marketplace.

With their temporary alliances and one-on-one interactions, human smugglers can effectively cope with uncertain market conditions, reduce exposure to law enforcement activities, and produce favorable financial returns. However, they also face many operational hazards. First of all, the enforcement of contracts and assignments relies heavily on informal social control in a cultural environment that promotes shared expectations and understanding of the smuggling tasks. Familial relations, speaking the same dialect, or sharing the same ancestral township thus become important elements of this informal social control. One's social position and network hinge heavily on the delivery of promised services. Second, without a hierarchy and clear chain of command, accountability and disciplinary actions are impossible. Smugglers often find loyalty and trust insufficient for self-protection and profit guarantee. This peculiar tension between trust and suspicion, coupled with an unpredictable business environment, seems to explain the fact that human smuggling is best suited for freelance operators.

Chapter 7

Trafficking of Women and Children[1]

Sexual exploitation of women and children is not just a social vice limited to third world, tourism-dependent countries. It is happening right inside the U.S. mainland. On December 17, 2005, Attorney General Alberto Gonzales announced the breakup of a large prostitution ring involving more than thirty children as young as twelve forced to have sex at truck stops, hotels, and brothels. Multiple indictments were made against traffickers in states including Michigan, New Jersey, and Pennsylvania for bringing children across state lines for prostitution.[2]

There are two elements that make women and children particularly vulnerable to exploitation during illegal migration. First, because all illegal migrants must rely on their handlers to move across borders, they are vulnerable to the unprincipled who take advantage of the weak and the desperate. Women and children thus become prime prey for abuses by unscrupulous smugglers and other criminal entities. Second, because being illegal means they have no access to the legal job market, smuggled women and children are forced to enter the illegal labor force. Numerous jobs are readily available to illegal migrants, as these jobs have been rejected by the native workforce because the pay is too low, the working conditions are too harsh, or, as in prostitution, the endeavor itself is illegal.

HUMAN TRAFFICKING—DEFINITION, EXTENT, AND CAUSES

Human trafficking has found supporters throughout the world who hold fundamentally differing views toward the rights and welfare of human beings. Both developed and developing countries have this problem to some extent. Together with human smuggling, human trafficking is considered the third-largest criminal industry in the world as of 2006, behind only drugs and firearms trafficking, with profits reaching billions of dollars each year[3] According to U.S. government estimates, human smuggling and trafficking generates $9.5 billion annually.[4] It is an enterprise that shows no prejudice toward race, gender, or geography, except for a general preference toward children and women. Trafficking victims are a diverse group, ranging from those eager to improve their lives to those desperate to escape civil unrest. Some leave their home countries on their own, whereas others, often children and women, are "given" or sold to related or unrelated adults who promise education and jobs. Invariably they fall victim to forced or bonded labor. Of the trafficked victims, children draw particular attention from human rights organizations and law enforcement agencies because of their inability to seek aid or protect themselves.

For many years, researchers, journalists, and even government agencies used *human trafficking* and *human smuggling* interchangeably to describe any organized illegal transportation of persons from one country to another. These two terms are still being used interchangeably in reports issued from public and private entities. To the general public, these two terms often appear to mean the same thing. Whether it is trafficking or smuggling, all such activities imply clandestine movement of human beings with the intention to evade or circumvent authorities. Only in recent years have deliberate efforts been made to differentiate the two terms.

Human smuggling involves willing and fee-paying illegal immigrants who are in search of opportunities to improve their lives. The term *human trafficking* or *trafficking in persons* carries a sinister connotation.[5] Human trafficking encompasses the additional elements of coercion and fraud. Under trafficking, the illegal entry is for the purpose of economic or sexual exploitation of the immigrants. Trafficking activities generally fall into two categories: first, sex trafficking, in which migrants are transported with the intent to perform sexual services at destination countries and in which the smuggling process is enabled through the use of force, fraud, or coercion; second, trafficking of individuals through the use of force, fraud, or coercion, for the purpose of involuntary servitude, peonage, debt bondage, or slavery. Specifically, the United Nations issued an official definition for human trafficking in December 2000 with the signing in Italy of the *UN Protocol to Prevent, Suppress, and Punish Trafficking in Persons:*

> Trafficking in persons' shall mean the recruitment, transportation, transfer, harboring or receipt of persons, by means of threat or use of force or other forms of coercion, of abduction, of fraud, of deception, of the abuse of power, or of a position of vulnerability or of the giving or receiving of payments or benefits to achieve the consent of

a person having control over another person, for the purpose of exploitation. Exploitation shall include, at a minimum, the exploitation of the prostitution of others or other forms of sexual exploitation, forced labor or services, slavery or practices similar to slavery, servitude or the removal of organs.[6]

This current definition of human trafficking has evolved over a long period of time and with much debate. In order to call governments to action and to force them to pay attention to the growing global sex and pornography industries, advocacy groups have pushed most Western governments to recognize human trafficking as a human rights issue. By defining trafficking as a violation of human rights, UN member states cannot shed their obligations to deal with cross-border trafficking activities.[7] The fight against trafficking therefore takes on a moral as well as political urgency, more so than measures against regular street crimes.

Victims of trafficking are primarily exploited for labor. A study by the International Labor Organization (ILO) estimated that fewer than 10 percent of the millions of victims of forced labor in Asia are trafficked for commercial sexual exploitation.[8] As a result, the ILO has constructed its own definition of human trafficking to emphasize the slavery persuasion: (1) the work or service is extracted under the menace of penalty and it is (2) undertaken involuntarily."[9] Because of its shock value, trafficking for commercial sex often commands a larger audience in the political arena.

Feminists in the early twentieth century were active in lobbying government agencies in the Western countries to abolish brothels and end all forms of prostitution.[10] Their successful political activism eventually tied prostitution to trafficking and subsequently led to the passage of the United Nations' *International Convention for the Suppression of the Trafficking in Persons in 1949* that called on all states to "suppress not only trafficking but also prostitution, regardless of whether or not they occur with the consent of the women involved."[11] This view was later modified with the arrival of another group of feminists that "sees prostitution as a possible option or a strategy of survival taken by women, which should be respected."[12]

Despite its wide acceptance, the interpretation and policy operation of the UN definition of human trafficking remains a messy process, and the term continues to be used to describe various groups of people.[13] Organized activities in moving people across borders involve both willing and unwilling participants. The willing participants pay a fee to be smuggled to countries that offer better economic opportunities. The fundamental issue in human smuggling lies in the voluntary relationship between the smugglers and the smuggled.[14] Others are trafficked for the purposes of sexual exploitation or indentured labor. In practice, however, it is often difficult to tell where smuggling ends and trafficking begins, as few victims are abducted outright by force from their homes.[15] Most would agree that when force, fraud, and coercion are used to force migrants into any type of bondage and indentured labor, the nature of the smuggling business is changed. Because human smuggling and trafficking often overlap, not only in transportation but also in delivery phases, creating a workable differential definition has been a challenge for the world community.

If abuse and exploitation are key definitional ingredients, many smuggled migrants are also trafficking victims (i.e., they are forced to work off smuggling debts). One can see how this definitional exercise can become slippery. It is possible that during the transportation process smugglers may subject their clients to worse travel conditions than what they had promised, or smugglers may charge extra fees or impose a more stringent payment schedule than that detailed in the original agreement. There have been many news stories and government reports of such abuses. Unfortunately, it is a recurrent theme in countless smuggling operations in which illegal immigrants find themselves time and again subjected to physical and psychological abuses in the hands of their handlers. Upon arrival, they are often forced to do jobs that they did not want or get paid far less than they had been promised. To what extent such exploitation qualifies as trafficking is open to debate.

How Serious Is the Problem?

In addition to definitional challenges, exposing the extent of human trafficking remains largely guesswork. For obvious reasons, empirical data are hard to obtain on the ebb and flow of human trafficking anywhere in the world. Despite the secretive nature of the business, many government and nongovernmental agencies somehow have managed to produce estimates that vary widely. Few empirical sources are available to verify these estimates. Kevin Bales, a sociology professor at Roehampton University in London, is one of the few researchers who has conducted field research to gauge the extent of modern-day slave labor worldwide. He estimates that approximately 27 million slaves exist globally.[16] According to Bales's estimates, India and Pakistan led the world in the number of trafficking victims. India was estimated to have 20 million slaves; and Pakistan, 3 million. The next closest countries for comparison were Mauritania, Nepal, and China, each having an average of 275,000 slaves per country.[17] The remaining countries had a range of 10,000 to 20,000 slaves.

Other global estimates of trafficking victims range from approximately 1 to 4 million annually. According to the International Organization for Migration, the number of victims trafficked both internally and across national borders in 1997 was 4 million. It is estimated that around 300,000 trafficked women, mostly from eastern European and African countries, are currently working as prostitutes in western Europe alone.

The U.S. government has for years produced various estimates of the extent of human trafficking around the world in its annual *Trafficking in Persons Report* (or the TIP report). In 1998 the U.S. government estimated that 700,000 people were trafficked annually across countries worldwide for sexual exploitation and forced labor, and 45,000 to 50,000 people were trafficked into the United States. These estimates were later revised. For instance, in 2003 the U.S. government estimated that 18,000 to 20,000 people were trafficked annually into the United States, and the world-wide number was 800,000 to 900,000.[18] Then, in 2004, the number of trafficked victims in the United States was estimated to be about 17,500 to 18,500.[19] By 2005, the estimated number of trafficked victims into the United States became 14,500 to 17,500, whereas the worldwide figure remained the same.[20] However, the 2005 TIP report recorded only 611 victims found by government agencies in the four years between 2002 and 2005 nationwide.[21] Needless to say, there is a considerable discrepancy between the numbers of observed and estimated victims of human trafficking.

In the 2006 TIP report, the U.S. State Department estimated that between 600,000 and 800,000 men, women, and children were trafficked across international borders.[22] Furthermore, in all TIP reports, little information was disclosed as to the methodological procedures for arriving at these estimates, let alone any explanation for the precipitous drop over such a short period of time in the absence of any major successful social or governmental campaigns.[23]

Fluctuations in estimates may result from the mixed interpretations of the definition of human trafficking applied by researchers at governmental agencies and nongovernmental organizations (NGOs) during data gathering. Definitions vary from sexual exploitation, to a form of payment for a collateral debt, and to nonsexual, coerced labor. Some indentured labor lasts a short period of time, whereas other labor appear to be lifelong bondage. A village boy was seized by Arab raiders and forced to herd livestock until he escaped ten years later. Young women from Macedonia who responded to advertisements for work in Italy were forced into prostitution. Children were sold by their parents into pedophile rings in Thailand for a percentage of the returns.[24] To complicate the problem further, estimates on the extent of human trafficking vary because of the political persuasion of the organization compiling the data. For instance, NGOs have a tendency to inflate numbers in an attempt to force governments to take action. Outlandish claims intended to incense the audience are therefore passed on as if they were based on solid empirical data.

One reference used widely to gauge the severity of the trafficking problem in a nation is the tier rank system of the TIP report. The U.S. State Department has created a three-tier system based on the Trafficking Victims Protection Act of 2000. The report rates countries based on their

Table 7.1 TIP Tier Ranking

Year	Tier 1	Tier 2	Tier 2 Watch List	Tier 4	Country Totals
2001	12	47	—	23	82
2002	18	53	—	19	90
2003	26	75	—	15	116
2004	25	54	42	10	131
2005	24	77	27	14	142

compliance with what the State Department calls minimum standards.[25] The first tier applies to countries that have a trafficking problem but are complying with minimum standards to combat trafficking, such as the United Kingdom, Norway, Lithuania, and the Czech Republic. The second tier includes countries that are not fully meeting the minimum standards but are making an effort to comply, such as Croatia, Kazakhstan, Paraguay, and Cyprus. The majority of countries are listed in this tier. The third tier is reserved for countries that are deemed to have a trafficking problem but are doing little or nothing to combat the problem, such as Burma, Jamaica, Saudi Arabia, and Venezuela. Placement on the third tier results in U.S. economic sanctions. The State Department also created an additional tier in 2003 (reported in 2004) called the "Tier 2 Watch List" that falls between Tiers 2 and 3; it is used for countries that are making significant efforts to move out of the third tier but that have not quite made it. Table 7.1 provides a summary of the number of nations in each category over the past five years.

The TIP tier system has come under much international criticism because it is often used by politicians in the United States to tie foreign aid to countries' efforts to combat human trafficking. Many countries' placements in the tier system are also rather perplexing. Countries such as Greece and Turkey, both U.S. allies and NATO members, have failed to get better than a Tier 2 rating over the past five years. Countries believed by many researchers and NGOs to have serious trafficking problems, such as Russia and Pakistan, receive higher ratings for political reasons.[26] Furthermore, the United States does not subject itself to this rating system.

Despite its many shortcomings, the TIP report provides one major open source of information for researchers and policy analysts. It attempts to examine not only the levels of human trafficking in different countries but also governmental and legislative efforts to combat the problem. Countries with well-articulated legislation and bona fide enforcement agencies for pursuing human traffickers are usually placed in Tier 1. Finally, the report helps the State Department determine the level of financial aid to foreign countries to curb human trafficking.

Causes of Human Trafficking

The problem of human trafficking touches every country in some aspect. There are sending countries, where prospective victims are recruited and transported; transit countries that serve as way stations; and destination countries, where vice lords eagerly await fresh supplies of women and children. The traffic typically flows from developing nations to affluent ones. This observation has led researchers to believe that human trafficking is causally related to poverty. Many researchers have used poverty and its concomitant factors such as lack of education and job opportunities to explain why women and children fall prey to human traffickers, particularly those of eastern European origin. For instance, in the aftermath of the Balkan war, women in Romania, Moldova, and other countries driven by poor social and economic conditions were enticed by promising advertisements for overseas opportunities.[27] Traffickers took advantage of their desperation and lured them into countries that did not have the support services or law enforcement capabilities to prevent sexual exploitation. Many governments and nongovernmental organizations have also come to believe that alleviating poverty is the key to eradicating this social ill.

Globalization is another common explanation for human trafficking. Improvements in transportation have simplified international travel as well as human trafficking activities. Increases in global commerce have also increased the awareness of disparities in standards of living and have produced a sense of despair for those trapped in impoverished regions. High demands in the worldwide sex trade also take advantage of the cultural subordination of women in many societies. These societies view women as an economic burden and tolerate the selling of daughters and acceptance of brothels as an employment outlet.[28] Some researchers argue that, although globalization may aid human traffickers, it may also improve international collaboration in spotting and fighting such abuses.[29] Furthermore, globalization may improve the standard of living in developing countries and promote the awareness of basic human rights, thus making it harder for predators to recruit unsuspecting victims.

Corruption as a Major Contributor

In recent years, however, a small but growing number of researchers have begun to examine the role of corruption not only as a sustaining factor, but also as an enabling factor in human trafficking activities. Poverty may explain much of the initial motivation for outward migration, but official corruption may offer a greater impetus in facilitating the trafficking process. These researchers have begun to explore the linkage between official corruption and human trafficking activities and argue that corruption should be considered the most significant indicator of human trafficking in countries when compared to other factors such as poverty.[30]

In general, corruption is defined as irregular conduct by government officials for personal gain. In the context of human trafficking, corruption simply means that public officials seek financial reward by either looking the other way or by actively facilitating trafficking activities, such as issuing travel documents in sending countries, allowing easy pass at transit and destination countries, or providing cover in red-light districts. Corrupt officials can be found in many countries and occupy high-ranking positions, such as consulate officials, border patrol officers, or local law enforcement agencies in districts infested with vice activities. Corrupt officials can also be found in intelligence and security services, armed forces, and private businesses such as travel agencies, airlines, and financial institutions. A report from the Program against Corruption and Organized Crime in South Eastern Europe (PACO) found that almost all countries in southeastern Europe had corruption problems directly linked to human trafficking and asserted that "trafficking cannot take place without the involvement of corrupt officials."[31] These corrupt acts range "from passivity (ignoring or tolerating), to actively participating in or even organizing trafficking of human beings, that is, from a violation of duties, to corruption or organized crime."[32] In many countries, local police officers are frequent customers of brothels where trafficked victims are kept.[33] Visa and immigration officials receive free sexual services in exchange for overlooking fraudulent documents presented by human traffickers.[34]

There are no practical ways to gauge how corrupt a government is. One of the most frequently quoted sources is the Corruption Perception Index (CPI) from Transparency International.[35] Transparency International has conducted the CPI study for many years and has expanded it to include 146 countries in its most recent analysis. It has become a respected "index that assembles expert perceptions vis-à-vis corruption" and a widely used source for researchers in various fields.[36] The CPI uses a ranking system, in which each country is assigned a number from 1 to 10, with 10 being the least corrupt and 1 being the most corrupt. The CPI data are typically compiled from eighteen different sources and by twelve different institutions.

Based on public data, a correlation table is presented in Table 7.2 to illustrate how poverty, corruption, and human trafficking are connected to each other. Correlation analysis examines how different factors may change in a corresponding manner. For instance, years of education tend to correspond with levels of future earnings. Religiosity tends to correspond well with frequency of church attendance. Poverty here contains four measures: (1) per capita income based on a country's gross domestic product (GDP), (2) infant mortality rate under age five, (3) percentage of primary education available to the general population, and (4) life expectancy.[37] Per capita income is the combined output within a country's

Table 7.2 Pearson Correlation of Poverty, Corruption Index, and TIP Ranking

	1	2	3	4	5	6
1. Tier ranking	—	.230*	−.435**	−.414**	−.286	−.081
2. Infant mortality	.230*	—	−.446**	−.448**	−.928**	−.541**
3. Corruption	−.435**	−.446**	—	.845**	.534*	.235*
4. Per capita income	−.414**	−.448**	.845**	—	.552**	.252**
5. Life expectancy	−.286**	−.928**	.534**	.552**	—**	.591**
6. Primary education	−.081	−.541**	.235*	.252**	.591	—

Source: The World Bank, UNICEF, UN Population Division, and the UNESCO Institute for Statistics.
*$p < .01$; **$p < .001$.

economy in one year divided by the population. Infant mortality is measured per 1,000 live births; it indicates the quality of medical care and access to public health services. Percentage of primary education is measured by the number of children with access to the primary educational systems inside a country. Life expectancy is the average number of years people in a nation are expected to live.

As Table 7.2 indicates, both corruption and poverty-related measures are significantly correlated with the TIP ranking, except for the percentage of the population with access to primary education. Of all variables, corruption and per capita income have the strongest correlation with the TIP ranking. The greater the transparency in government operations (i.e., less corruption), the lower the rank in the TIP tier system (i.e., less problem with human trafficking), and the greater the per capita income, the lower the TIP rank.[38] A close examination of the latest TIP report and the CPI study seems to confirm these patterns. Countries accused of high levels of corruption also tend to be those exerting little effort against human trafficking, whereas states low in official corruption mostly strive to combat human trafficking.

Poverty is an important enabling factor, but official corruption may be more pertinent. The lack of government transparency, official ineptitude, and collusion are likely to facilitate and enable human trafficking to a greater extent than factors related to poverty. The policy implication is clear—any effort to curb human trafficking must address its symbiotic relationship with the regulatory environment. Although there is no denying that women and children, allured by financial incentives, often become victims of human trafficking, the sociocultural circumstances that permit and sustain the initial deception and subsequent enslavement of prospective victims may have more to do with governmental ineptitude or downright corruption.

Trafficking and victimization trends often vary from region to region, and that variance makes it hard to develop coherent and consistent causal patterns. The fact that most victims come from less-developed countries has led researchers to focus almost exclusively on the role of poverty in the trafficking business. The poverty theory makes sense because the lack of economic opportunities most often provides the initial impetus for prospective victims to fall prey to human traffickers. However, in order for human traffickers to mount successful and continuous operations, a regulatory environment conducive to the trafficking trade and related vice industry is required. This regulatory environment deserves greater attention if researchers hope to gain insight into not just factors contributing to the onset of human trafficking but also, more importantly, what sustains and perpetuates this enterprise.

Human Trafficking as a Business

The brokers and facilitators of human trafficking come in many shapes and forms. Some traffickers work with just one or two associates and rely on an informal network of entrepreneurs for referrals as well as for services. Others have developed elaborate networks of partners that operate in a highly organized manner. By most accounts, outright kidnapping or transporting victims in shackles is rare. The vast majority of women and children become victimized by people they either trust or come to depend on for survival in the foreign country. Allured by the prospect of a brighter future, victims often embark on a journey to America or to other developed countries, either on their own initiative or at the urging of their families. With few employable skills and little education, many women are often forced into jobs that they had never thought of taking. The sex industry often plays a role in the trafficking of young women to countries, both in the West and in the developing world that depends heavily on tourism. The sex industry demands a continuous supply of prostitutes, young and different, which often cannot be supplied locally. Brothel operators must recruit women from other places. Foreign women are often cheaper, younger, and, most importantly, easier to control than local prostitutes. As a result, sex trade operators are increasingly turning to traffickers and smugglers to recruit women and girls from poor countries.

In one such case in July 2005, following extensive investigations and in collaboration with the Labor Department and authorities of Honduras, the U.S. government broke up a large trafficking operation, indicting ten of its members.[39] The perpetrators allegedly recruited young women, some as young as fourteen, from poor rural villages in Honduras and smuggled them into the United States. They were promised legitimate jobs as waitresses in restaurants but, upon arrival, they were forced to work off their smuggling debt as female companions in bars in Hudson County, New Jersey. These women were subjected to physical and sexual assaults and forced to work up to seven days a week in bars owned by the ringleader.

Threats to harm their family members back in Honduras were also used to keep these women in line. Despite being underage, many of these women were forced to drink continually and dance with male customers in order to make money to pay for smuggling fees ranging from $10,000 to $20,000. When some of the young women became pregnant by their handlers, they were forced to terminate pregnancies so they could continue to generate income. The gangster boss, a fifty-year-old U.S. citizen and native of El Salvador, hired recruiters in Honduras to locate young, attractive women in poor villages, mostly in their teens and early twenties, and then used the *coyotes* to smuggle them into the United States. A group of enforcers made sure these women worked and obeyed instructions. Despite the fact that these women were able to bring in $250 to $500 a week working at the bars, they were required to turn in all their earnings and were given only $240 for forty-eight hours of work per week, plus a percentage of the profits from the sale of alcoholic drinks to customers.

Because the United States is one of the most sought-after destination countries, brokers and facilitators involved in human trafficking activities come from all corners of the world as well as from inside the country. In 2005 a Russian woman was charged with introducing her eighteen-year-old niece to prostitution after paying $6,000 for a fraudulent visa to bring her to the United States and then forcing her to have sex with men in Las Vegas and Los Angeles.[40] In Livonia, Michigan, two residents were arrested for forcing at least four women from Ukraine to work as dancers at a local strip club.[41] These women were recruited with promises of legitimate jobs as waitresses. They were smuggled into the United States for $12,000 each and forced to work at the strip club for twelve hours a day, six days a week. All their earnings were taken by the traffickers to pay for the so-called travel expenses and the additional fees required for identification papers. They lived in an apartment with no telephone and were beaten and threatened with death if they attempted to escape.

In another case in New York, three men pleaded guilty to federal charges for trafficking Mexican women for prostitution and subjecting the victims to violence and forced abortions. One man forced his girlfriend to have an abortion so she could continue to do her prostitution work in Brooklyn and Queens, while another man threatened to kill his own wife's family in Mexico if she did not continue to have sex with twenty men a night. The three men admitted that they went down to Mexico and recruited women with promises of jobs and marriages. Once in the United States, these women were routinely subjected to beatings for being reluctant to engage in prostitution. None of the money from prostitution was given to the women. Two of the three men were brothers who worked through their relatives in Mexico to recruit young women from impoverished areas through deception and fraud, which included gifts, chocolates, and even marriages.[42]

The exploitation of women and children knows no boundary. A brief review of the news releases of ICE operations indicates that human trafficking occurs in most states. For instance, a Wisconsin couple used threats of serious harm and physical restraint to hold a Filipina woman as a domestic servant in their home for nineteen years.[43] The woman was forced to work long hours, seven days a week, with little or no pay. She was confined within the house most of the time, and she could not leave unsupervised. She was required to hide in the basement whenever non-family members were present, and she was not allowed to socialize or communicate freely with anyone outside.

Human trafficking is not limited to slave labor or sexual services. Recently authorities in Baja California uncovered a baby-trafficking operation. A group of seven individuals allegedly bought babies in Mexico and sold them in the United States for adoption.[44] One of the seven traffickers was a U.S. citizen from New Jersey; the others included Mexican nationals and a mother (who sold her two children to adoption agents in the United States). The traffickers allegedly paid a $1,000 finder's fee to recruiters to find parents willing to give up their babies. The scheme came to the attention of authorities when two of the suspects offered to buy a boy from a man in Tijuana for $5,000 plus a rent-free apartment for a year. The man reported it to the police.[45]

SEX TRAFFICKING—KOREAN STYLE

Although some traffickers are nothing more than "street vendors" or "hustlers" who peddle their "merchandise" to whoever seeks their services, others are far more organized in their business conduct and coordinated in their executions. When it comes to organization and execution, few come close to the level of sophistication of Korean sex traffickers. The following two case studies illustrate how Korean sex traffickers operated lucrative prostitution businesses in the United States using women trafficked from their home country.

Operation Gilded Cage[46]

Korean prostitutes in the United States have traditionally worked in massage parlors, skin-care treatment centers, or acupressure clinics. They are found in many urban centers, such as Los Angeles, San Francisco, and New York. These women typically entertain Korean tourists as well as local clients. In June 2005 approximately one thousand federal and local law enforcement officers conducted raids simultaneously in Los Angeles and San Francisco. They made dozens of arrests in the two cities, seizing $3 million in illicit proceeds. The nine-month investigation, which was code-named Operation Gilded Cage, broke up one of the largest prostitution rings in San Francisco and Los Angeles that allegedly trafficked hundreds of Korean women into the United States for prostitution.

In Los Angeles, where there is a large Korean community, twenty-four persons were arrested and charged with trafficking hundreds of South Korean women into the United States to work as prostitutes. Twenty-eight business and private residences across the greater Los Angeles area were searched. These sites included brothels and safe houses where authorities seized more than $1.8 million in bank deposits, cash, and checks.

In San Francisco, federal and local law enforcement authorities arrested twenty-seven members of an organization that allegedly transported and found work for about one hundred Korean sex workers and held their passports until their debts were paid. Approximately fifty brothels and several private residences were searched. About $2 million was seized. The brothel operators in the Bay Area and Los Angeles appeared to know each other and shared sex workers with each other.

The investigation centered on the Jung Organization in Los Angeles. The ringleaders, Young Joon Jung and Ho Kyung Kim, allegedly recruited prostitutes in South Korea and smuggled them across the Mexican and Canadian borders or fraudulently obtained visitors' visas. Traffickers reportedly enticed women from the impoverished areas of South Korea by offering them jobs as waitresses and bar hostesses in the United States, and charged them fees ranging from $10,000 to $15,000. The brothel owners reportedly paid traffickers the trafficking fees for each of these prostitutes but held their passports until the fees were paid off. During this period, brothel owners collected and maintained control of all prostitution proceeds. These Korean-run massage parlors, located throughout Los Angeles and the Bay Area, were often in older buildings that attracted little attention from passersby. Most had buzzers to let clients in and were tightly controlled by the owners.

Brothel owners and members of the Jung Organization worked together to schedule and transport these prostitutes to work on different shifts at various locations. The transportation was provided by a network of underground Korean "taxi" services associated with the Jung Organization. These brothels advertised their services through local Korean-language papers and the Internet. The Jung network extended their operations to Las Vegas, Dallas, Boston, and New York.

Chiropractic Licenses for Rent—The Luly Case[47]

After five years of investigation, the Los Angeles County Sheriff's Department broke up an organized prostitution ring that operated under the guise of chiropractic offices. The main suspect in this case, John Luly, a chiropractor licensed in California, was arrested on December 31, 2004, as he disembarked from a plane that had just arrived from the Philippines.

His two main coconspirators, also licensed chiropractors, were arrested on February 11, 2005. The Luly operation attracted attention from the vice squad of the Los Angeles County Sheriff's Department because he and his coconspirators became careless in their business expansion.

Indoor prostitution in Los Angeles County has traditionally been run inside spas, massage parlors, skin-care clinics, or nightclubs. Because of aggressive crackdowns in recent years, sex services in these traditional locations have been greatly reduced. In response, brothel owners have increasingly looked elsewhere for alternative business outlets. They have adapted by changing massage parlors and skin-care clinics to chiropractic offices, and they pay licensed chiropractors to hang their certificates inside their business locations. Because California law allows unlicensed massage therapists to work under the supervision of licensed chiropractors, this strategy accomplishes two things for the brothel owners: they now have a legitimate business front, and the sex workers can work as massage therapists under "supervision."

Luly and his partners soon became the "owners" of many chiropractic clinics. But the real owners were mostly Koreans, and the sex workers inside the offices were Koreans and Hispanics. The business was lucrative. It was estimated that each location could generate up to $2 million a year in prostitution proceeds.

Wiretaps and undercover investigations were carried out on many of these suspicious chiropractic offices. It was discovered that the majority of the prostitutes were smuggled in across the Canadian or Mexican border. The brothel owners moved their sex workers from state to state to escape prosecution or to fill in other locations. Many of the females were kept in safe houses maintained by the owners and were picked up by a taxi service also operated by the brothel owners. Massage therapist certificates were obtained for the prostitutes by the owners, who would pay up to $1,000 per certificate.

In August 2002 Luly and his partners operated a total of fifty-four chiropractic locations in five Southern California counties. They were paid between $1,200 and $2,000 a month, in cash, from each location by the actual owners, although the actual monthly payment varied depending on the size of the operation. The minimum was $1,000 to hang a copy of the chiropractor license on the business premises. The proceeds were divided among Luly and his two partners. An associate who allowed his license to be posted in a location received one-quarter of the monthly fee, and an associate who sat in the office (pretending to be working there) for two to six hours would get $100 in cash from the manager of the location. Patients who entered these locations were always male. Occasionally new patients arrived and asked to be assessed by the chiropractor on duty. The prescription was always a massage. If a female accidentally wandered into the office and inquired about services, she would be turned away by the manager. There was no insurance billing. No credit cards were accepted. It was a cash-only business.

A "shell game" was often played by the involved chiropractors, in which they switched licenses from business to business to confuse city license officials, police officers, and the state chiropractic board. None of these locations even bothered to display anything resembling a piece of chiropractic equipment. About the only thing chiropractic was a copy of the license on the wall, and only five chiropractors were ever present at any of the dozens of locations during the investigation.

Advertisements for the businesses were placed in adult newspapers. Password-protected Web sites were set up for current and prospective "patients" to share and describe various types of sex acts and associated fees at different locations. Descriptions of explicit sex acts and services were also posted on Web sites and in local adult publications. Male patrons were provided with details of sex services when they entered the clinics. Most locations charged an entry fee of about $50 for half an hour and $80 for one hour of massage therapy. Actual sex services, for which the customers would pay extra, were introduced and negotiated during the massage session.

Luly and his associates were no strangers to law enforcement agencies. Prior to their apprehension, a total of 117 arrests had been made for prostitution and other sex-related crimes at their business locations, as well as forty-seven massage-related violations. Their earliest encounter with the police was back in 1997 in Huntington Beach, California. Despite numerous visits by law enforcement and regulatory agencies about the prostitution activity at their business locations, Luly and his partners showed little interest in responding to the complaints and continued to expand their business locations instead. By July 2001 Luly had posted satellite certificates at eleven locations, despite the fact that there had already been forty-two arrests for various sex crimes and twenty-seven arrests for massage violations at his "clinics. By August 2002 Luly and his two coconspirators had put their licenses in fifty-four locations where an additional sixty-two arrests for various sex crimes and twenty arrests for massage violations had occurred.

COMBATING HUMAN TRAFFICKING

Human trafficking is a multidimensional issue involving immigration, labor, criminal behavior, health, and human rights. Its transnational character demands that origin, transit, and destination countries work together to effectively deal with this problem. Unfortunately, these countries rarely see things the same way. Destination countries tend to view trafficked victims the same way they do illegal migrants, regardless of their life circumstances, and want to get rid of them. Origin and transit countries pay little attention to these victims because they have few resources to offer. The lack of jobs for women and the absence of welfare protection for children in many developing countries leave these groups particularly vulnerable to human traffickers.

The UN has spearheaded many efforts to encourage member states to introduce legislation to specify and increase penalties against human trafficking, to train law enforcement agencies to recognize and aggressively prosecute trafficking cases, and to improve international collaboration in joint crackdown efforts. Interpol has taken the lead in organizing international law enforcement training conferences and establishing mechanisms whereby police officials of different countries can share intelligence and assist in each other's investigations. Unfortunately, the majority of developing countries cannot afford to place human trafficking high on their national agenda or to invest manpower or money. Moreover, due to official corruption and ineptitude, enforcement has remained weak and sporadic.

The United States, on the other hand, has been in the forefront of the fight against human trafficking, and the topic has attracted much political attention in the United States. Secretary of State Condoleezza Rice called trafficking in human beings a modern-day slave trade and said the United States bears "a particular duty to fight this scourge because trafficking in persons is an affront to the principles of human dignity and liberty upon which this nation was founded."[48] The President's Interagency Task Force (PITF), established in 2001, was chaired by the secretary of state and attended by senior officials from the departments of State, Homeland Security, and Justice. In 2003 a senior working level group, the Senior Policy Operating Group (SPOG), was created to follow up on PITF initiatives and to implement U.S. government antitrafficking policies and guidelines. Congress passed the Trafficking Victims Protection Act of 2000 that aimed at curtailing human trafficking worldwide. In January 2006 Congress renewed the bill with an expansion to include measures to combat prostitution inside U.S. borders, providing funds to local and state law enforcement agencies to go after pimps and johns, the core client base for the human trafficking business.

Diplomacy and Human Trafficking

The aggressive domestic antitrafficking policies, however, have not translated well in the United States' dealings with other countries. The battle against transnational human trafficking is a politically and diplomatically sensitive issue. Many countries that have close political and economic ties with the United States are also countries that have long histories of human rights abuses, including Saudi Arabia, Kuwait, and the United Arab Emirates. Over the years the United States has accused many countries of not doing enough to stop the modern-day slave trade in prostitutes, child sex workers, and forced laborers. But at the same time, the U.S. government does not want to cause excessive diplomatic friction with countries where vital U.S. interests lie.

For instance, the TIP report in 2005 alleged that Saudi Arabia failed to comply with the minimum standards for the elimination of trafficking and was not making significant efforts to do so. The oil-rich country has long been accused by human rights groups of turning a blind eye to the problem of exploiting foreign laborers and of holding them in servitude-like working conditions. It is widely known that Saudi employers physically and sexually abuse women housekeepers from South Asia, Africa, and other places. Many of these domestic workers were raped and impregnated. Children born out of these sexual assaults are not recognized by the Saudi government. However, Saudi Arabia's poor standing in the TIP report did not prevent the United States from forging a tight alliance built on economic and military cooperation. Nor did it prevent President Bush from inviting Crown Prince Abdullah, ruler of Saudi Arabia, to the Bush family ranch in Crawford, Texas, in April 2002.

The Problems of the TIP Report

The TIP report has been widely used and quoted by government agencies, NGOs, and researchers, despite its many flaws. Few have the access to examine who decides what to include in this report. Recently, however, the U.S. Government Accountability Office (GAO; formerly the General Accounting Office) raised questions about the accuracy and methodology of the estimates in the TIP report. The GAO study challenged the figures issued by the U.S. government on the number of persons being trafficked across international borders annually. The GAO report poignantly stated, "The U.S. government's estimate was developed by one person who did not document all his work, so the estimate may not be replicable, casting doubt on its reliability. Moreover, country data are not available, reliable, or comparable. . . . The U.S. government has not yet established an effective mechanism for estimating the number of victims or for conducting ongoing analysis of trafficking-related data that resides within government entities."[49] The report also pointed out that the explanations for the tier system established by the U.S. State Department are incomplete and that the system is not consistently used to develop antitrafficking programs. The many problems associated with the ranking system undermine the TIP report's credibility and usefulness as a diplomatic tool, as well as its utility to guide U.S. government funding effectiveness on antitrafficking programs.

The GAO report also criticized the federal government for its lack of a coordinated strategy for combating trafficking abroad or a mechanism to gauge the outcomes of its programs overseas. Although the U.S.

government has established coordination mechanisms, roles and responsibilities have not been spelled out for the multiple agencies that are supposedly working together. Nor are there any performance measures or evaluations to gauge the overall impact of antitrafficking programs abroad, thus preventing the U.S. government from determining the effectiveness of its efforts or improving its assistance to foreign governments.

Questions That Need Answers

The involvement of organized crime in the clandestine enterprise of human smuggling has been well documented. News stories, government reports, and academic studies have found extensive involvement by criminal gangs, entrepreneurial businessmen, and even ordinary citizens along the entire smuggling routes providing services to facilitate smuggling operations. None thus far have examined the differences between criminal organizations involved in human smuggling and those involved in trafficking women and children. There is little information to indicate whether these are the same groups of people or whether they each operate their own routes.

Much of the current discourse on human trafficking has not been guided by empirical research. The increased urgency in U.S. government policy and funding priority to combat trafficking in women and children has been influenced more by a moral panic that continues to gain momentum rather than by solid and systematic assessment of the problem.[50] Research on human trafficking remains challenging due to its secrecy and political sensitivity. The existing body of literature is plagued with methodological and analytical flaws. Researchers often drew conclusions or generalized findings based on biased samples (e.g., street prostitutes only, but no call girls or other indoor workers), interviews in shelters or jails, and anecdotal stories.[51]

Because of the lack of empirical guidance, there are several key questions that remain unanswered about the trafficking business and the socioeconomic circumstances that give rise to trafficking activities. These questions include the configurations of factors (e.g., economic, sociocultural, legal, personal) that form the main driving force behind cross-border trafficking in women and children from the source countries to the United States, the process of the trafficking trade that turns job-seeking women into victims of sexual exploitation, and possible strategies to prevent trafficking and assist the victims. One would assume that international cooperation would be required to examine the flow of migrants from the source countries to the United States, particularly the investigations of trafficking activities. Surprisingly no such studies can be found in the literature. Such studies are greatly needed to provide policy-relevant knowledge that will guide the battle against this global problem.

Current research and available data offer little information on where and when the victimization process of trafficking actually begins. Such determinations are easy to make if parents sell their daughters to traffickers who in turn transport these women across borders and eventually sell their "merchandise" to brothels. However, women oftentimes leave home on their own in search of jobs. They are lured by traffickers and then sold to sex traders for profits. These women are not "trafficked" at the beginning but become so in their self-initiated cross-border migration.[52] There are other urgent questions that need empirical answers:

The process and modus operandi of becoming trafficked. First of all, victims must at some point become available as commodities and be sold to either traffickers or recruiters for trafficking purposes. There is little research on how this process works. Although such occurrences are possible, most victims are not kidnapped or forcefully removed from their villages and sold to the human traffickers. Therefore, questions remain regarding what strategies and schemes traffickers or relatives and family members of the victims use to initiate the transformation.

The trafficking process. Transporting human beings is different from smuggling drugs or other contraband. Food, water, shelter, transportation, and checkpoints at border crossings are only some of the logistical challenges that traffickers must overcome. Little is known about the common strategies used by traffickers to transport and shelter their clients. Discussions on how traffickers plan their transportation routes, arrange their transfers, and dispose of their "merchandise" (either through local gangsters or through brothel owners) have been mostly speculative. Furthermore, little is known about the financial arrangements between sellers and buyers.

Fighting human trafficking is no easy task and requires the commitment and cooperation of both sending and receiving countries. More importantly, policy makers should be guided by empirical evidence rather than simply try to be politically trendy.

Chapter 8

Hitchhiking: Human Smuggling and Terrorism

On December 14, 1999, U.S. Customs inspector Diana Dean was conducting a routine inspection of a motorist passenger who had just arrived in Port Angeles onboard a ferry from Victoria, British Columbia.[1] The passenger, Ahmed Ressam, appeared nervous and hesitant in his response to Dean's questions. Sensing that something was not right, Dean ordered the passenger to a secondary inspection where additional Customs inspectors joined in and found bags of bomb materials and timing devices hidden inside the vehicle's spare tire compartment. Ahmed Ressam was on his way to plant and set off explosives at the Los Angles International Airport during the new millennium celebration. He was later convicted and sentenced to twenty-two years in prison, plus five years of supervision upon release.

Algerian-born Ressam entered Canada in 1994, using a forged French passport. When he was stopped by immigration officials at the Montreal airport, he applied for political asylum, citing political persecution and torture if he were to be returned. As with all asylum applications in Canada, a formal hearing was scheduled to determine the merit of his claim. Also like the vast majority of asylum seekers in Canada, Ressam disappeared. A warrant was subsequently issued for his arrest and deportation, which meant little to him or to anyone else among the thousands upon thousands of asylum seekers who skipped their hearings. However, Ressam was actually arrested, finger-printed, photographed, and, above all, was given another court date and released back onto the streets. When his welfare checks ran out, Ressam turned to petty crimes to support himself. He shoplifted, snatched purses, stole unattended luggage, and pickpocketed. He was arrested again and again. Each time he was released on fines and probation. Ressam later managed to obtain a Canadian passport using the false name, Benni Noris. In 1998 he traveled to a terrorist training camp in Afghanistan and learned how to handle explosives, among other things.

THE TERRORISM-ORGANIZED CRIME NEXUS[2]

More than a decade ago, on March 12, 1993, a series of bombings rocked Bombay, India, killing and injuring close to a thousand people. Subsequent investigations traced the bombings not to a terrorist but to a mafia boss whose widespread syndicate and racketeering activities helped transport the explosives and weapons to the terrorists who staged the bombing incident.[3] In this case, the terrorist organization used the black market and underground transportation network controlled by the mafia boss to acquire and transport materials needed to stage the attacks. Was this a formal declaration of the convergence of two different social organizations?

Like all social organizations, there are two basic functions a terrorist organization must fulfill in order to remain viable. The first is financial capacity—a system of funding apparatus must be established and maintained to raise money for terrorist operations and organizational needs. The second function is a distribution capacity—a transportation system whereby leaders and soldiers of an organization, as well as equipment and materials (e.g., weapons and explosives), can be moved from one location to another without attracting attention from the authorities.

Although in the early decades of the twentieth century a number of states openly or secretly supported fringe organizations, state-sponsored terrorist organizations are becoming few these days. Without state sponsorships, extremist groups are becoming dependent on the goods and services provided by illicit enterprises found in many parts of the world. Financially, terrorist organizations in the Middle East or elsewhere may continue to receive funding from their wealthy donors and "charity" functions. However, any transactions through legitimate channels are closely monitored by governments. Illegal commerce thus becomes the ideal market place where terrorists can raise and transfer money, come into contact with one another, and carry out necessary organizational functions, from purchasing terrorist equipment and materials to moving operatives to their strategic locations across international borders.

Law enforcement officials believe that the convergence of organized crime and terrorist groups has already taken place. Because both organized criminals and terrorists rely on an underground economy to raise and move money, their interests and activities inevitably intertwine in this illicit market place. Money launderers move and hide proceeds for drug traffickers. In turn, drug trafficking groups sell weapons to terrorists, and terrorists engage in cigarette and jewelry smuggling or credit card fraud to raise money for their operations.[4]

Investigations by federal and local law enforcement agencies have revealed a series of such convergence cases involving potential terrorists and ordinary, financially driven criminal organizations. In July 2000 federal and local law enforcement agencies broke up a cigarette smuggling operation in Charlotte, North Carolina.[5] Eighteen suspects were arrested in this multi-agency operation, codenamed "Smokescreen." Smugglers in this case took advantage of differential taxes levied by Michigan and North Carolina by buying cigarettes in one state and transporting them to another. Inside the warehouse where the smuggled cigarettes were kept, authorities also found cash, weapons (including shotguns, rifles, and an AK-47), and documents written in Arabic. The smuggling scheme was simple. North Carolina had low cigarette taxes, five cents a pack, while Michigan levied seventy-five cents a pack. Smugglers would purchase hundreds of cartons of cigarettes with cash and transport them from Charlotte to Detroit and sell them to Arab-owned convenience stores in Detroit. The proceeds were then shuttled back to Charlotte. Although cigarette smuggling as a racket is nothing new, an alarming aspect of this case was that part of the proceeds were sent to the Middle East to support the activities of *Hezbollah* (or the "Army of God" in Arabic), the terrorist organization in Lebanon that kidnapped two Israeli soldiers and sparked a month-long war in the Golan Heights in August 2006. Hezbollah has long been listed by the U.S. government as a terrorist organization, responsible for firing rockets at civilian targets in Israel and supporting the Al-Aqsa Martyrs Brigades in recruiting and training suicide bombers.

The ring leader, Mohamad Youssef Hammoud, allegedly sent money to members of Hezbollah in Lebanon and met frequently with Hezbollah members in the Charlotte area, including Mohamad Harb, a Lebanese-born, naturalized U.S. citizen. According to U.S. Justice Department documents, Harb was raising money and purchasing supplies for Hezbollah. The materials that Harb sent to Hezbollah included night-vision goggles; cameras and scopes; surveying equipment; global positioning systems; mine and metal detection equipment; video equipment; advanced aircraft analysis and design software; laptop computers; stun guns; radios; mining, drilling, and blasting equipment; radars; ultrasonic dog repellents; and laser range finders. Federal agents believed these supplies were purchased with profits from the cigarette smuggling business.

Terrorism and Geographical Mobility

In a broad sense, to accomplish whatever political goals, terrorists must be able to travel. Geographical mobility enables terrorist groups to acquire weapons and explosives and to recruit and move personnel to strategic locations. The business of human smuggling fulfills the vital function of geographical mobility. Terrorists travel abroad to foster ties with potential allies, to conduct training, to raise money, and to attract political support for their causes. Most importantly, they need to travel to plan and carry out attacks.

Aside from the September 11 events, Islamic extremists affiliated with Al-Qaeda have long demonstrated their ability to plan and carry out attacks against U.S. interests in a wide range of geographical locations. On February 26, 1993, Islamic fundamentalists detonated a cargo van packed with 1,500-lbs. of explosives in an underground garage below the World Trade Center in New York City. The explosion killed six people and injured 1,042. The foundation of Tower One was damaged and so were several subway tunnels. On August 7, 1998, well-coordinated explosions were set off simultaneously at U.S. embassies in Kenya and Tanzania, killing 257 people and injuring more than 4,000. On October 12, 2000, USS Cole docked in Aden harbor in Yemen for a routine refueling stop. A small craft packed with explosives rammed the port side of the destroyer. The explosion punctured a forty-by-forty-foot hole and led to flooding in the engineering spaces. Seventeen sailors were killed, and thirty-nine others were injured.

TERRORISM, ILLEGAL MIGRATION, AND GLOBALIZATION

The rising tide of globalization has also brought along Islamic extremism and organized crime. With the help of modern aviation, telecommunication, email, and cell phones, entrepreneurs as well as their criminal organizations have followed the advance of legitimate economy to carve out niche markets around the world. Business opportunities have thus multiplied for transitional criminal organizations, including telemarketing frauds, banking and financial scams, identity theft, intellectual property piracy, corporate espionage, and the trafficking of weapons and human beings.

Along with the expansion of both legitimate and criminal enterprising opportunities, globalization has also reduced the distances between nations and cultures, creating tensions, frictions, and confrontations. The United States, as an advocate and dominant player of the market economy, has overshadowed the world with its ideological and economic presence and thus become the prime target for many radical groups. Anything that symbolizes the American or Western culture becomes a fair target for explosion or bombing. These include skyscrapers, shopping malls, bridges, airplanes, and major metropolitan areas such as New York and Los Angeles. Rapid and clandestine mobility thus become a key operational requisite for fringe groups to remain viable.

There are two ways to achieve clandestine mobility. First, terrorists can blend into the regular commercial traffic and travel by plane, bus, or train. Although this method is convenient, it relies on the acquisition of forged or fraudulently obtained identity papers, such as those used by Ahmed Ressam. Individuals with skills to manufacture or alter such documents are therefore highly sought after. The second method, albeit less convenient, will be blending into the global traffic of illegal migration, taking advantage of loosely guarded international borders such as those between the United States and its two neighboring countries. Human smugglers provide a convenient conduit for terrorists to move around the world to their strategic positions and into the United States. It is not only possible but logical for terrorists to make use of the established network of transportation across borders and into the United States.

Terrorist groups need more than the border crossing service. Ahmed Ressam was able to cross international borders with impunity primarily because of his role in an underground counterfeit business, in which he stole passports from tourists visiting Canada. The value of a well-altered identification paper is well understood by both criminal and terrorist organizations. Human smugglers and document vendors have long developed partnerships that feed on each other's business needs. Much of this symbiotic relationship serves as a lubricant to the cogs of the global underground economy, because counterfeit documents and clandestine transportation networks enable entrepreneurs of all kinds to meet and exchange goods and services. The use of fraudulent documents can be as benign as landing a janitor job at Wal-Mart or as serious as gaining employment at mission-sensitive facilities such as airports, shipyards, and defense industries. In June 2005 twenty-six illegal immigrants were discovered working at Northrop-Grumman's shipyard in Pascagoula, Mississippi.[6] These illegal immigrants all used false documents to gain employment at this warship building facility. Some of them had been previously deported but re-entered the country with a different identity.

When it comes to illegal transnational migration, there are numerous groups of entrepreneurs around the world who will gladly provide fee-paying customers with services as simple as walking across unguarded borders or as sophisticated as a combination of by-air, by-land, and even by-sea transportation operations. Human smugglers, such as the Chinese snakeheads, have developed reliable international networks with way stations and safe houses that can systematically transport illegal migrants to their desired destinations. Other criminal elements in the underground economy, including corrupt officials, travel agencies, lawyers, and even unscrupulous bankers, can provide a wide array of services from passports and visas to transportation and border crossing. It is only a matter of time before extremists find a way to tap into the network of illicit service providers that can meet their organizational needs.

Disturbing Trends in Human Smuggling

As the nineteen hijackers on September 11, 2001, amply demonstrated, it is not difficult to infiltrate the United States through legal and illegal channels. Sightings of illegal migrants from high-risk parts of the world at the U.S.-Mexican border have been reported with increased frequency in recent years. For example, in 2004 Border Patrol agents from Arizona and Texas encountered scores of males "of Middle Eastern descent" believed to have trekked through the Chiricahua Mountains with the help of *coyotes* as part of a larger group of illegal immigrants. Many of them were released from immigration detention centers due to lack of space.[7]

Similarly, in a series of investigations by the Associated Press in 2005, illegal migrants from countries rife with extremists were entering the United States through illegal border crossings. These countries included Iran, Lebanon, Jordan, Egypt, Iraq, and Pakistan. The majority of illegal migrants exploited smuggling channels in Latin America. Some of the human smugglers were ethnic Arabs who helped their countrymen for a fee, but many others were Mexicans. In addition to reviewing court indictments, congressional testimonies, and government reports, the Associated Press reporters conducted dozens of interviews in Mexico and the United States that revealed an alarming trend of illegal border crossings. The following were some of the cases reported by the Associate Press:[8]

- In May 2005 federal agents arrested a thirty-nine-year-old Iranian man in a sting operation for trying to smuggle other Iranians into the United States over the Arizona-Mexico border. Zeayadali Malhamdary, who owned a tailoring business in Mesa, Arizona, offered an undercover agent $12,000 to insert fraudulent Mexican visas into Iranian passports to help illegal migrants enter Mexico first and then cross overland into the United States. The undercover agent was also instructed to pick up the Iranian migrants at the Mexico City airport and take them to the border town of Nogales for illegal border crossing. Malhamdary allegedly had smuggled about sixty Iranians into the United States using similar schemes.
- In September 2004 five individuals were charged in Michigan for smuggling more than two hundred illegal migrants from Iraq, Jordan, and other Middle Eastern countries into the United States from 2001 to 2004. The scheme involved flying illegal migrants from the Middle East with counterfeit passports and other fake documents to South American countries including Peru and Ecuador, and then onto Dulles International Airport outside of Washington, D.C. The smugglers allegedly received assistance from corrupt officials in these South American

countries. Two of the defendants, Neeran "Nancy" Hakim Zaia and Basima "Linda" Sesi, were Iraqi-born naturalized U.S. citizens and held regular jobs prior to their arrest. Zaia, who operated a U.S.-based travel agency, recruited her clients via Arab-language media outlets in Detroit. Sesi, an assistant ombudsman for the city of Detroit, recruited clients for Zaia, charging fees between $9,500 and $12,000 per person.

• In July 2004 an Egyptian man and his Guatemalan wife were arrested at the Miami International Airport on charges of human smuggling. Ashraf Ahmed Abdallah and Sara Luz Diaz Gamez worked with recruiters in Egypt and transporters in South American countries to move illegal migrants toward the U.S.-Mexican border. The husband-and-wife team, based in Guatemala City, established way stations in Ecuador, Nicaragua, Brazil, Costa Rica, Guatemala, and Mexico. Illegal Egyptian migrants, paying $8,000 a person, were flown directly into Latin American countries on tourist visas and then transported to Guatemala City to prepare for the last leg of journey to Mexico, where they would be smuggled across the border into Texas, New Mexico, and Arizona.

Although most illegal border crossings occur in the south, the U.S.-Canadian border is not free from infiltration by illegal migrants from countries with terrorist ties. In April 2006 U.S. and Canadian authorities broke up a human smuggling ring that transported illegal migrants from India and Pakistan into Washington State through British Columbia.[9] The smuggling organization exploited loopholes between patrolled ports to slip migrants across the border. The smugglers bought maps of the border and asked local residents about border patrol and police enforcement activities in the area. Twelve U.S. and Canadian men were arrested. Approximately fifty illegal migrants paid $35,000 a person to be smuggled into the United States.

In another case, in October 2004 Pakistani cab driver Muhammad Qasum Lala received a seventeen-month prison sentence for smuggling his countrymen over the border from Canada into the United States. Acting on tips, Border Patrol agents staked out a bed-and-breakfast in Blaine, Washington, that Lala used as a safe house. Lala, who lived in Surrey, British Columbia, allegedly transported six to ten people several times a week from Canada into Blaine. The ride across the border cost about $3,000 a person.

Although these illegal migrants were just as likely to look for better economic opportunities as those from other countries, one can never tell if and when extremists were among them. According to one FBI affidavit, an illegal migrant from Lebanon admitted spending time in the United States raising at least $40,000 to support Hezbollah.[10]

INTERACTIONS BETWEEN TERRORISTS AND ORGANIZED CRIMINALS

There is no systematic research examining the interaction between terrorist groups and regular criminal organizations. But speculations abound. Many in the intelligence community as well as in the news media believe with much certainty that such a nexus already exists. It makes logical sense. Islamic extremists will not rely on growing corns and vegetables to support their organizational needs. They have to find efficient ways to raise money, purchase and distribute explosives and weapons, and send operatives to their target locations. Instead of developing their own channels and working out their own logistics, it will be convenient for them to simply tap into existing illegal channels established by other entrepreneurs to acquire and distribute goods and services necessary for their survival and missions. The question is how these two groups initiate contact and conduct transactions or whether terrorists and organized crime groups engage in similar or identical criminal activities. This is an important empirical question that bears significant policy and law enforcement implications. It will be interesting to examine empirically just what types of economic activities tend to attract extremist groups.

On the other hand, organized crime groups have long been known to apply terrorist tactics in their business practices, such as violence or threat of violence, extortion, bombing, and even direct armed confrontations with rival gangs and law enforcement agencies. However, these terrorist tactics are not used for achieving political objectives but for protecting or seizing territory. Violence for instrumental purposes has always been a staple for drug traffickers and human smugglers. Drug traffickers and producers in Latin American or the Golden Triangle in Southeast Asia have long been known for organizing armed resistance against government anti-trafficking campaigns. Again, it remains an empirical question if these two groups will converge in some deliberate way so that they can assist and benefit from one another.

Conditions Conducive to the Terrorism-Organized Crime Nexus

Because of the lack of empirical research on the nexus between organized crime and terrorism, one can only speculate how such collaboration can take place. One must begin with an assumption that terrorists and organized criminals can find each other. From human smuggling to loan sharking, and from drug trafficking to labor racketeering, one can think of many forms of organized criminal activities in many major urban centers around the world. One can perhaps find a cab driver to get in touch with a mafia boss or go to a barber's shop to get some leads. It is easier said than done. With few exceptions, such as fencing stolen goods and prostitution where there are visible store fronts and strangers are allowed, most racketeering activities are controlled by criminal organizations that shun strangers. Business transactions are typically carried out between people who know each other directly or through trusted go-betweens. For terrorist groups to get in touch with criminal organizations or to secure their services, one must have dual membership in both sectors or rely on referrals that can be trusted by both sides. On the other hand, those who are familiar with organized criminals should know, it may be easy to get in touch with them and get favors initially, but not so easy to get rid of them.

There are, however, broader conditions that may encourage the growth of extremism and their possible collusion with criminal organizations. First, because of the entrepreneurial nature of illicit enterprises, extremist groups can easily find and choose willing participants to acquire the needed goods and services. The underground market place is after all an equal opportunity environment where money reigns. As enterprising agents, human smugglers or firearms dealers do not discriminate against any fee-paying customers. As one group of entrepreneurs pursues financial gains, another group of "entrepreneurs" seeks ways to advance its political interests in different parts of the world through violence and mayhem.

Second, the U.S.-led war and subsequent occupation in Iraq has fueled anti-American sentiments in many parts of the world. The U.S. global strategy in its war on terror has led to accusations of human rights violations, hence deeper resentment among Muslim countries and weariness among allies. For fear of agitating or radicalizing otherwise moderate members of the Muslim community, some governments have been slow in taking steps to investigate and pursue terrorist suspects. A few governments are simply reluctant to be perceived as playing to U.S. influence. In short, the United States may have produced a lot more hostile and extreme groups around the world, whose bases are not necessarily in the Middle East. Their scattered presence makes it easy to tap into the diverse world of illicit enterprises and access resources wherever available.

Third, the globalization of commerce and information has also increased contacts between Muslims from the Middle East and their counterparts in other parts of the world. The export of clerics and their practices from the Middle East has reached many parts of the Western world and will likely influence a new generation of believers who are susceptible to the radical version of Islam. Radicalization of Islam is also likely to persist along with perceived social injustice and unfair treatment of Muslim minorities in parts of the world outside the Middle East. Unless these social conditions can somehow be addressed adequately, fringe groups will emerge to pursue radical changes. Such is the case in the Philippines where the Muslim minorities grieve over their unfair treatment by the mainstream society and perceive their plight as a direct consequence of those whose values and practices are an affront to their belief system.

Conditions Hindering the Terrorist-Organized Crime Nexus

Despite the aforementioned factors, terrorist groups may not find it easy to work with regular criminal organizations. Any cooperation between criminal organizations and terrorist groups is most likely a one-way proposition, where illegal enterprises blinded by their financial interests unwittingly take on unscrupulous hitchhikers with a different agenda. The nexus between organized crime and terrorism is at best a tenuous one. This is mainly because criminal organizations and terrorist groups are diametrically different social entities. In fact, criminal organizations, whether they are loosely connected groups of human smugglers or well-organized drug cartels, cannot be more dissimilar to terrorists along two dimensions—ideological and operational. Ideologically, organized crime by definition is an irregular form of profit seeking entity, not a political machine. Although some organized criminals may be sympathetic to the causes of extreme groups, criminal organizations in general do not have a political agenda other than protecting their financial interests. Their involvement in enterprising activities is solely profit oriented.

On the contrary, the fundamental agenda of terrorist organizations is to overthrow the existing political system and drastically change the socio-economic environment, which they consider unjust and immoral. However, the reason that organized crime exists is precisely because of the inadequacies or inefficiencies of the existing economic and political system. Any disruption to the existing socio-economic arrangement will threaten the profit making activities of criminal organizations. Obviously, it serves no criminal organizations' interests to abandon or destroy existing socio-economic arrangements from which they derive their profitable existence. This fundamental ideological difference determines that any connection between the criminal organizations and extremist groups is likely to be coincidental rather than deliberate, and the extent of collusion is likely to be limited.

Operationally, most criminal organizations do not want attention from the public or authorities. Nor do they intentionally seek confrontations with the police. They typically keep a low profile and would prefer making money quietly. Most will do everything to avoid public exposure, thus minimizing unwanted attention. This is a main reason that youth gangs are rarely integrated into organized crime groups. They are raucous and unruly and often draw attention from the police. Extremists are the opposite. They crave attention from the public or anyone who would listen. When they strike, their targets are mostly chosen to maximize the exposure and to draw the most attention. In fact, all terrorist attacks share one goal—drawing as much attention as possible to their political causes.

Researching the Unknown

There is no shortage of possibilities for terrorist groups to exploit existing illegitimate market opportunities and channels to move arms and explosives as well as operatives to strategic locations. It is not only logical but possible. But there are also reasons to believe that most criminal organizations will try to avoid doing business with extremist groups, or at least will not do business with them on purpose. The question is how and when, in spite of their divergent interests, their paths may cross each other.

One major problem with our current understanding of the nexus between organized crime and terrorism is the lack of any systematic and empirical studies. Obviously it is extremely difficult for anyone to engage in field work either to observe criminal organizations to see if and how they interact with people of extreme political inclinations or to study how extremists use illicit enterprises to further their political causes. Hardly anyone has conducted systematic field work or published any findings on such a topic. Most published works on this subject matter come from anecdotal stories in the news media or government reports. Their sources of information are either too secretive to verify or too sporadic to document for research purposes. Before there is enough empirical support for such a nexus, people can only assume that such a relationship seems logical and possible.

In the end, although organized criminals may not form strong partnerships with terrorists, their unintentional convergence still deserves grave concerns from the governments of all nations. Determined and aggressive efforts must be applied to control illicit enterprises because of their potential for being used as a conduit to facilitate terrorists' activities. It is fair to say that behind each terrorist attack, there is a tie to some form of illicit enterprising activities, be it human smuggling or transportation of controlled materials. It is therefore imperative for policy makers to recognize the lethal consequences of such a nexus and begin integrating the fight against organized crime into the war on terrorism.

TERRORIST THREAT FROM SOUTHEAST ASIA

Following the September 11 events, the anti-terrorism focus has been on Afghanistan, Iraq, and the rest of the Middle East. The recent discovery of the plot to blow up U.S.-bound passenger planes from London was a reminder that extremist groups can form, activate, and launch attacks from anywhere and on their own schedule. While much of the world focuses on the unraveling situation in Iraq, little attention has been paid to Southeast Asia, another hotbed for fringe activities and anti-Western sentiments. Members of Al-Qaeda were once active in Southeast Asia. Al-Qaeda has become a symbol for instigating violence against American influence and presence.

There have been several terrorist incidents in Southeast Asia since the September 11 attacks. The worst incident was the Bali bombings of October 12, 2002, which killed 202 mostly foreign tourists and injured another 209. Jemaah Islamiyah, a native terrorist organization allegedly affiliated with Al-Qaeda, was blamed for the incident. On August 5, 2003, a car bomb exploded outside the lobby of the JW Marriott Hotel in Jakarta, killing twelve people and injuring more than 150. The thirty-three-story five-star hotel was frequented by American businesspeople and officials. The hotel suffered major damages to its lower floors and was closed for five weeks. Jemaah Islamiyah was blamed for the incident. In February 2004, in the Philippines, a ferry caught fire after an onboard explosion that left 180 passengers missing. The Philippine terrorist organization Abu Sayyaf claimed responsibility as an act of revenge against the government's mistreatment of Muslims in the Mindanao region.[11]

As discussed earlier, organized criminal activities possess the optimal structural and operational facilities for terrorist activities. Extremist groups will have a difficult time planning, coordinating, and staging terrorist operations without their parasitic dependence on the established network of illicit enterprises that provide the logistics and even access to potential targets. Southeast Asia is known for its less regulated market economies and lax border control. Among the most widely known illicit enterprises dominated by criminal organizations are heroin trafficking, human smuggling, trafficking in women and children, and the piracy of goods on the high seas. Related to these illicit enterprises are shady financial and charity organizations that help launder illegal profits and conduct financial transactions to facilitate the illegal market.

Major Organized Crimes in Southeast Asia

Drug Trafficking

Southeast Asia has long been the major drug trafficking and distribution region in the world because of its proximity to the Golden Triangle, one of the world's largest opium-cultivation and heroin-producing locations. The Golden Triangle is a 150,000-square-mile mountainous area located where the borders of Myanmar (Burma), Laos, and Thailand meet.[12] This region once produced more than 50 percent of the world's raw opium and refines as much as 75 percent of the world's heroin.[13] For most of the 1990s, the Golden Triangle enjoyed the infamous reputation of being the "breadbasket" of the world's heroin trade.[14] It was only in recent years that the status of the Golden Triangle as the world's heroin supplier was eclipsed by Afghanistan. However, Myanmar has recently become a primary source of amphetamine-type stimulants, producing hundreds of millions of tablets annually for exports to Southeast Asia and other parts of the world.[15] Easy access to chemical precursors in the region has also made Southeast Asia a prime location for methamphetamine production and distribution. In recent years, law enforcement agencies in the Philippines, Malaysia, Taiwan, Fiji, and Indonesia have uncovered so-called mega-labs capable of producing thousands of pounds of methamphetamine on a weekly basis.[16]

The main drug trafficking route up to the mid-1980s was through Thailand overland and then to Hong Kong on Thai fishing trawlers. From there, drugs were dispersed further to the United States, Europe, and Australia. Hong Kong was, and still is, the organizational and financial center for the region's heroin trade.[17] Since the mid-1980s, drug traffickers have developed alternative routes through China (mostly along China's southern provinces) bordering with Myanmar, Vietnam, and Laos. The rapid development in drug trafficking in southern China was brought about by two reasons. First, drug traffickers developed routes from the Golden Triangle along China's southern provinces (i.e., Yunnan, Guangxi, Guangdong, and Fujian) to move their cargoes to the exit points in Hong Kong or Taiwan on their way to the Pacific region. Second, China has developed a booming drug consumption market since its economy took off in the 1980s. Now the Chinese government openly acknowledges that every province and all major urban areas have drug problems. China is no longer just a transit country favored by transnational drug traffickers, but also a large consumption market. Australia, New Zealand, Japan, and Korea are other major drug markets that draw their supplies from Southeast Asia. Governments in the region and elsewhere are increasingly concerned that Southeast Asia will soon become the world supplier of methamphetamine, ecstasy, and other synthetic drugs.

Human Smuggling

All nations in Southeast Asia are either sending or transit nations in the global human smuggling trade. Lax border control and minimum visa requirements in the region (for religious and tourist purposes) have made most Southeast Asian nations ideal places for human smugglers to conduct their business. Indonesia, the Philippines, Cambodia, Vietnam, Thailand, and Singapore are widely known to U.S. law enforcement agencies as transit nations for human smuggling organizations, where safe houses and way stations are set up to receive and forward illegal immigrants. Ethnic Chinese communities in the region are booming with travel agencies and hosting businesses. Lax banking regulations in the region allow proceeds from human smuggling as well as drug trafficking to be laundered.

Recent human smuggling activities in Southeast Asia have also revealed alarming trends in the kind of people that are either entering or transferring through the region. According to Interpol, Australia (which has long been a desired destination for transnational human smuggling activities) is now facing an influx of illegal immigrants from Islamic nations. The top sending countries of illegal immigrants to Australia are now Afghanistan, Iraq, Iran, Pakistan, and Sri Lanka. Keis Asfoor, the principal of an Iraqi crime syndicate based in Indonesia, was recently sentenced to twelve years in prison and fined $1 million for masterminding a series of large-scale human smuggling activities to Australia.[18] Abu Quassey, an Egyptian, was also recently sentenced to seven years in Indonesia for organizing human smuggling activities to Australia.[19] The illegal movements of the masses from countries with links to Islamic extremists are likely to present opportunities to terrorist groups that want to place their members into specific countries.

Trafficking in Women and Children

Riding along the wave of regular economic migrants are groups of women and children being trafficked abroad for slavery labor, sex trade, and brokered marriages. Of all known trafficking cases, it is estimated that 225,000 victims are trafficked annually from Southwest and Southeast Asia, especially the Mekong Subregion countries including Myanmar, Laos, Cambodia, China, and Vietnam, onward to other popular tourist destination countries.[20]

The growth of sex tourism in the region demands a steady supply of young women and girls. Thailand, Cambodia, and the Philippines are known to the world as the most popular sex tourist destination countries. Thailand alone has some 200,000 sex workers. China, especially Yunnan and Guongxi (two provinces in the border area), is one of the major suppliers of young women and children for the sex trade in Thailand because of their geographic proximity. In recent decades, there has been a continued demand for women from Yunnan Province in southern Thailand (Bangkok, Pattaya, and Phuket), where lighter-skinned women are highly sought after by brothels to serve ethnic Chinese Malayans visiting the popular tourist spots.[21] Between 200,000 and 500,000 Chinese women and girls have reportedly been trafficked into or through Thailand, mainly by way of Myanmar.[22] Many of these young women are from the minority tribes in Yunnan Province.[23] Human traffickers are using many of the same routes as other human smugglers to move women and children across borders. Along their treacherous routes are way stations and safe houses, which can be easily exploited by hitchhikers of other enterprises.

Piracy

Piracy of goods on the high seas in many parts of the waterways in Southeast Asia has long been a serious maritime hazard and is notably the worst in the world. Indonesia leads the world in the number of piracy incidents, accounting for about one in five attacks on commercial shipping, followed by Bangladesh.[24] Most of the reported incidents were for robberies and kidnappings for ransom.

According to the International Maritime Bureau, there were 344 maritime piracy attacks in the first nine months of 2003, compared to 277 in all of 2002, a jump of 19 percent.[25] Pirates can operate from ordinary ports and shores along the six hundred-mile Malacca Straits. Maritime law enforcement authorities (coast guard, marine police, and port police) in the region are facing mounting challenges to ensure safety and security in this important international water way.[26] Despite the many known incidents of maritime piracy, regional governments are slow to take aggressive steps to safeguard ports and seaways, and this vulnerability to piracy is an open invitation to terrorists looking for an easy yet spectacular target.[27] Latest intelligence suggests that terrorist groups may be seeking targets on global shipping along the six hundred-mile-long Malacca Straits, where oil tankers or major cargo ships may be commandeered to ram commercial seaports.[28]

Terrorist Groups in Southeast Asia

Islamic extremists have existed in Southeast Asia for decades. Al-Qaeda established and used its Southeast Asian cells to help organize and finance its global activities, including the September 11 attacks, and provide safe haven to its operatives.

Osama bin Laden's brother-in-law (Mohammed Jamal Khalifa) ran a network of Islamic charities in the southern Philippines and the proceeds were funneled to local Muslim militants.[29] Ramzi Yousef planned the 1993 World Trade Center bombing from a safe house in Manila. Five years before the September 11 attacks, Philippine investigators uncovered a terrorist plot to fly a plane into CIA headquarters, but no one took it seriously.[30] The Philippine terrorist organization Abu Sayyaf is still fighting from jungle hideouts. Each nation in the region faces its own unique set of problems.

Indonesia

The most populous Muslim country in the world, Indonesia provides a fertile ground for Islamic militants. One of the most active terrorist groups in Indonesia is Jemaah Islamiyah, which is believed responsible for dozens of attacks in Indonesia in the past several years, including the bombings on the resort island of Bali in October 2002. The group allegedly has close ties to Al-Qaeda.[31]

Malaysia

Malaysian authorities are worried that another Bali-style bombing could happen in their country. Members of Jemaah Islamiyah have used Malaysia extensively in the past decade as a base of operations.[32] Because of lax visa control, Malaysia has been used by Islamic militants from both the Middle East and Southeast Asia as a haven for meeting and planning purposes. Police in Malaysia alleged that members of an international criminal organization were once in collusion with Abdul Qadeer Khan of Pakistan (a key figure in that country's nuclear program) to produce centrifuge parts for Libya's once fledgling nuclear program.[33]

Singapore

In December 2001 members of the Jemaah Islamiyah were plotting to bomb the U.S., Australian, and Israeli embassies in Singapore. They also planned to steal and fly a jet into the terminal at Singapore's Changi airport, as well as attack a visiting U.S. warship at Singapore's naval port. Singaporean authorities got wind of the plots and terminated them before they could be carried out.[34]

Thailand

Because of its lax visa requirements, coupled with porous borders with neighboring countries and an "anything-goes" attitude, Thailand has become the ultimate "country of convenience." Thai officials conceded that the mastermind of the Bali bombing, Hambali, planned the attacks during a meeting in Thailand.[35]

Islamist Movements in Southeast Asia

Islam in Southeast Asia is considered moderate in comparison to the doctrine practiced in the Middle East. Introduced not by Arab armies but by Sufi mystics in the middle of the fourteenth century, Islam in Southeast Asia has incorporated elements from Hinduism and Buddhism as well.[36] There have been few Islamic extremists in Southeast Asia. The Moros of Mindanao and the Sulu Archipelago (areas of extreme poverty and geographical isolation), however, are an exception. They have fought for more than a century to establish a separate Islamic state.[37] By and large, Muslims in Southeast Asia are less resistant to modernity than their orthodox counterparts in the Middle East and North Africa. For instance, secular governments in

Indonesia and Malaysia were able to create significant economic development in the last few decades, while similar efforts were less successful in Egypt and Algeria.[38]

Economic development, however, has not spread wealth evenly in the region. Extreme poverty persists among Muslims in Indonesia and Malaysia, as well as in Singapore, the southern Philippines, and southern Thailand. They were left out of the economic benefits enjoyed by either the mainstream societies or non-Muslim groups.

Economic disparities have bred discontent and given rise to Islamic separatist movements that call for independence from the exploitative secular governments. Land rights and jobs are at the core of these disputes.

Political repression by the authoritarian regimes in the region also fueled the Islamist movements. For instance, Abu Bakar Ba'asyir, the spiritual leader of Jemaah Islamiyah, was detained by the Suharto regime from 1978 until 1982. Three years later, he and his followers fled to Malaysia where his influence expanded and Malaysia became a gathering ground for Islamist groups from all over the world. Ferdinand Marcos declared martial law in 1972 to crack down on Muslim secessions led by the Moro Islamic Liberation Front (MILF), which later brought forth its splinter terrorist organization Abu Sayyaf. Finally, the frustrations over Israeli occupation in the West Bank and Gaza Strip and perceived American bias towards the Israelis have also fueled the desire to form a separate state.[39]

Jemaah Islamiyah (the Islamic Community), the most widely known Islamic militant group in the region, was formed in the 1940s and 1950s and sought to establish "one great Islamic state" that would incorporate Malaysia, Indonesia, Singapore, Brunei, and the Mindanao-Sulu region of the Philippines.[40] Its membership is estimated to be about three thousand across Southeast Asia, mostly residing in urban centers or rural religious schools.[41] Jemaah Islamiyah has survived various crackdowns by the Indonesian authorities and gained ground after the fall of the country's long-time ruler, President Suharto, in 1998. Since Megawati became president in 2001, following the impeachment of her predecessor, Abdurrahman Wahid, Indonesia had been slow to crackdown on extremist groups until the Bali bombing. Members of Jemaah Islamiyah typically target businesses or buildings either representing Western influence or catering to Westerners.

Al-Qaeda's influence in Southeast Asia mostly takes two forms. First, because of the large and well-dispersed Muslim populations in Southeast Asia, it provides a haven for Islamic extremists to meet and plan global terrorist activities, including the bombing of the World Trade Center in 1993 and then the September 11 attacks. Second, Al-Qaeda uses its organizational capacities, financial support, and technical expertise (e.g., handling weapons and explosives) to recruit and support regional extremist groups.

Controlling Islamic Extremism in Southeast Asia

Governments in Southeast Asia face many challenges in dealing with regional extremist groups. The Bali bombing in 2002 sent a profound shockwave through regional governments to the realization of how close they were to danger. For the last few years, many countries in the region have been striving to improve social and economic conditions to address the root causes of Islamist movements in Southeast Asia. Rapid economic development in Indonesia and Malaysia, as shown on the labels of many consumer products in the global market, is a testament of the regional commitment to economic growth. The concomitant improvement in the standards of living for millions of Muslims in Southeast Asia will likely discourage the spread of extremism and thwart the growth of fringe groups. The active development of the Asia Pacific Economic Cooperation (APEC) provides further impetus to improve commerce in the region. Leaders of APEC nations and their affluent neighboring countries (e.g., Australia, the United States, Japan, South Korea, and China) are contemplating a free trade zone in the region, which will further spur economic growth.

Aside from economic growth, there is a more fundamental factor that may serve to limit the extent of radicalization of Islam in the region. Historically and culturally, Muslims in Southeast Asia have been living amid people of different faiths and cultures and are thus more tolerant than their counterparts in the Middle East. Moreover, the Islamic communities in Southeast Asia have never been ruled by radical clerics who dictate people's lives and influence the political process, as those in the Middle East have. Muslims in Southeast Asia are also aware of the extreme social norms and practices imposed by powerful clerics in the Middle East, thanks to advances in telecommunication technologies. These extreme social practices and the cruel treatment of women do not resonate well in moderate countries such as Indonesia where a woman (i.e., President Megawati Sukarnoputri) could rise to political prominence and give orders to men. The series of terrorist acts worldwide have produced neither sympathy nor support among the Muslim populations in the region. Instead, Muslim leaders in the region have called for "strong action" against the bombers and for death sentences to be handed down to convicted terrorists.

Most Islamic militant movements in Southeast Asia have been headed by former Asian "mujahedeens" who fought in Afghanistan during the Soviet occupation. These individuals are exceedingly difficult to find and replace. With the fall of the Taliban, Osama Bin Latin nowhere to be found, and Al-Qaeda relentlessly pursued by multinational forces, remaining extremists in Southeast Asia face a serious shortage of leaders with relevant war experience and technical expertise.

Finally, the Bali bombing has significantly improved the collective response of the governments for chasing terrorist suspects. This time, they are not doing it because of pressure from the United States, but for their own political and economic stability. In fact, Southeast Asian leaders all agree that terrorism threatens regional economic development and therefore must be dealt with seriously. At the October 2003 APEC summit in Bangkok, Thailand, leaders from fifteen countries agreed to eradicate transnational terrorist groups fully and immediately.[42] Economic development and serious efforts by regional governments may be just what it takes to contain the spread of Islamic extremism in Southeast Asia.

Chapter 9

Combating Human Smuggling

Human smuggling is parasitic to the flow of transnational human migration. Human smuggling emerges as an illicit but inevitable response to a much more complex social context involving the informal labor market, the illicit underground economy, and the unmet demand created by legal migration regulations. Like all illicit enterprises catering to unmet demands, human smugglers have carved out their own niche market.

THE POLITICS OF ILLEGAL IMMIGRATION

Illegal immigration has always been part of the U.S. demographic landscape. For decades the problem was viewed mostly as a nuisance, and it was tolerated to some extent. Public opinion flares up when immigrants arrive in large droves.[1] Anti-immigration advocates fear that endless population growth will lead to social fragmentation, deteriorating welfare and working conditions for the native workforce, and mounting burdens on the environment.[2] Cultural entrepreneurs fear that the presence of large numbers of immigrants, particularly Latinos, will alter the national identity.[3] Labor-intensive industries, however, fight back with statistics and examples of how immigrants, illegal and legal, are the main reason that the country enjoys its wealth and standard of living.

Congress, in response to public sentiment, has passed legislation to provide Band-Aid solutions, while ignoring any fundamental changes in the nation's economic undercurrents. U.S. policies toward illegal immigration and corresponding law enforcement efforts against human smuggling have reflected the nation's ambivalence and conflicting views toward the problem. The events of September 11, 2001, have altered this perception.

Unlawful entries, particularly those facilitated by human smugglers, are now considered a threat to national security because surreptitious routes and smuggling strategies can also be exploited by terrorists and other criminals.

Labor Shortage and Economic Development

The force of the market economy is hard to ignore. Labor demands fluctuate with the cycles of economic growth. When certain market sectors suffer chronic labor shortages, incentives will rise for entrepreneurs to exploit irregular channels to import labor. Human smuggling thus becomes a lucrative enterprise. Most developed countries, these days, are busying themselves with erecting walls and reinforcing borders to stop the influx of illegal migrants. Few have tried to understand the tensions and forces between transnational commerce and transnational labor and to devise strategies to manage competing demands. Quick at learning the rules of the game, human smugglers instead become brokers and facilitators who assume a role governments have neglected to fulfill.

The United States continues to lead the world in job creation, skilled and unskilled, attracting a steady flow of illegal immigrants, which in turn sustains the business of human smuggling. Since 1970, the total number of jobs created among the ten major developed countries has been concentrated in three countries, with the United States far ahead of the pack, followed by Japan and Canada.[4] Demographic changes in the United States and other Western countries, however, have become a drag on the economy because fertility rates have been declining, and people are living well beyond their productive years. The decline in fertility and the increase in longevity are inevitably exerting exceeding pressure for an array of social services from pensions to health care. Fresh labor thus must be brought into the market to sustain the economic growth and provide relief.[5] The U.S. economy has become dependent on (even addicted to) the cheap labor provided by illegal immigrants—so much so that New York City's sanctuary policy to protect illegal immigrants, which was created by an executive order in 1989 under Democrat mayor Ed Koch, has been upheld by every mayor since.[6] The current mayor, Michael Bloomberg, again affirmed this sanctuary policy when he was elected in 2001. Under this policy, New York City officials are barred from handing over illegal immigrants to federal agencies for deportation proceedings, and illegal migrants also enjoy rights to education and other social services. The tension between local and federal responsibilities highlights the conundrum and competing interests of people of different regions and socioeconomic sectors. By extending largely the same rights and services enjoyed by U.S. citizens to illegal immigrants,[7] the mayor of New York implicitly acknowledges that the city's economy will not function without the large contingent of cheap workers, to which the wealthy have become accustomed.

On the other hand, many sending countries have also become dependent on the money sent by migrant workers from the United States and other developed countries. According to a recent international migration report issued by the United Nations Population Division, remittances by migrants are a major source of foreign exchange earnings for some countries and are an important component of their economy, amounting to more than 10 percent of the gross domestic product in nine countries.[8] Therefore, there is an incentive for the migrant-sending nations to continue to encourage the emigration of their labor forces.

Politically, naturalized immigrants and native-born children of all immigrants have become a force that politicians cannot afford to ignore. The number of Hispanic immigrants eligible to vote has increased significantly in recent decades. The Hispanic bloc received its biggest boost under the Immigration Reform and Control Act (IRCA) of 1986. Although Hispanic citizens accounted for only 5 percent of all voters in the 2000 national elections, the true power of the so-called Hispanic vote will soon be felt, as 12 million U.S.-born Hispanics are not yet of voting age, and 9 million have not yet become naturalized citizens but will someday.[9] Furthermore, migrants from Latin America, who have historically settled in major urban centers such as Los Angeles and Houston, are now following jobs to suburbs and even to small rural towns. Many are undocumented migrant workers pursuing a variety of job opportunities in meatpacking and produce processing plants, construction, and other labor-intensive industries in the South and the Midwest.

Although some politicians in Washington call for an ordered transformation that brings illegal immigrants into the mainstream society, others consider any such attempt an amnesty, alluding to the consequences of the IRCA in 1986. Senators John McCain of Arizona and Ted Kennedy of Massachusetts floated a bill that would give undocumented immigrants and their families temporary legal status for up to six years, after which they could gain permanent legal status if they met a work requirement and paid a fee of $1,000. Senators John Corny of Texas and Jon Kyl of Arizona wanted instead to provide temporary legal status to undocumented workers to allow them to work in government-approved jobs, but they would be fined $2,000 after the first year if they did not leave the United States. The fine would be increased each subsequent year if they chose to stay. The two competing immigration bills did not advance far in the 109th Congress, which ended in December 2006, when the Republicans ceded control to Democrats following the midterm election. If history offers any indication, few should expect Congress to pass similar bills without creating a host of other unintended consequences.

The Future of the Human Smuggling Enterprise

The arrival of each wave of immigrants, legal and illegal, contributes to the infrastructure that supports further newcomers. Human smuggling as a business builds upon this infrastructure. Newly arrived immigrants rely on those who have established residences and businesses. One need not develop substantial social networks to provide smuggling services such as shelter, food, and work that enable illegal immigrants to continue their journey or settle down.

Few disagree that government efforts are needed to fight the exploitation and abuse inflicted by those who seek to profit from illegal migrants. Ironically, tighter immigration and border control only lead to a greater demand for smuggling services and encourage smugglers to use more daring transportation schemes and dangerous routes. At the same time, illegal migrants are becoming more dependent than ever on their handlers. This increased dependency emboldens human smugglers, some of whom have shown a reckless disregard for human life. Financial exploitation, physical assaults, and rapes are becoming more common, and hazardous transportation methods are being employed more frequently. Of particular concern to law enforcement agencies along the southern border in recent years is the increasing use of firearms by human smugglers. Violence erupts from time to time among rival gangs fighting to control smuggling routes, turfs, and clients. In some cases, these gangs have gone so far as to seize hostages and even kill the migrants they have been paid to smuggle in order to deny profit to their competitors. In a recent raid, federal agents seized illegal weapons, including AK-47s, military-grade assault rifles, and a .50-caliber Desert Eagle automatic handgun.[10] Although smugglers mostly arm themselves against other smugglers or bandits in remote border regions, these firearms increase the risks both to migrants and to border patrol officials.

It will be unrealistic to expect the United States or any other country to eliminate human smuggling activities as long as the underlying sociopolitical causes that give rise to illegal migration remain unchanged. Illegal migration occurs neither randomly nor evenly across the board from developing countries to developed countries. Instead it follows well-established patterns as a response to insufficient and inadequate legal immigration.[11] As research has shown, most immigrants do not intend to settle permanently in their host countries; rather they are interested in making enough money to send back to their home countries, often with some specific financial goals in mind (e.g., building a house, buying a piece of land, setting up a business, or getting married).[12] The more difficult it is to get into a destination country, the more human smugglers will likely charge their clients. Consequently, the longer illegal migrants will have to work to pay off their smuggling debts, the less likely they will be to return to their home countries.[13] With an illegal population of 12 million and growing, the nation's political establishment has again found itself in a quagmire.

THE CHALLENGES OF COMBATING HUMAN SMUGGLING

Fixing the nation's borders and the immigration system is no easy task. Many politicians and policy makers have tried, only to find that the problem of illegal immigration not only has persisted but has also grown. There have been many historical examples, including the Naturalization Act of 1790, which barred anyone but free whites of "good moral character" from becoming citizens; the Chinese Exclusion Act of 1882, which targeted for the first time a specific racial group from entering the country; and, more recently, the IRCA, which was intended to solve the illegal immigration problem once and for all. Illegal immigration has not stopped. Instead, twenty years later, the illegal population has practically exploded. Employers continue to hire illegal immigrants with impunity. In fact, of the estimated 12 million undocumented immigrants living in the United States, 40 percent of them came within the past five years.[14] The September 11 events, the War on Terror, and the swelling population of undocumented immigrants have besieged legislators on Capitol Hill, who are once again struggling to decide what to do about the nation's immigration and border control problems.

Guarding the Porous Border

Guarding the nation's land borders is a daunting task. The U.S.-Canadian border is close to four thousand miles long, and the U.S.-Mexican border is about two thousand miles long. With more than 1 million Mexican nationals arrested for illegal crossing each year (to say nothing about those who cross undetected), the focus of the current debate on illegal migration is on the U.S.-Mexican border. Politicians, pundits, talk show hosts, and many others who have access to a public forum compete to offer solutions, ranging from intensifying border patrol to creating a moat nation surrounded by high-tech electronic fences and military guard towers. A columnist even produced specific figures on what it would take to secure the southern border with Mexico: it would require a complete fence along the U.S.-Mexican border and 15,000 troops, averaging three shifts of seventeen men each mile per day, plus a fleet of 225 helicopters to deliver immediate response; and the fence, outfitted with surveillance components available in ordinary stores, could be constructed in less than six months.[15] Other estimates are less optimistic. One source puts the cost of constructing triple-layer fences along hundreds of miles of the busy sections of the border at about $3 million per mile.[16] If vehicle barriers are added to these sections, another $1.3 million is needed for each mile. Unguarded fences are certainly of little use. Border patrol agents need to be hired, trained, and equipped in large numbers. The estimated cost is $170,000 per agent.

In late 2006 Congress got serious and passed a bill to build 700 miles of fences along the southern border. These fences will be of dual-layer construction, equipped with sensors, and surrounded by a buffer zone north of the border. An additional twenty-five new official points of entry will be opened along the route to improve legal border crossings. This bill and other proposals to build fences have met with strong condemnations from Mexican politicians, who view militarization of the border as a hostile gesture toward a friendly neighbor and as counterproductive. Many on the U.S. side believe that militarizing the border is precisely what the nation needs. In a rare prime-time national broadcast on May 15, 2006, President Bush announced his plan to send thousands of National Guard troops to reinforce the U.S.-Mexican border and to impose order on unruly and anything-goes border regions, where human smugglers and drug traffickers crisscross with little hindrance. Although the number of troops (some ten thousand guardsmen) involved in border patrol duties is more symbolic than substantial, the announcement was nonetheless a drastic gesture at a time when the guardsmen were already stretched thin in Iraq.[17]

Watching the Exit

Exactly six months after the September 11 attacks, the former U.S. INS notified a Florida flight school that the student visas for two of the hijackers had been approved.[18] This embarrassing event highlights the difficulty of guarding the nation's entry points while struggling to meet the demand for regular immigration services. As fences and sensors are increasingly used, human smugglers will seek greater use of regular immigration channels.

Hardening the border may make it more difficult for undocumented migrants to cross into the United States on foot, but the problem of counterfeit documents or of visitors simply overstaying their visas is difficult to handle. No one knows how many foreign nationals first enter the United States legally and then overstay their visas. Although many illegal migrants come from Mexico, millions of foreign nationals enter the country on temporary visas each year, and immigration authorities have little idea of when or if they actually leave. The US-VISIT, a behemoth computer system that tracks visitors' biometrics (e.g., personal information, fingerprints, photographs), is only partially operational; Congress has spent $900 million on it thus far. The system allows participating agencies to gather biometric features to identify foreign visitors and check against criminal records and terrorist watch lists. Although the system tracks visitors who arrive at international airports and seaports and all major border crossings, it does not have a corresponding exit system.[19] The system collects fingerprints and photographs of only about 2 percent of all people entering the country because Americans and most Canadians and Mexicans are exempt.

Congress ordered the creation of the US-VISIT system more than a decade ago and considers it vital to national security and an important barrier to illegal immigration. One congressional report estimated that one-third of all illegal immigrants currently in the United States are foreigners who have overstayed their visas.[20] However, the logistics of catching those who overstay their visas have proved prohibitively expensive. The Department of Homeland Security (DHS) recently conceded that the agency lacked money and appropriate technology to meet the deadline to install exit-monitoring systems at the fifty busiest land border crossings (as most foreign visitors come from Mexico and Canada) by December 2006. Gathering biometrics at the exits and matching them with those collected at the entry points requires a massive buildup of infrastructure and hiring of immigration personnel, something that the government has no money for. The DHS believes that it will take five to ten years to develop the technology needed to implement the exit portion of a border security plan without major disruptions to existing cross-border commerce. Although the agency has been testing a program using radio frequency identification (RFID) technology rather than biometrics,[21] a fundamental flaw of the RFID technology is that it tracks only documents entering or leaving a checkpoint, not the documents' owners, who could be anywhere.

Punishing Softly the Smugglers

The U.S. judicial system treats human smuggling differently from most other organized crimes. Penalties are light for most human smuggling cases, although the law may appear harsh on paper. The Violent Crime Control and Law Enforcement Act of 1994 allows up to ten years of imprisonment for convicted human smugglers. The penalty can increase to twenty years per smuggled immigrant when bodily injury occurs or life is in jeopardy during smuggling. If death occurs during the smuggling of a migrant, life imprisonment or even the death penalty may apply. In practice, such harsh punishment is rarely doled out.

Federal prosecution guidelines have recently been updated to encourage human smuggling prosecutions, particularly in cases involving smugglers who have prior criminal records or who transport clients in hazardous conditions (such as concealment in the trunk of a car). Furthermore, U.S. attorneys can prosecute smugglers on felony illegal reentry charges when they do not meet the standard for smuggling charges. The prosecution guidelines have made it easy to charge human smugglers, but the enforcement of these statutes has lagged far behind. A senior U.S. attorney in the San Diego District lamented,[22]

> It is not that we are not treating human smuggling seriously. Our judicial system simply is not equipped to handle the volume of human smuggling cases except for the very serious ones. If one is caught smuggling a couple of illegal immigrants through the Otay Mountains, or even five or six of them, it is unlikely we will pursue any serious prison time against him. We have far more serious crimes that take up much of our time than transporting illegal migrants. Cases involve drug cartels, contracted murders, and a whole host of other serious crimes in the region. And most human smugglers know this.

Court systems in other countries show far less enthusiasm for human smuggling. Most governments do not view the transportation of willing migrants who seek better economic opportunities in another country as a crime that warrants serious punishment. In Thailand, a country favored by many smugglers in Asia for transit purposes, the maximum punishment for forging official documents or possessing stolen passports is a $240 fine.

Despite repeated requests and pressure from the U.S. government and the negative public image portrayed in news coverage, most sending countries, particularly Mexico, have shown little enthusiasm for counter-smuggling measures. It is hard to blame any of the sending or transit countries, because there are few reasons to assist the United States in cracking down on human smuggling activities. Mexico, the biggest sending country, is often criticized for not doing enough to stop its people from moving north. Little progress has been made for decades. Mexican officials often invoke their constitution, which prohibits authorities from imposing restrictions on the free movements of its citizens, to deflect U.S. criticism. Although transporting migrants across international borders for a fee is a crime, no Mexican authority can prevent people from gathering near the border. The truth is that it will be very unpopular for Mexico's political system to do anything to impede the movement of migrants to the north. Mexico depends on the infusion of $20 billion sent home each year by its people living in the United States. More than one-fifth of Mexican households live on such remittances each year.[23] In sum, Mexicans do not view illegal immigration and human smuggling as a problem, certainly not as their problem.[24]

COMBATING HUMAN SMUGGLING AT THE MACRO LEVEL

There are two basic approaches to fighting human smuggling activities—macro-level changes initiated by the U.S. government, and tactical or micro-level strategies devised and implemented by law enforcement agencies. At the macro level, many structural and legislative changes are needed to address socioeconomic factors fundamental to the influx of illegal immigration; most politicians recognize that illegal immigration is a problem, but they disagree on the proper course of action.

The Guest Worker Program

The idea of a guest worker program with Mexico has been around for some time. The Bush administration has been trying for years to please the opposing sides of the president's political base—business leaders who want more flexible immigration policies to recruit foreign labor into the United States and the cultural conservatives who feel threatened by the continuing influx of foreigners.[25] His guest worker program, proposed soon after he came to the White House in 2000, was derailed by the post–September 11 hysteria to shut down the border. His efforts to revive the plan have thus far made little progress.

Many other countries, on the other hand, operate some form of labor importing program. The Bracero program, in operation from the 1940s through the 1960s in the United States, did not eliminate illegal immigration, but it did address much of the labor shortage at the time. Canada has been operating a guest worker program for its agricultural business for decades. Much can be learned from the Canadian experience. The Bracero program had its shortcomings and catered mostly to agricultural interests; a new mechanism needs to be introduced to address labor demands in other sectors of the economy.

Guest worker programs often make conceptual sense, but in practice they are difficult to administer. There are many pitfalls. For instance, it is difficult to manage large numbers of migrants regarding where they should work or whether they can raise a family. Soon after World War II, many farmers left Italy, Spain, Portugal, and Greece to work in countries such as Germany, France, and Belgium. Soon these southern European countries began to experience their own labor shortages following rapid postwar economic development, and they thus sought to recruit "temporary" workers from places such as North Africa to meet the labor demand.[26] These workers were expected to return to their native countries when the labor shortage eased. Instead, many chose to settle permanently in Europe and began petitioning for the entry of their spouses, children, and other relatives, creating additional unintended waves of immigrants.[27]

Some countries have devised strict policies, such as those in the Persian Gulf states, to keep their guest workers from becoming long-term residents and thus creating a permanent underclass. Other countries, such as Japan, have long-held immigration rules restricting foreigners from settling permanently or becoming citizens. The riots by many descendants of immigrants in the suburbs of Paris in 2005 illustrate the increasing wariness of receiving countries with large immigrant communities regarding the ramifications of clashes between cultures, religions, and racial identities.[28]

Reducing Outward Migration through Economic Growth

A joint study by the International Organization on Migration (IOM) and the United Nations found that the international community can alleviate illegal immigration (or irregular migration) through investment, trade, and aid to improve the economic conditions of the sending countries. Citing poverty and a lack of employment opportunities as the main causes of transnational migration, the IOM study claimed that economic growth in sending countries can reverse the current torrent of illegal migration. Increases in employment opportunities and standard of living will keep prospective migrants from leaving. The creation of jobs and global trade will slow down outward migration, because an accelerating economy draws both skilled and unskilled labor.[29] There are many historical examples of reversals in transnational migration, such as Japan, Korea, and all southern European countries that changed from sending to receiving countries.

At the current rate of globalization, the growing world economy and transnational commerce may actually cause illegal immigration to decrease on its own. If the flow of illegal migration slows down, so will the need for human smuggling services. As more countries open up their economies and markets, it will become easier for people of various socioeconomic strata to enter the marketplace, collaborate, and compete.[30] Through various international trade agreements, major migrant-sending countries such as Mexico and China are breaking down trade barriers and accelerating economic growth at an unprecedented pace. With both Mexico and China (already the top two trading partners with the United States) competing for greater access to the world's largest economy and consumer market, the concomitant growth in jobs and the standard of living in both countries will curtail the flow of illegal population migration.[31]

In a report issued at the G8 conference in 2000, China was touted as a model country in making outstanding strides in eliminating poverty in its population.[32] It is obvious that there is a close relationship between economic development in a sending country and its outward migration. As jobs become abundant, and wages improve as a result, fewer people will want to leave their home countries. Cultural familiarity (e.g., the comforts of home, the tastes of local cuisine, one's social circle and physical surroundings) and the low cost of living in the sending countries will further reduce the incentive for prospective migrants to leave.

Economic growth can be viewed as a self-limiting factor for the human smuggling enterprise. Much of the political discourse these days alludes to the dark fantasy that if the U.S. government does not take forceful and drastic measures, illegal immigration and concomitant human smuggling activities will spin out of control, and the streets will be flooded with illegal migrants, who will disrupt social order and drain social services. No one wants to take chances on these doomsday predictions; thus Congress and the White House are under pressure to do something, anything, to stop illegal immigration. It is true that human smuggling will continue for a long time and may even increase from time to time. But it is unlikely that the enterprise will grow at an uncontrollable rate. Research has shown that human smuggling as a business fluctuates tremendously depending on the market demand for illegal labor, changes in legal and political conditions, and law enforcement activities. Demand for illegal immigrants does not remain constant.

Improving International Collaboration

The complexity of combating human smuggling and trafficking in persons requires the involvement of multiple government and law enforcement branches, which poses integration challenges. Acting on the September 11 Commission's recommendations, Congress passed the Intelligence Reform and Terrorism Prevention Act of 2004, which established the Human Smuggling and Trafficking Center, housed inside the State Department, to integrate and coordinate efforts previously carried out by different federal agencies.[33] Such attempts to pool resources and share intelligence should improve the overall effectiveness of law enforcement activities.

A logical extension of this emphasis on integrating domestic government agencies is to increase international cooperation. An effective anti-smuggling strategy requires such collaborations not only between sending and receiving countries but also with transit countries. Although there may not be much enthusiasm in sending countries to stop illegal migration, law enforcement agencies generally assist one another in investigating criminal organizations. Liaison offices for intelligence sharing and joint operations are much more effective than efforts put forth by one nation fighting on its own. For example, an extensive international network of drug enforcement agencies has been established to foster global antidrug investigations and interdiction activities. Similar structures can also be established to monitor and fight human smuggling and trafficking activities, particularly at a time of heightened concern of terrorist organizations taking advantage of established human smuggling channels. Since the 1990s, the U.S. government has deployed immigration officials in its overseas posts (e.g., the INS Operation Global Reach Program). The agency has worked with Mexican, Honduran, and Thai officials to break up major human smuggling rings. The agency also works with domestic and overseas airlines and other foreign carriers to enlist their help in combating human smuggling activities. Because international carriers often face financial penalties for carrying unauthorized migrants, there are incentives for private companies to work collaboratively with government agencies.

One major aspect that this international cooperative effort needs to focus on is improving intelligence and regular information-sharing mechanisms on identification paperwork, as counterfeit documents are most often produced on foreign identification papers. Greater emphasis should be placed on helping sending countries to produce trustworthy identification documents, so that destinations countries can have confidence. However, such efforts require the investment of resources in technologies and the creation of protocols for sharing document manufacturing technologies, identification procedures, and technical training. There are few standards in identifying and verifying identification papers among governments. Such cooperation can concentrate limited resources on targeted populations or goods from foreign countries while expediting most passengers and goods through points of entry.

The recent voluntary participation in a cargo shipping certification program is a good example. Shipping lines and foreign governments that voluntarily implement strict procedures for container inspections prior to loading can be certified by U.S. Customs, and as a result their cargo containers can be expedited through U.S. ports. Similarly, people who wish to come to the United States to work or visit can also go through a certifying process. A large-scale temporary work program can thus be implemented if governments can reach this level of cooperation.

Enforcing Employment Authorization

As one scholar opined, the best strategy—and the one that most people agree on—to reduce the flow of undocumented immigrants is to enforce labor laws already on the books.[34] But serious workplace enforcement takes great political will and tenacity. Most politicians are unwilling to confront the industries that profit from the cheap labor provided by illegal immigrants. The bottom line is that the United States has a labor shortage in several industries. This is not just a U.S. problem. It exists in much of the developed world, particularly in Western Europe. Employer violations remain the largest loophole in the fight against illegal immigration. This is the elephant in the room that most politicians would rather not see, and rightly so. The images of individual homeowners hiring day laborers to do lawn work or odd repair jobs are obscuring the fact that it is the large employers in industries such as hospitality, agriculture, and construction that provide the persistent draw to illegal migrants. Employers who occasionally hire day laborers at the corners of Home Depots do not generate a sufficiently stable employment environment to sustain the flow of illegal immigration.

Many people point their fingers at federal law enforcement agencies for failing to enforce federal employment laws in the workplace. But workplace enforcement is more about political will than it is about law enforcement's tactical capabilities.

In one such example, federal agents raided six meatpacking facilities owned by Swift & Company, and arrested 1,282 illegal immigrants, who allegedly had used false identification papers to gain employment.[35] In contrast to past workplace raids, this operation was carried out in the name of breaking up identify theft schemes and protecting the privacy rights of innocent Americans. In a rather unusual public display, Homeland Security Secretary Michael Chertoff, Assistant Secretary for Immigration and Customs Enforcement (ICE) Julie L. Myers, Federal Trade Commission (FTC) Chairman Deborah Platt Majoras, and Cache County (UT) Attorney N. George Daines appeared in a joint press conference on December 13, 2006, to make the announcement, which drew wide attention from the nation.

The Swift investigation began in February 2006 and uncovered hundreds of meatpacking workers who had allegedly assumed the identities of U.S. citizens and used their Social Security numbers and other identity documents to gain employment at the packing facilities. Criminal organizations around the country obtained and sold genuine birth certificates and Social Security cards belonging to U.S. citizens to these illegal migrants. In some cases, these criminal organizations stole legitimate identity documents and Social Security cards from unwitting U.S. citizens. In other cases, these documents were purchased from U.S. citizens willing to sell their identities for money, including homeless people and individuals in jail. Several members of the organizations were arrested in Minnesota, Texas, Utah, and Puerto Rico.

As discussed in Chapter 3, the practice of assuming someone else's identity has been known for decades in immigrant communities. It is not uncommon to find people who are willing to rent out their Social Security numbers and other identity papers for a fee. They are simply happy to have others contributing toward their Social Security savings. By using valid Social Security numbers and birth certificates, illegal immigrants can defeat the employment verification program (i.e., the Basic Pilot Employment Eligibility Verification system, or Basic Pilot), a federal computer database designed to help employers detect unauthorized workers.

There are many political pitfalls in enforcing immigration laws in any of the industries that employ large numbers of illegal immigrants. Such raids often cause uproars from employers, who complain about production disruptions. Civil rights organizations also accuse the government of racial profiling and harassing Mexicans and others from Central America. Although industry representatives claim to have procedures in place to determine employment eligibility, they have also long maintained that it is difficult to verify the false documents provided by job applicants. After the Swift raid, consumer groups and experts sounded alarms immediately, predicting an adverse impact on meat prices. Some critics suggest that such massive raids at workplaces are merely for show because the government cannot afford to continue this practice when prices in supermarkets, restaurants, and hotels begin to climb. Others, including academics and industry experts, quote figures suggesting that such raids tend not to have a lasting impact on production activities overall.[36] Some even suggest that such raids may actually benefit the labor-intensive industry because rising wages will attract domestic job applicants and strengthen labor unions.

COMBATING HUMAN SMUGGLING AT A TACTICAL LEVEL

Law enforcement strategies proven to be most successful are those that emphasize disrupting human smuggling activities. Over the past decade or so, a wealth of knowledge and experience has been accumulated by federal agents who have worked on antismuggling details. Unfortunately, there are few channels available to federal and local law enforcement agencies to accumulate and share such tactical knowledge and expertise. The following presents a few of these effective antismuggling strategies.[37]

Disrupting Smuggling Networks

The traditional law enforcement strategy of looking for "godfathers" in human smuggling organizations should be abandoned. Much of the anti–human-smuggling energy has been spent on tracking down the kingpins or large smuggling organizations, when in reality most smuggling activities are carried out by loosely affiliated enterprising agents. Law enforcement resources can be most effective when concentrated on disrupting these small groups of entrepreneurs (or task forces), as mounting empirical evidence suggests that nontraditional criminals are responsible for transporting the majority of illegal immigrants. The various market and socio-legal constraints dictate not only that there are few big smugglers but also that few last long in this business.

A hierarchically structured criminal organization can be best dealt with by removing its leadership (i.e., the strategy of going after the big boss). Small entrepreneurial groups, as are most human smuggling rings, are most sensitive to the disruption of their resources. The removal of any one linkage along a transportation route will severely disrupt or even terminate an entire operation. This book has devoted much space to explaining how human smuggling networks operate and how smugglers deal with one another. The series of one-on-one relationships between and among members of a smuggling organization are a product of operational requisites designed to minimize risk and manage market uncertainties. By employing various defense measures to mitigate the risks inherent in the business, human smugglers also expose their Achilles' heel—that to complete a smuggling operation, all links in a network must succeed in completing their individual tasks. If law enforcement agencies can fully understand and appreciate the intricacies and vulnerabilities of these dyadic relationships, a great deal of success can be achieved by simply removing any one individual smuggler in the chain. Once a smuggler is arrested, all smuggling operations going through this person will either fall apart or be put on hold while other partners, now disjointed, spend time and resources to reconnect the chain.

Unfortunately, federal agency administrators still believe that investing manpower and resources and engaging in long-term investigations will lead to the discovery and crackdown of large criminal organizations. There is no doubt that in this business some smuggling groups are more successful than others and have thus grown in size and reputation. However, the removal of one or two such large smuggling groups produces little impact on the smuggling business as a whole because the survival of the enterprise relies not on one or two major smuggling cartels but on the collective behaviors of the masses of small-time smugglers.

Monitoring Legitimate Businesses That Provide Auxiliary Services

The channels exploited by human smugglers are also those through which ordinary visitors and businesspeople arrive in this country. Auxiliary services that enable regular and legitimate movement of foreign nationals in and out of the country are also vital to the success of smuggling operations. They are no less important than the services provided by corrupt officials. These services—provided by lawyers, paralegals, travel agencies, temporary employment agencies, and motels—are used by human smugglers to arrange legal business documents, establish business entities, and provide coverage for their smuggling activities.

Increasing Detention Facilities

Most Mexican nationals caught crossing the border are quickly deported. However, because of a lack of detention space, unless the apprehended migrants are deemed a threat to national security (i.e., are on a terrorist watch list) or to public safety (i.e., with prior or outstanding criminal records), they are typically released on bond or recognizance (i.e., on an Order of Recognizance, or ROR). Most immigrants simply vanish into the ethnic enclave and start earning money. Therefore nothing discourages prospective migrants more than reduced chances of earning a living once they arrive in the United States. Annually, some one hundred thousand undocumented immigrants benefit from a de facto "catch and release" policy because there are not enough beds for them.[38] Illegal migrants often accrue significant debts in getting themselves smuggled into the United States. Depending on the country of origin, undocumented migrants, such as those from China and Korea, pay tens of thousands of dollars, taking on debts that often require years of hard work and savings to repay. By holding apprehended migrants in detention facilities, time spent waiting for hearings is wasted. Stories of prolonged detention and reduced chances of bails or releases will travel back to the sending countries and discourage other would-be migrants.

Similarly, even though the issue is politically sensitive, the United States must face the fact that its political asylum system is defunct. It saves few truly persecuted, but it shelters many who exploit the good intentions of the American people. Illegal immigrants from around the world have for decades exploited the asylum system. Federal officials, immigration examiners, and even lawyers who make money off filing these petitions know that most asylum stories are fraudulent, and supporting documents are fabricated. For instance, a study based on extensive fieldwork found that in New York City the majority of Chinese asylum claims are fraudulent.[39] However, the ideology-driven asylum system does not seem capable of judging the veracity of numerous Chinese applicants who file petitions on such grounds as China's draconian one-child policy and religious persecution (e.g., for practicing Falun Gong, a religious sect combining principles of Buddhism and Taoism that is considered a subversive movement by the communist government).[40] More recently, Chinese asylum seekers have made claims that they were persecuted by the Chinese government for harboring North Korean migrants escaping the Stalinist regime.[41]

One fundamental question is whether the courts or the public can stand deporting a genuine asylum seeker only to find him or her persecuted later in the hands of a brutal foreign government, or whether it would be better to err on the safe side by admitting thousands of immigrants, hoping to save one or two potential victims. By most accounts, asylum seekers are by no means at any risk of being persecuted by their home countries; many asylum seekers return to visit their home countries as soon as they are granted temporary residency, even though only U.S. citizenship can protect them from being persecuted.

Migrants from countries other than Mexico (or OTMs) are supposed to be held while they await hearings regarding their deportations or asylum petitions. The shortage of detention space is more about political will than about fiscal and logistical capacity. Many strategies can be developed to change the "catch and release" policy. Recently ICE implemented two programs to keep track of these apprehended immigrants: electronic monitoring devices (EMD) and the Intensive Supervision Appearance Program (ISAP).[42] ICE has also created the National Fugitive Operations Program (NFOP), with teams of agents deployed around the country tracking down and arresting undocumented immigrants who have failed to appear in court as promised. Since their creation in March 2003, the Fugitive Operations Teams have arrested more than ten thousand fugitives. These efforts, although laudable, are likely to produce a limited effect on the millions who are in the country illegally. More resources should be spent on expanding detention capacity to ensure that most, if not all, illegal immigrants are held until their cases are decided in court. By holding apprehended illegal immigrants regardless of whether they pose a threat to national security or community safety and thereby denying them the opportunity to work and make money, federal agencies can achieve a significant deterrence effect. The hearing process can be significantly improved if additional judges are on loan from other federal courts and special court sessions are held in extended hours.

Expedient Deportation Procedures

In addition to expanding immigration detention facilities, officials must also overhaul deportation proceedings so that an overwhelmed detention system does not release illegal immigrants into the street. Expedited procedures should be established to allow Border Patrol officials to deport most illegal immigrants, granting them the same power they have now over Mexican nationals. For others, such as those who have filed political asylum petitions, judges must be made available to work on extended hours or even around the clock, just as the immigration and customs agents do, to process and decide on deportation petitions. All detained illegal migrants should be held in custody while waiting for their deportation hearings; this would be a strong deterrent for potential illegal migrants, for they would have to face the prospect of wasting time in jail instead of making money.

On August 10, 2004, the DHS announced that OTMs would also be deported within a few days rather than held for a hearing in most cases.[43]

The DHS claimed that one of its top priorities was to end the practice of "catch and release." Although expedited deportation proceedings have been implemented at official ports of entry since 1997, the DHS announcement expanded this practice to those caught entering illegally by land elsewhere, within one hundred miles of either border and within fourteen days of arrival. It sounded like progress, but there are two problems with this renewed enthusiasm. This policy applies only to illegal migrants who have the misfortune of being caught close to the border (within one hundred miles) and who are dumb enough to admit that they have arrived only recently (within fourteen days). Such a Band-Aid approach is unlikely to have any measurable effect.

For illegal migrants from Mexico, several repatriation strategies have been tried by the U.S. government over the years. The problem remains the same—how to keep the repatriated illegal immigrants from crossing the border again. Mexican nationals who are apprehended at the border and who have no criminal records are typically dropped off on the Mexican side of the border, through a port of entry. However, most immediately get in touch with their smuggling handlers to arrange for another attempt. In the summer of 2004, the U.S. government experimented with a so-called interior repatriation program. Illegal migrants were flown back home to the interior of Mexico. For a total of about $15 million, 14,067 migrants were returned to Mexico City or Guadalajara from Tucson.[44] The program was repeated in the summer of 2005 with a goal of repatriating 33,900 illegal migrants to the Mexican interior. The program was intended to disrupt human smuggling operations by making it more difficult for the migrants to return to border regions. The project, which started in the Tucson sector, was expanded to cover the Yuma sector in 2005, where apprehended migrants were bused to Tucson for the flights. There have been no empirical studies to verify just how effective such repatriation strategies are. It will be difficult to sustain financially such free flights when the U.S. Border Patrol catches around 1 million Mexican nationals each year. Far less expensive methods of transportation to the Mexican interior perhaps should be explored, such as chartered passenger trains or buses. The idea remains the same—taking migrants back to their hometowns or farther away from the border, thus increasing the costs of crossing attempts.

Going after the Money

No antismuggling strategies can become successful without an aggressive pursuit of the financial assets of those who profit from the business. Asset forfeiture has become a powerful tool to bring down traditional criminal organizations. As with all illicit enterprises, asset forfeiture is the ultimate deterrent to those who seek to profit from human smuggling activities. According to ICE estimates, during a six-month period in early 2003, more than $160 million was funneled into Phoenix through money transmitting businesses, and much of the money was believed to be payments for smuggling fees. Federal agencies have only in recent years intensified their efforts in pursuing the money trail to disrupt human smuggling activities.

Although Congress authorized the use of RICO legislation on human smuggling activities in 1996, asset seizures have not been a priority in the fight against human smuggling until recently. For instance, in 2004, ICE seized more than $7 million nationwide from organizations involved in human smuggling and human trafficking activities. One year later, in 2005, asset forfeiture more than tripled to nearly $27 million.[45] In November 2005 federal agents broke up a network of underground motels that catered to smuggling operations in Arizona. Thirteen owners and former owners of six motels in Mesa, Arizona, were charged with harboring illegal migrants and providing safe houses to human smugglers.[46] The breakup of these safe houses was the result of an undercover investigation that began in February 2005, with federal agents posing as human smugglers and renting rooms from the motel operators. The motel operators allegedly coached the undercover officers on how to conceal their smuggling activities, advising them to register under false names, rent multiple rooms, and park their vehicles in less visible places to avoid attention. The federal prosecutor in this case was seeking forfeiture on five of the six motels.

In another case, during New Year's weekend in 2000, twenty-five Chinese immigrants were found inside a container on a freighter docked at the Port of Vancouver, British Columbia.[47] The ship had left Hong Kong on December 20 and was heading for Seattle but was diverted to Vancouver because of a port backlog in the United States. Acting on a tip from U.S. authorities, Canadian Customs and Immigration agents searched the freighter and heard voices coming from one of the hundreds of containers on board. The Canadian authorities fined the shipping company, New Jersey–based NYK Line North America, $375,000 for the incident, the largest penalty ever handed out by Canada Immigration. The ship was not allowed to leave until the fine was paid. Although it was unlikely that the ship's crew had conspired with the smuggler, the fact that the ship was held accountable for the contents of the containers on board would serve as a reminder to other commercial ocean liners to step up security procedures to prevent such incidents.

PAUCITY OF EMPIRICAL KNOWLEDGE

One major problem with U.S. antismuggling efforts is the paucity of empirical research. Little research has been done on this topic, either by government analysts or by academic researchers. Frankly, few policy makers and law enforcement agency administrators know much about the people who are involved in human smuggling or trafficking activities. For instance, despite the fact that Mexican coyotes have been active along the U.S. southern border for decades, providing logistic support and navigational assistance to U.S.-bound migrants of all nationalities, research on these entrepreneurs and their organizations is surprisingly limited. Other than anecdotal stories and sporadic interviews by news reporters, there has not been a single study involving systematic data collection of any sizable scale that examines human smuggling operations in Mexico or the United States. Researchers and law enforcement agencies do not know whether these coyotes are mostly border residents or urban dwellers. There is also little information about how Mexican human smugglers form alliances with smugglers from the interior or other nations to recruit and transport clients.

Most U.S. law enforcement activities are built on the outdated model that formal criminal syndicates are behind smuggling operations; thus they are ill-suited to fighting the masses of entrepreneurs who form temporary alliances and engage in sporadic criminal activities. Agency administrators prefer to concentrate their resources on fighting one group of smugglers at a time, preferably a large one.

Since the September 11 events, billions of dollars have been invested in hiring Border Patrol agents and acquiring hardware and technologies. It is difficult to gauge the effectiveness of these recent border enforcement efforts because few studies have been carried out. One may suggest that the rise in smuggling fees can be used as an indicator of the increased difficulties involved in entering the country. Human smuggling fees have indeed increased many fold since the 1980s and 1990s. For instance, in the mid-1990s it cost only $200 to $300 for a Mexican national to be smuggled from Tijuana to Los Angeles. Today, the going rate exceeds $2,000 for the same trip, and for Chinese migrants it typically costs about $6,000 or more. Increased risks in apprehension certainly contribute to higher smuggling costs, but higher prices may also reflect greater market demand for human smuggling services.

The U.S. government does not engage in systematic assessment of its antismuggling policies and practices. Most antismuggling strategies reflect either the political climate of Washington, D.C., or the convictions of agency administrators. The knowledge of those fighting in the trenches is not gathered, analyzed, and shared in any systematic fashion. The cumulative knowledge of experienced investigators quickly disappears when they retire or move on to other posts. Unfortunately, misguided policy makers in Washington continue to devise antismuggling programs in the absence of empirical guidance or, worse, implement policies for publicity purposes. For instance, the DHS deployed ICE investigators and uniformed customs and border patrol agents throughout Los Angeles International Airport (LAX) in 2004, as part of a highly publicized anti-smuggling operation.[48] The LAX operation was an extension of the Arizona Border Control Initiative, a Homeland Security enforcement operation to curb cross-border smuggling activity. There were three objectives: (1) to curb human smuggling activity at the facility; (2) to interdict and arrest suspected smugglers; and (3) to gather intelligence about smuggling methods. It is doubtful that any of these objectives could be accomplished through such an exercise because LAX is not a major redistribution center. Even if federal agents were on guard at all regional airports in Southern California, the impact on human smuggling activities would be negligible. The reason is simple: Most undocumented immigrants, once inside the United States, do not travel by air. Of the few who fly, their smuggling handlers will most likely supply documents good enough to pass the airport's security.

It would be of great value to evaluate these operations to identify problems and assess their impact on smuggling activities. More importantly, empirical research needs to be carried out on a systematic basis to guide future decision making and strategizing. Armed with the knowledge of how human smugglers operate, policy makers can devise strategies accordingly or improve existing ones.

The scale of illegal immigration has been so great in the past few decades that it has produced profound changes to the American demographic composition. Human smuggling and trafficking are intimately tied to a host of other social, cultural, and economic factors, and therefore its discussion and possible solutions must be placed in a broader context. For anyone who thinks there are straightforward solutions to this problem and advocates them as such, plenty of lessons in humility will be waiting.

Notes

PREFACE

1. Onell R. Soto, "Four Men Linked to Immigrant Smuggling Arrested in County," *San Diego Union-Tribune*, December 7, 2004, B2.

2. Donald L. Barlett and James B. Steele, "Who Left the Door Open?" *Time*, September 20, 2004, 51–66.

CHAPTER 1: HUMAN SMUGGLING AND IRREGULAR POPULATION MIGRATION

1. International Organization for Migration, "Foreign Direct Investment, Trade and Aid: An Alternative to Migration," *News Release No. 781*, jointly issued with the United Nation Conference on Trade and Development (November 19, 1996), http://www.itcilo.it/english/actrav/telearn/global/ilo/seura/iom2.htm.

2. United Nations, *International Migration Report 2002* (New York: United Nations, Department of Economic and Social Affairs Population Division, 2002), 2.

3. Ibid.

4. Ibid.

5. United Nations Commission on Population and Development, "Concise Report on World Population Monitoring, 1997: International Migration and Development," *Report of the Secretary-General*, http://www.itcilo.it/english/actrav/telearn/global/ilo/seura/migwod2.htm.

6. Ibid.

7. National Intelligence Council, *Global Trends 2015: Dialogue about the Future with Nongovernment Experts* (Washington, DC: NIC, 2000), 23, http://www.cia.gov/nic/NIC_globaltrend2015.html.

8. *International migrant stock* is a term commonly used by population researchers to describe the number or percentage of residents who are foreign-born.

Estimating the number of foreigners in a country is difficult. It is even more daunting to separate legal residents from illegal residents. Censuses often provide the main source of data for estimating foreign-born residents in a nation, based on gathered information on places of birth. Sometimes when information on the place of birth is not available, citizenship information is used. International migrants are therefore the same as foreign-born residents, legal or illegal.

9. United Nations, *International Migration Report 2002*, 4.

10. Douglas S. Massey, "Foreword," in *Smuggled Chinese: Clandestine Immigration to the United States*, by Ko-lin Chin (Philadelphia: Temple University, 1999), ix.

11. Douglas S. Massey, Joaquin Arango, Graeme Hugo, Ali Kousaouci, Adela Pellegrino, and J. Edward Taylor, *Worlds in Motion—Understanding International Migration at the End of the Millennium* (Oxford: Clarendon Press, 1998), 4.

12. Thomas J. Espenshade, "An Analysis of Public Opinion toward Undocumented Immigration," *Population Research and Policy Review* 12 (1993): 189–224; Thomas J. Espenshade, "Contemporary American Attitudes toward U.S. Immigration," *International Migration Review* 30 (1996): 535–670.

13. United Nations Commission on Population and Development, "Concise Report on World Population Monitoring, 1997: International Migration and Development," *Report of the Secretary-General*, http://www.itcilo.it/english/actrav/telearn/global/ilo/seura/migwod2.htm.

14. Ibid.

15. Ibid.

16. Kevin O'Neil, Kimberly Hamilton, and Demetrios Papademetriou, "Migration in the Americas" (paper prepared for the Policy Analysis and Research Program of the Global Commission on International Migration, Washington, DC: Migration Policy Institute, 2005), 5, http://www.gcim.org/en/ir_experts.html.

17. The terms *immigrant* and *foreign-born person* are often used interchangeably. The U.S. Census Bureau uses the term *foreign-born* to identify residents (irrespective of their legal status) who were born outside the United States and not to a U.S. citizen parent. Native-born people are those born in the United States, Puerto Rico, or U.S. Island Areas, as well as those born in a foreign country with at least one parent who was a U.S. citizen. A list of basic demographic terminology used by the Census Bureau is available at http://www.census.gov/Press-Release/www/2002/dp_comptables.html.

18. O'Neil, Hamilton, and Papademetriou, "Migration in the Americas," 5.

19. Audrey Singer, "The Rise of New Immigrant Gateways," *The Living Cities Census Series* (Washington, DC: Brookings Institution, February 2004), 5, http://www.brookings.edu/metro/publications/20040301_gateways.htm.

20. O'Neil, Hamilton, and Papademetriou, "Migration in the Americas," 5.

21. Jeffrey S. Passel, *Size and Characteristics of the Unauthorized Migrant Population in the U.S.* (Washington, DC: Pew Hispanic Center, 2006), i–ii, http://pewhispanic.org/files/reports/61.pdf.

22. Sylvia Moreno, "Flow of Illegal Immigrants to U.S. Unabated—Mexicans Make Up Largest Group; D.C. Area Numbers Up 70 Percent since 2000," *Washington Post*, March 22, 2005, A2.

23. Jessa M. Lewis, "Strategies for Survival: Migration and Fair Trade-Organic Coffee Production in Oaxaca, Mexico" (working paper no. 118, Center for Comparative Immigration Studies, University of California, San Diego, 2005), http://www.ccis-ucsd.org/PUBLICATIONS/wrkg118.pdf.

24. Wayne A. Cornelius, "Controlling 'Unwanted Immigration': Lessons from the United States, 1993–2004," *Journal of Ethnic and Migration Studies* 31, no. 4 (2005): 789.

25. Douglas S. Massey, Joaquin Arango, Graeme Hugo, Ali Kousaouci, Adela Pellegrino, and J. Edward Taylor, "Theories of International Migration: A Review and Appraisal," *Population and Development Review* 19, no. 3 (1993): 431–66.

26. John R. Harris and Michael P. Todaro, "Migration, Unemployment, and Development," *American Economic Review* 60, no. 1 (1970): 126–42; Sarah Mahler, *American Dreaming: Immigrant Life on the Margins* (Princeton: Princeton University, 1995).

27. Massey et al., *Worlds in Motion*, 13.

28. Douglas S. Massey, Jorge Durand, and Nolan J. Malone, *Beyond Smoke and Mirrors: Mexican Immigration in an Era of Economic Integration* (New York: Russell Sage Foundation, 2002), 9.

29. Michael J. Piore, *Birds of Passage: Migrant Labor in Industrial Societies* (New York: Cambridge University, 1979).

30. Oded Stark and David Bloom, "The New Economics of Labor Migration," *American Economic Review* 75 (1985): 173–78.

31. Oded Stark, *The Migration of Labor* (Cambridge, UK: Basil Blackwell, 1991).

32. Ewa Morawska, "The Sociology and Historiography of Immigration," in *Immigration Reconsidered: History, Sociology, and Politics*, ed. Virginia Yans-McLaughlin (New York: Oxford University, 1990), 187–239.

33. Anup Shah, *Poverty Facts and Stats*, updated on June 11, 2005, available at http://www.globalissues.org/TradeRelated/Facts.asp.

34. United Nations Development Program, *Human Development Report 1999* (Oxford: Oxford University Press, 1999), 22.

35. Lewis, "Strategies for Survival: Migration and Fair Trade-Organic Coffee Production in Oaxaca, Mexico."

36. In the mid-1980s, the Mexican government introduced market-oriented reforms to its economy. Banking institutions, among other major players, were privatized and investment and credit lending became less restricted. As a result, the country's economy grew at a reasonably healthy pace and inflation was brought down. These positive changes in the Mexican economy began to attract large foreign investments, especially during a period when the U.S. interest rates were low. The influx of large capital took place without strict banking regulations and oversight. Soon banking liabilities and bad loans exceeded asset reserves. In December 1994 the Mexican government abandoned its currency control and let the peso exchange rate float freely against the U.S. dollar. The value of the peso plunged. A financial market meltdown ensued, with mass industrial layoffs and several well-publicized suicides.

37. World Bank, *Poverty in Mexico: An Assessment of Conditions, Trends and Government Strategy* (Mexico: The World Bank [Report No: 28612-ME], 2004).

38. Personal interview.

39. Oded Stark, "Migration Incentives, Migration Types, the Role of Relative Deprivation," *Economic Journal* 101 (1991): 1163–78.

40. Rakesh Kochhar, *Survey of Mexican Migrants—Part Three* (Washington, DC: The Pew Hispanic Center, December 6, 2005), 16, http://pewhispanic.org/files/reports/58.pdf.

41. Bian Yanjie, "Chinese Social Stratification and Social Mobility," *Annual Review of Sociology* 28 (2002): 91.

42. David Barboza, "Meatpackers' Profits Hinge on Pool of Immigrant Labor," *The New York Times*, December 21, 2001, A26.

43. John Ritter, "Finding Labor for the Fields a Trying Task—California's Building Boom Is Pulling Workers Away from Agriculture," *USA Today*, October 10, 2005, 3A.

44. Ibid.

45. Ibid.

46. Ronald Skeldon, *Myths and Realities of Chinese Irregular Migration*, IOM Migration Research Series, No. 1 (Geneva, Switzerland: International Organization for Migration, 2000).

47. Jane Wardell, "British Panel: Raise Retirement Age to 69," *San Diego Union Tribune*, December 1, 2005, A3.

48. Ibid.

49. Information regarding long-term financing problems was obtained from the official Web site of the Social Security Administration: http://www.ssa.gov/pubs/10055.html#future.

50. United Nations, *Living Arrangements of Older Persons around the World* (New York: United Nations, Department of Department of Economic and Social Affairs, Population Division, 2005), xiii.

51. Ibid., 18.

52. Kochhar, *Survey of Mexican Migrants*, 9, http://pewhispanic.org/files/reports/58.pdf.

53. U.S. Department of Justice, *Press Release* on December 19, 2001, http://www.usdoj.gov/opa/pr/2001/December/01_crm_654.htm. Later Tyson was acquitted on all charges by a federal jury in Chattanooga, Tennessee, on March 26, 2003.

54. Barboza, "Meatpackers' Profits Hinge on Pool of Immigrant Labor," A26.

55. Massey et al., *Worlds in Motion*, 29.

56. Frank N. Pieke, "Introduction: Chinese Migrations Compared," in *Internal and International Migration—Chinese Perspectives*, ed. Frank N. Pieke and Hein Mallee (Surrey, UK: Curzon, 1999), 9.

57. Jason Bennetto, "Gang Held over Smuggling 100,000 Turks into Britain," *The Independent*, October 12, 2005, http://news.independent.co.uk/uk/crime/article318866.ece.

58. Ibid.

59. Ibid.

60. *International Crime Threat Assessment*, a report prepared by a U.S. government interagency working group in support of and pursuant to the President's International Crime Control Strategy. Materials in this report came from the Central Intelligence Agency; Federal Bureau of Investigation; Drug Enforcement Administration; U.S. Customs Service; U.S. Secret Service; Financial Crimes Enforcement Network; National Drug Intelligence Center; the Departments of State, the Treasury, Justice, and Transportation; the Office of National Drug Control Policy; and the National Security Council. http://www.fas.org/irp/threat/pub45270chap2.html#4.

61. Ibid.

62. Marlowe Hood, "The Taiwan Connection," *Los Angeles Times Magazine*, October 9, 1994.

63. Willard H. Myers III, Testimony on April 21, 1994, before the Senate Foreign Relations/Terrorism, Narcotics and International Operations, U.S. Law Enforcement and Foreign Policy, Federal Document Clearing House, 1994.

64. Roger Thompson, "Fukienese Alien Smuggling" (paper presented at the Second Annual Southeast Regional Asian Crime Symposium, Clearwater, FL, 2000).

65. Kevin Sullivan and Mary Jordan, "Mexico Becomes World's Anteroom: Immigrants from around Globe Seek Back Door into U.S.," *The Washington Post*, June 7, 2001, A1.

66. Ibid.

67. Wayne A. Cornelius, "Thinking Out Loud/IMMIGRATION; There's No Point in Flailing at This Piñata; Scapegoating Mexico Is Easy, but It Doesn't Get Us Anywhere," *Los Angeles Times*, May 29, 2005, M3.

68. Cornelius, "Controlling 'Unwanted Immigration,'" 790.

69. Wayne Cornelius, "Death at the Border: The Efficacy and Unintended Consequences of U.S. Immigration Control Policy, 1993–2000" (working paper no. 27, Center for Comparative Immigration Studies, University of California, San Diego, 2000), http://www.ccis-ucsd.org/PUBLICATIONS/wrkg27new.pdf.

70. Onell R. Soto, "Case against 2 Sailors Detailed: Document Say Old Port of Entry Was Used to Smuggle Immigrants," *San Diego Union-Tribune*, February 3, 2006, B2.

CHAPTER 2: HUMAN SMUGGLING THROUGH LEGAL CHANNELS

1. Immigration and Customs Enforcement (ICE), "Two Sentenced for Smuggling Operation That Left Eleven Dead in Iowa Railcar," news release, November 21, 2005, http://www.ice.gov/pi/news/newsreleases/index.htm.

2. The information on immigration and visa application procedures presented in this chapter is intended to provide only a context for the discussion of human smuggling activities and should not be taken as legal advice.

3. The United States also allows refugees to immigrate on humanitarian grounds.

4. Although family and employment are the two primary venues for foreign nationals to immigrate to the United States, there is another, somewhat obscure, venue for immigration. This is the so-called diversity category, which provides a small number of immigration opportunities to countries that are not the principal sources of current immigration.

5. United Nations' Commission on Population and Development, "Concise Report on World Population Monitoring, 1997: International Migration and Development," *Report of the Secretary-General*, 13th Session, February, 24–28, 1997, http://www.itcilo.it/english/actrav/telearn/global/ilo/seura/migwod2.htm.

6. Sharon LaFraniere, "Many Women Snared in Fake Marriages in South Africa," *New York Times*, September 5, 2004, A3.

7. Ibid.

8. Susan Saulny, "Here Comes the Bride. Again, and Again..." *New York Times*, July 10, 2003, A1.

9. Ibid.

10. Ibid.

11. Federal Bureau of Investigation, "Under the Cover of Romance: Breaking the Heart of Chinese Immigration Fraud," news release, July 29, 2003, http://www.fbi.gov/page2/july03/072903chinaimm.htm.

12. U.S. Attorney General, "California Man Pleads Guilty to Marriage Fraud Charges," news release, February 23, 2004, http://www.state.gov/m/ds/rls/29972.htm.

13. U.S. Immigration and Customs Enforcement (ICE), "Federal Grand Jury Indicts 12 for Marriage Fraud, International Alien Smuggling," news release, September 15, 2005, http://www.ice.gov/pi/news/newsreleases/index.htm.

14. Exceptions are allowed if a couple can demonstrate "good cause" for any late filing of the petition.

15. Personal interview with the smuggler in Log Angeles in the summer of 2000.

16. James A. Jones. "The Immigration Marriage Fraud Amendments: Sham Marriages or Sham Legislation?" *Florida State University Law Review* 24, no. 3 (1997): 685.

17. Besides business activities, B1 visas are also given to a few other categories of people, such as lawyers in cross-national litigation, professional athletes, and clergy.

18. Personal interview in the fall of 2005 in Sacramento, California.

19. Rachel L. Swarns and Eric Lipton, "U.S. Is Dropping Effort to Track If Visitors Leave," *New York Times*, December 15, 2006, A1.

CHAPTER 3: THE GAME OF COUNTERFEIT DOCUMENTS

1. Immigration and Customs Enforcement, "Counterfeit Document Ringleader Sentenced to 5 Years," news release, December 8, 2003, http://www.ice.gov/graphics/news/newsreleases/.

2. Leslie Berestein, "Immigration Loophole Leads to Spread of Fake-ID Mills," *San Diego Union Tribune*, February 19, 2006, A1.

3. ICE, "Four Arrested in Counterfeit Document Scheme—An Array of Fake Documents and Sophisticated Machinery Uncovered," news release, November 14, 2003, http://www.ice.gov/graphics/news/newsreleases/.

4. Eduardo Porter, "Social Security Numbers Offered for Rent," *San Diego Union Tribune*, June 7, 2005, A1.

5. Ibid.

6. Government Accountability Office (GAO), *State Department—Improvements Needed to Strengthen U.S. Passport Fraud Detection Efforts* (testimony delivered by Jess T. Ford, Director of International Affairs and Trade, before the Committee on Homeland Security and Governmental Affairs, U.S. Senate, on June 29, 2005, Document No.: GAO-05-853T).

7. Ibid., 2.

8. Ibid., 5.

9. Mae M. Ngai, "Legacies of Exclusion: Illegal Chinese Immigration during the Cold War Years," *Journal of American Ethnic History* 18, no. 1 (1998): 3–35.

10. Paul J. Smith, "The Terrorists and Crime Bosses behind the Fake Passport Trade," *Jane's Intelligence Review*, no. 13 (July 2001): 42–44.

11. Ibid., 11.

12. The State Department, since February 2004, requires that children aged fourteen years and under appear with their parents when applying for a passport

so that submitted photographs can be compared and verified in front of family members.

13. GAO, Ibid., 2005, 2.

14. Mark Stevenson, "Mexico a Portal to U.S. for Fake-Passport Users," *San Diego Union Tribune*, August 8, 2005, A25.

15. Ibid.

16. Countries that participate in the visa-waiver program (VWP) with the United States must meet a list of stringent requirements. Currently twenty-seven countries have visa-waiving agreements with the United States and are posted at http://travel.state.gov/visa/temp/without/without_1990.html. Many other countries not in the VWP also allow visa-free entries for U.S. passport holders. For detailed foreign entry requirements, check http://travel.state.gov/travel/tips/brochures/brochures_1229.html.

17. Because of the frequent occurrence of stolen or lost passports and green cards in China, the procedure for obtaining replacement documents has significantly tightened in recent years. The U.S. consulates require that all U.S. citizens or permanent residents who claim to have lost their travel documents in China file a formal report with the local Public Security Bureau (i.e., the police) where the loss occurred. To file for a replacement passport or green card, the applicant must appear in person with the original police report, proof of identity (i.e., birth certificate or original citizenship paperwork), and other supporting documents and forms. Americans are also warned not to "give away" or sell their passports in China, because it is a criminal offense in both countries.

18. Charles Harns, "Improved Travel Documents in the Context of the Overall Migration Management in Africa" (keynote speech at the International Travel Documents and Issuance Systems: Technical Review of Standards and Systems for East and Central African Governments, and Participating West African Governments, Nairobi [Kenya], February 6–8, 2006).

19. Susannah Price, "Sri Lanka's Human Smuggling Rings," *BBC News*, February 10, 2000, http://news.bbc.co.uk/1/hi/world/south_asia/637825.stm.

20. Glenn R. Simpson, "Tiny Pacific Island Is Big Worry for U.S.," *Wall Street Journal*, May 16, 2003, A4.

21. Roger Thompson, "Fukienese Alien Smuggling" (paper presented at the Second Annual Southeast Regional Asian Crime Symposium, Clearwater, Florida, 2000).

22. Daniel McGrory, "Lithuanian Gangs Forge Ahead in Britain," *Times*, February 21, 2005, http://www.timesonline.co.uk/article/0,,2-1493053,00.html.

23. Ibid.

24. Ibid.

25. Scott MacLeod, "New Zealand Plans Law Switch on Stolen Passports," *New Zealand Herald*, May 2, 2003, A4.

26. Alisa Tang, "Thailand Emerges as Fake Passport Capital," Associated Press, September 8, 2005, http://web.lexis-nexis.com.

27. Ibid.

28. Ibid.

29. Ibid.

30. Personal communication with author.

31. Porter, "Social Security Numbers Offered for Rent."

32. Ibid.

33. Ibid.

34. Duncan Mansfield, "Tennessee Driver Certificates Lure Illegal Immigrants from Other States," Associated Press, January 29, 2006, http://web.lexis-nexis.com.

35. Ibid.

36. Information related to obtaining a Certificate for Driving in the state of Tennessee is available at http://tennessee.gov/safety/driverlicense/dlmain.htm.

37. Anita Wadhwani, "Driving Certificates Turning into IDs," *Tennessean.com*, June 25, 2004, http://www.tennessean.com/government/archives/04/06/53319732.shtml.

38. Mansfield, "Tennessee Driver Certificates Lure Illegal Immigrants from Other States."

39. Ibid.

CHAPTER 4: SMUGGLING THROUGH ILLEGAL CHANNELS

1. U.S. Customs and Border Protection, "On a Typical Day. . .," *Fact Sheet*, http://www.cbp.gov/.

2. Donald L. Barlett and James B. Steele, "Who Left the Door Open?" *Time*, September 20, 2004, 51.

3. U.S. Immigration and Customs Enforcement, "2 Criminally Charged with Alien Smuggling," news release, May 6, 2005, http://www.ice.gov/pi/news/newsreleases/.

4. Ibid.

5. Onell R. Soto, "Four Men Linked to Immigrant Smuggling Arrested in County," *San Diego Union-Tribune*, December 7, 2004, B2.

6. Ibid.

7. Leslie Berestein, "Migrant Smugglers Drawn to Casinos," *San Diego Union Tribune*, December 19, 2004, A1.

8. Ibid.

9. Ibid.

10. Ibid.

11. U.S. Immigration and Customs Enforcement, "Laredo Marine Corps Recruiter Convicted of Alien Smuggling," October 14, 2005, http://www.ice.gov/pi/news/newsreleases/.

12. Ibid.

13. Julie Watson, "More Women Risking Rape, Death, Capture to Cross Desert into U.S.," Associated Press, April 28, 2006, http://web.lexis-nexis.com.

14. *Arizona Republic* (Online Print Edition), "In Altar, Teeming with Transients, Small Town Shares Arizona's Conflicts over Impact of Illegal Immigration," August 21, 2005, http://www.azcentral.com.

15. The Economist, "Migrants in Mexico: Waiting to Cross," *The Economist*, August 10, 2006, http://www.economist.com/; *Arizona Republic*, "In Altar, Teeming with Transients."

16. Arthur H. Rotstein, "Cell Phones Sometimes Provide a Lifeline for Illegal Immigrants Stranded in Desert," Associated Press, May 27, 2005, http://web.lexis-nexis.com.

17. Peter Andreas, *Border Games—Policing the U.S.-Mexico Divide* (Ithaca, NY: Cornell University Press, 2000), 85.

18. John L. Martin, *Operation Blockade: Bullying Tactic or Border Control Model?* (Washington, DC: Center for Immigration Studies, December 1993), http://www.cis.org/articles/1993/back993.html.

19. United States General Accounting Office, *Illegal Immigration: Status Report of Southwest Border Strategy Implementation* (report to Congressional Committees GAO/GGD-99-44) (Washington, DC: U.S. General Accounting Office, 1999), http://www.gao.gov.

20. U.S. Department of Justice, "Operation Gatekeeper: An Investigation into Allegations of Fraud and Misconduct" (*USDOJ/OIG Special Report*, Washington, DC: U.S. Department of Justice, Office of Inspector General, 1998), http://www.usdoj.gov/oig/special/9807/.

21. John L. Martin, *Can We Control the Border? A Look at Recent Efforts in San Diego, El Paso and Nogales* (Washington, DC: Center for Immigration Studies, 1995), http://www.cis.org/articles/1995/border/index.html.

22. U.S. Department of Justice, "Reno Announces New Agents and Resources to Boost Operation Safeguard and Cut Illegal Immigration," news release, January 5, 1995, http://www.usdoj.gov/opa/pr/Pre_96/January95/.

23. U.S. Attorney General, *An Investigation of Travel Reimbursements in Connection with the INS's Operation Safeguard* (Washington, DC: U.S. Department of Justice, Office of the Inspector General, December 2002), http://www.usdoj.gov/oig/special/0301/index.htm.

24. U.S. Border Patrol, "Freight Train Apprehensions Dramatically Reduced," news release, January 15, 2003 (Washington, DC: U.S. Department of Justice, Border Patrol [McAllen Sector]), http://www.cbp.gov/.

25. U.S. Department of Homeland Security, "Fact Sheet: Arizona Border Control Initiative—Phase II" (released on March 30, 2005), http://www.dhs.gov/xnews/releases/press_release_0646.shtm.

26. U.S. Immigration and Customs Enforcement, "Feds Vow to Use 'Ice Storm' Tactics in Other Cities as Phoenix Sees Progress in Human Smuggling Crackdown," news release, May 18, 2004, http://www.ice.gov/pi/news/newsreleases/.

27. Pia M. Orrenius, "Illegal Immigration and Border Enforcement along the U.S.-Mexico Border: An Overview," *Economic & Financial Review* 1 (2001): 7.

28. Ibid., 7.

29. Leslie Berestein, "Record Numbers Have Died Trying to Cross Border," *San Diego Union Tribune*, September 4, 2005, 3A.

30. Olga R. Rodriguez, "Migrants Forgo Smugglers to Enter U.S.," Associated Press, May 19, 2006, http://web.lexis-nexis.com.

31. Ibid.

32. Dennis Wagner, "Illegals Dying at Record Rate in Arizona Desert," *USA Today*, August 19, 2005, 1A.

33. Berestein, "Record Numbers Have Died Trying to Cross Border."

34. Migrants Rights International, *Background on U.S. Border Militarization: Failed Immigration Enforcement Strategy Is Causing More Migrant Deaths*, July 2003, http://www.migrantwatch.org/mri/background_doc_to_press_statement.htm

35. U.S. Customs and Border Protection, "CBP Launches Operation Desert Safeguard Aimed at Preventing Migrant Deaths: Effort Focuses on Dangerous Sonoran Desert Area," press release, June 3, 2003, http://www.cbp.gov.

36. Michelle Malkin, *Invasion: How America Still Welcomes Terrorists, Criminals, and Other Foreign Menaces to Our Shores* (Washington, DC: Regnery Publishing, 2002).

37. Sherrie Kossoudji, "Playing Cat and Mouse at the U.S.-Mexico Border," *Demography* 29, no. 2 (1992):159–80; Douglas S. Massey, Jorge Durand, and Nolan J. Malone, *Beyond Smoke and Mirrors: Mexican Immigration in an Era of Economic Integration* (New York: Russell Sage Foundation, 2002).

38. Karl Eschbach, Jacqueline M. Hagan, and Nestor P. Rodriguez, "Deaths during Undocumented Migration: Trends and Policy Implications in the New Era of Homeland Security," *In Defense of the Alien* 26 (New York: Center for Migration Studies, 2003).

39. Ibid.

40. Anita Snow, "Cuban Authorities Shoot Suspected Smuggler," Associated Press, April 7, 2006, http://web.lexis-nexis.com.

41. Ibid.

42. U.S. Department of Homeland Security, "Homeland Security Agencies Thwart Unusual Human Smuggling Scheme Involving Luxury Sailing Yacht," news release, September 1, 2004, http://www.uscg.mil/pacarea/News/newsreleases/index04.htm.

43. U.S. Immigration and Customs Enforcement, "South Bay Man Pleads Guilty to Smuggling Aliens and Tropical Fish into United States," news release, September 9, 2005, http://www.ice.gov/pi/news/newsreleases/.

44. Edward J. M. Rhoads, "White Labor vs. Coolie Labor: The Chinese Question in Pennsylvania in the 1870s," *Journal of American Ethnic History* 21, no.2, (2002): 3.

45. Erika Lee, *At America's Gates: Chinese Immigration during the Exclusion Era, 1882–1943* (Chapel Hill: University of North Carolina, 2003), 169–70.

46. Rose Hum Lee, *The Chinese in the United States of America* (Hong Kong: Hong Kong University, 1960).

47. Marlowe Hood, "The Taiwan Connection," *Los Angeles Times Magazine,* October 9, 1994, 20.

48. Edward Barnes, "Two-Faced Woman," *Time*, July 31, 2000, 48–50.

49. Ed Offley and Joel Connelly, "U.S., Canada Casting High-Tech Net to Catch Smugglers of Chinese," *San Diego Union Tribune*, October 8, 1999, A29.

50. Personal interview in the summer of 2000.

51. Reuters, "China Refugees Found on Canadian Island," *San Diego Union Tribune*, August 13, 1999, A17.

52. Personal interview with Mexican immigration authorities in Tijuana in August 1999.

53. Robert L. Jamieson, Jr., "Illegal Entry into U.S. Has a Long, Dangerous History," *Seattle Post-Intelligencer*, January 11, 2000, http://seattlepi.nwsource.com/local/dang11.shtml.

54. Ian Bailey and Mark Hume, "Stowaways Land as Anti-smuggling Planning Starts: Seattle-Bound Chinese Discovered When Ship Diverted to Vancouver," *National Post*, January 5, 2000, A5.

55. Robert Jablon, "30 Chinese Arrested for Illegal Entry to U.S.," *San Diego Union Tribune*, December 30, 1999, A3.

56. Sam Howe Verhovek, "22 Chinese Stowaways Found at Cargo Facility in Seattle," *Los Angeles Times*, April 6, 2006, A5.

57. Sam Howe Hervocek, "Deadly Choice of Stowaways: Ship Containers," *New York Times*, January 12, 2000, A1.

58. Personal interview in the fall of 2006 in Los Angeles.

59. Madeline Baro Diaz, "Cuban Mails Herself to Miami, and to Freedom Airport: Workers Find Woman Alive in Crate," *South Florida Sun-Sentinel*, August 26, 2004, 1A.

60. David Ovalle, "Stowaway Found on Plane at Miami International Airport," *Miami Herald*, March 5, 2004, http://www.latinamericanstudies.org/dominican-republic/stowaway.htm.

61. Karen Gaudette, "Missing Chinese Girl Turns Up on East Coast with Kin," *San Diego Union-Tribune*, August 4, 2002, A3.

62. Personal interview in the summer of 2000 in Fuzhou, China.

63. Personal interview in the summer of 2000 in Fuzhou, China.

CHAPTER 5: SISTER PING—THE SNAKEHEAD QUEEN

1. Materials included in this case study came from personal interviews with human smugglers in the United States and China, from federal investigators familiar with Sister Ping's smuggling operations, and from published reports from U.S. government sources and the news media.

2. U.S. Immigration and Customs Enforcement, "Sister Ping Sentenced to 35 Years in Prison for Alien Smuggling, Hostage Taking, Money Laundering and Ransom Proceeds Conspiracy," news release, March 16, 2006, http://www.ice.gov/graphics/news/newsreleases/.

3. Edward Barnes, "Two-Faced Woman," *Time*, July 31, 2000, 48–50.

4. Federal Bureau of Investigation (FBI), "The Case of the Snakehead Queen: Chinese Human Smuggler Gets 35 Years," news release, March 17, 2006, http://www.fbi.gov/page2/march06/sisterping031706.htm.

5. Ibid.

6. Barnes, "Two-Faced Woman."

7. Mata Press Service, "Mother of All 'Snakeheads' Gets 35 Years in Jail," *Asian Pacific Post*, March 27, 2006, http://www.asianpacificpost.com.

8. Ibid.

CHAPTER 6: THE ENTERPRISE AND ORGANIZATION OF HUMAN SMUGGLING

1. For a detailed discussion of how the Chinese human smugglers are perceived, see chapter 3 of Ko-lin Chin's *Smuggled Chinese* (Philadelphia: Temple University Press, 1999).

2. Daniel Gonzalez and Sergio Bustos, "'Coyotes': Criminals to the U.S. but Heroes to Many Immigrants," *USA Today*, November 30, 2003, 19A.

3. Leslie Berestein, "Record Numbers Have Died Trying to Cross Border," *San Diego Union Tribune*, September 4, 2005, 3A.

4. Associated Press, "Smuggler Sentenced in Immigrant Deaths," November 22, 2005, http://web.lexis-nexis.com.

5. Angela Lau and Sandra Dibble, "Illegal Chinese Immigrants Found in Baja— At Least 82 Have Been Detained," *San Diego Union Tribune*, August 25, 1999, A3.

6. U.S. Immigration and Customs Enforcement, "55 Charged in Federal Probe Targeting Large-Scale Human Smuggling Network," news release, October 11, 2006, http://www.ice.gov/pi/news/newsreleases.

7. Diego Gambetta, *The Sicilian Mafia: The Business of Private Protection* (Cambridge, MA: Harvard University Press, 1993).

8. Christian Geffray, "Introduction: Drug Trafficking and the State," *International Social Science Journal* 53, no. 3 (2001): 421–26; Francisco E. Thoumi, "Illegal Drugs in Colombia: From Illegal Economic Boom to Social Crisis," *Annals of the American Academy of Political & Social Science* 582 (2002): 102–16.

9. Gary W. Potter, *Criminal Organizations: Vice, Racketeering, and Politics in an American City* (Prospect Heights, IL: Waveland, 1994).

10. Olga R. Rodriguez, "Mexico Falls Short on Crack Down Promise," Associated Press, July 26, 2004, http://web.lexis-nexis.com.

11. U.S. Department of Justice, "Inspector General Announces Arrest of INS Official in Alien Smuggling Ring," press release, July 16, 1996, http://www.usdoj.gov/opa/pr/1996/July96/339ig.htm.

CHAPTER 7: TRAFFICKING OF WOMEN AND CHILDREN

1. The author would like to acknowledge Samuel L. Pineda for his contributions to the data gathering and analysis of the materials presented in this chapter.

2. Associated Press, "Major Child Prostitution Rings Broken: 31 Indicted," *San Diego Union Tribune*, December 17, 2005, A7.

3. Morrissey Siobhan, "Sinister Industry," *ABA Journal* 92, no. 3 (2006): 59; Francis T. Miko and Grace (Jea-Hyun) Park, *Trafficking in Women and Children: The U.S. and International Response* (Washington, DC: The Library Congress, Congressional Research Service, 2002), 1.

4. U.S. Immigration and Customs Enforcement, "ICE Agent Testifies before Congress on Growing Threat of Human Trafficking," news release, June 24, 2003, http://www.ice.gov/pi/news/newsreleases/.

5. Human Smuggling and Trafficking Center, *Fact Sheet: Distinctions between Human Smuggling and Human Trafficking* (2005), http://www.usdoj.gov/crt/crim/smuggling_trafficking_facts.pdf.

6. United Nations, *Protocol to Prevent, Suppress and Punish Trafficking in Persons, Especially Women and Children, Supplementing the United Nations Convention against Transnational Organized Crime* (2000), http://www.unodc.org/pdf/crime/final_instruments/383e.pdf.

7. United Nations, *Protocol against the Smuggling of Migrants by Land, Sea and Air, Supplementing the United Nations Convention against Transnational Organized Crime* (2000), http://www.unodc.org/pdf/crime/final_instruments/383e.pdf.

8. David A. Feingold, "Think Again: Human Trafficking," *Foreign Policy Issue* 150 (2005): 26.

9. International Labor Organization, "A Global Alliance against Forced Labor," *International Labor Conference 93rd Session*, 2005, http://www.ilo.org/.

10. Joyce Outshoorn, "The Political Debates on Prostitution and Trafficking of Women, Social Politics," *International Studies in Gender, State and Society* 12, no. 1 (2005): 142.

11. Ibid.

12. Ibid., 145.

13. Elzbieta M. Gozdziak and Elizeabeth A. Collett, "Research on Human Trafficking in North America: A Review of Literature," *International Organization for Migration* 43, no. 1/2 (2005): 106.

14. Louise Shelley, "Russian and Chinese Trafficking: A Comparative Perspective," in *Human Traffic and Transnational Crime: Eurasian and American Perspectives*, eds. Sally Stoecker and Louise Shelley (New York: Rowman & Littlefield, 2005), 63.

15. Christina Arnold and Andrea M. Bertone, "Addressing the Sex Trade in Thailand: Some Lessons Learned from NGOs," *Gender Issues* 20, no. 1 (2002): 32.

16. Kevin Bales, *Understanding Global Slavery: A Reader* (Berkeley: University of California Press, 2005), 185.

17. Ibid.

18. U.S. Department of Justice, *Assessment of U.S. Activities to Combat Trafficking in Persons* (August 2003), http://www.usdoj.gov/ag/.

19. U.S. State Department, *Fact Sheet: Distinctions between Human Smuggling and Human Trafficking* (Washington, D.C.: Human Smuggling and Trafficking Center, 2005), 1, http://www.state.gov/p/inl/rls/fs/49768.htm.

20. U.S. Department of Justice, *Assessment of U.S. Activities to Combat Trafficking in Persons* (September 2005), http://www.usdoj.gov/ag/.

21. Ibid.

22. U.S. Department of State, *Trafficking in Persons Report*, Office to Monitor and Combat Trafficking in Persons, 2006, http://www.state.gov/g/tip/rls/.

23. Some discussion has been provided in recent years on the use of Bayesian models to estimate the number of trafficking victims in the United States. Statistical procedures such as Bayesian modeling can be used to produce estimates when missing values are present in the primary data. However, these estimates are suspicious when none of the missing values or the sources of the primary data were discussed in the report. To date, no explanation has been offered on how these estimates have been compiled over the years or on reasons for the sharp downward trend.

24. David Masci, "Human Trafficking and Slavery: Are the World's Nations Doing Enough to Stamp It Out?" *CQ Researcher* 14, no. 12 (2004): 275.

25. The purpose of the minimum standards is to place primary responsibility for the elimination of human trafficking on the government of a country of origin, transit, or destination. Governments in countries with significant trafficking problems are expected to make serious and sustained efforts to curtail trafficking activities and punish those involved. Details of these standards and criteria can be found at http://www.state.gov/g/tip/rls/tiprpt/2005/46770.htm.

26. Miko and Park, *Trafficking in Women and Children.*

27. Corene Rathgeber, "The Victimization of Women through Human Trafficking—An Aftermath of War?" *European Journal of Crime, Criminal Law & Criminal Justice* 10, no. 2/3 (2002): 152.

28. Francis Miko, *Trafficking in Women and Children: The U.S. and International Response*, Congressional Research Service Report, 98-649C, Foreign Affairs, Defense, and Trade Division, March 26, 2004.

29. Masci, "Human Trafficking and Slavery."

30. Bales, *Understanding Global Slavery*, 103.

31. PACO, *Trafficking in Human Beings and Corruption* (Program against Corruption and Organised Crime in South Eastern Europe, Economic Crime Division, Portoroz, Slovenia, 2002), 9.

32. Ibid., 7.

33. Andrew Cockburn, "21st Century Slaves," *National Geographic Magazine*, 2003, http://magma.nationalgeographic.com/ngm/0309/feature1/.

34. Osita Agbu, "Corruption and Human Trafficking: The Nigerian Case," *West Africa Review*, 2003, http://www.westafricareview.com/vol4.1/agbu.html.

35. The CPI scoring system measures corruption perceived by businesspeople and country analysts. The score ranges between ten (highly clean) and zero (highly corrupt). For instance, according to the 2005 CPI, Iceland, Finland, and New Zealand were ranked the cleanest countries, whereas Turkmenistan, Bangladesh, and Chad were the most corrupt in the world. Most Scandinavian countries were highly ranked. The United States was ranked seventeenth. The CPI gathers data from sources that span the last three years (for instance, the CPI 2005 includes surveys from 2003, 2004, and 2005). All sources measure the overall extent of corruption (e.g., frequency and/or size of bribes) in the public and political sectors. Data come from surveys as well as experts (risk agencies/country analysts). Each country is also provided a range of possible values (i.e., confidence intervals) that reflect how a country's score may vary. Nominally, the confidence intervals vary about 5 percent above and below the mean. Additional information on the methodology of the CPI can be found at http://www.transparency.org/policy_and_research/surveys_indices/cpi/2005/methodology.

36. Johann G. Lambsdorf, *Corruption Perceptions Index: Global Corruption Reports* (Ann Arbor, MI: Transparency International, 2005), 233.

37. Two other variables have also been considered: the official rate of poverty in a nation, and the percentage of child labor. Because of the difficulty in obtaining adequate data from official sources, they are excluded from the analysis.

38. The correlation coefficients for both per capita income and corruption exceeded $r = .41$, which indicate relatively strong connections. Additional multivariate statistical procedures were also conducted and found that official corruption was indeed the most powerful predictor of a nation's placement in the TIP tier system while controlling for all poverty-related measures.

39. Immigration and Customs Enforcement (ICE), "10 Charged in International Human Smuggling Ring That Lured Young Honduran Women to U.S. for Forced Labor," news release, July 21, 2005, http://www.ice.gov/pi/news/newsreleases/.

40. Associated Press, "Woman Faces Charges of Sex Trafficking," *San Diego Union Tribune*, May 8, 2005, A5.

41. ICE, "Ice Arrests Men Who Forced Women to Work as Strippers—Ukrainian Women Were Tricked into Traveling to the U.S., Then Forced to Work at Strip Club," news release, February 17, 2005, http://www.ice.gov/pi/news/newsreleases/.

42. William Glaberson, "Sex-Trafficking Pleas Detail Abuse of Mexican Women," *New York Times*, April 6, 2005, B3.

43. ICE, "Wisconsin Couple Indicted on Human Trafficking Charges: Brookfield Pair Is Charged with Holding a Woman in Servitude for 19 Years," news release, March 16, 2005, http://www.ice.gov/pi/news/newsreleases/.

44. Anna Cearley, "7 Charged with Trafficking Children," *San Diego Union Tribune*, November 26, 2005, B2.

45. Ibid.

46. This case study was based on press releases from the U.S. Department of Justice, U.S. Attorney's Office, Northern District of California. References include the following:
U.S. Department of Justice, "29 Charged in Connection with Alien Harboring Conspiracy," press release, July 1, 2005, http://www.usdoj.gov/usao/can/press/; U.S. Department of Justice, "More Charges in Operation Gilded Case: Man Charged with Alien Harboring and Money Laundering Offenses in Operating San Francisco Brothel," March 1, 2006, http://www.usdoj.gov/usao/can/press/; Jaxon Van Derbeken and Ryan Kim, "Alleged Sex-Trade Ring Broken Up in Bay Area—Police Say Koreans in Massage Parlors Were Smuggled In," *San Francisco Chronicle*, July 2, 2005, A1; Jason Sweeney, "FBI's Operation Gilded Cage Includes Knollwood Drive Raid," *Saratoga News*, July 27, 2005, http://www.svcn.com/archives/saratoganews/20050727/index.html; ICE, "24 Indicted in Korean Human Smuggling Scheme That Brought Prostitutes into the United States," news release, July 14, 2005, http://www.ice.gov/pi/news/newsreleases/.

47. This case study was based on the investigation report and an interview prepared by the lead detective from the Los Angeles County Sheriff's Office.

48. Condoleezza Rice, "Release of the Fifth Annual Department of State Trafficking in Persons Report," U.S. State Department, June 3, 2005, http://www.state.gov/secretary/rm/2005/47193.htm.

49. U.S. Government Accountability Office (GAO), *Human Trafficking: Better Data, Strategy, and Reporting Needed to Enhance U.S. Antitrafficking Efforts Abroad* (GAO-06-825) (Washington, DC: U.S. Government Accountability Office, July 2006), 2, http://www.gao.gov/new.items/d06825.pdf.

50. Ronald Weitzer, "The Growing Moral Panic over Prostitution and Sex Trafficking," *Criminologist* 30, no. 5 (2005): 1.

51. Ibid.

52. Arnold and Bertone, "Addressing the Sex Trade in Thailand," 26.

CHAPTER 8: HITCHHIKING: HUMAN SMUGGLING AND TERRORISM

1. The description of the incident was provided in a written statement prepared by Diana Dean for the Senate's Judiciary Committee. The statement can be found at http://judiciary.senate.gov/oldsite/21020dd.htm. Additional information about the "Millennium Bomber" was compiled based on a special report, "A Terrorist Within: The Story of One Man's Holy War against America," in the *Seattle Times*, by Hal Bernton, Mike Carter, David Heath, and James Neff, between June 23 and July 7, 2002, http://archives.seattletimes.nwsource.com.

2. *Terrorism* in this text pertains to organized activities instigated by individuals who share the same religious or political convictions, belong to self-identified and recognized organizations, and are determined to bring about social and political changes through the use of violent means, such as Al-Qaeda and Jemaah Islamiyah. Excluded from this definition are those who launch terrorist activities by themselves, such as Timothy McVeigh of the Oklahoma bombing on April 19, 1995, and the Unabomber, Theodore Kaczynski, who mailed explosive materials to selected targets from the late 1970s to the mid-1990s.

3. David E. Kaplan. "Paying for Terror—How Jihadist Groups Are Using Organized-Crime Tactics—and Profits—to Finance Attacks on Targets around the Globe," *U.S. News & World Report*, December 5, 2005, 41.

4. This assessment was made by Bruce Gebhardt, deputy director of the FBI, at the International Security Management Association Conference, Scottsdale, Arizona, on January 12, 2004, http://www.fbi.gov/pressrel/speeches/gebhardt011204.htm.

5. James A. Damask, "Cigarette Smuggling: Financing Terrorism?" Mackinac Center for Public Policy, Midland, Michigan, July 1, 2002, http://www.mackinac. org/article.aspx?ID=4461; FBI, "Suspected Hezbollah Cell Disrupted," *Terrorism 2000/200*, July 21, 2000, http://www.fbi.gov/publications/terror/terror 2000_2001.htm.

6. Immigration and Customs Enforcement, "26 Unauthorized Workers Arrested at Northrop Grumman Facility," news release, June 1, 2005, http:// www.ice.gov/graphics/news/newsreleases/articles/pascagoula060105.htm.

7. Emma Perez-Treviño, "Potential Terrorists Released due to Lack of Jail Space, Congressman Says," *Brownsville Herald*, July 23, 2004, http://www. brownsvilleherald.com/ts_comments.php?id=60297_0_10_0_C.

8. Associated Press, "Closer Look at Smuggling from Nations with Terror Ties," July 2, 2005, http://web.lexis-nexis.com.

9. Associated Press, "14 Indicted in Human Smuggling Ring on U.S.-Canada Border," April 13, 2006, http://www.lexis-nexis.com/.

10. Ibid.

11. *San Diego Union Tribune*, "Abu Sayyaf Claims It Is Responsible in Ferry Fire," February 29, 2004, A22.

12. United Nations International Drug Control Program, *World Drug Report* (New York: Oxford University Press, 1997).

13. Southeast Asian Information Network, *Out of Control 2: The HIV/Aids Epidemic in Burma* (1998), http://www.ibiblio.org/freeburma/drugs/ooc2/.

14. Peter Chalk, "Southeast Asia and the Golden Triangle's Heroin Trade: Threat and Response," *Studies in Conflict & Terrorism* 23 (2000): 89–106.

15. Pasuk Phongpaichit, Sungsidh Piriyarangsan, and Nualnoi Teerat, *Guns, Girls, Gambling, and Ganja: Thailand's Illegal Economy and Public Policy* (Bangkok: Silkworm Books, 1998); U.S. State Department, *International Narcotics Control Strategy Report* (Washington, DC: U.S. Department of State, Bureau for International Narcotics and Enforcement Affairs, 2006), http://www.state.gov/p/inl/ rls/nrcrpt/.

16. U.S. State Department, *International Narcotics Control Strategy Report* (Washington, DC: U.S. Department of State, Bureau for International Narcotics and Enforcement Affairs, 2005), http://www.state.gov/p/inl/rls/nrcrpt/.

17. Mark Gaylord, "City of Secrets: Drugs, Money and the Law in Hong Kong," *Crime, Law & Social Change* 28 (1997): 91–110.

18. This information was obtained from the Interpol at the 7th Meeting on Project Bridge at the Interpol headquarters in Lyon, France, February 25–36, 2004.

19. Ibid.

20. U.S. Department of State, *Trafficking in Persons Report* (Washington, DC: U.S. Department of State, Office to Monitor and Combat Trafficking in Persons, 2003), http://www.state.gov/g/tip/rls/.

21. Christina Arnold and Andrea M. Bertone, "Addressing the Sex Trade in Thailand: Some Lessons Learned from NGOs," *Gender Issues* 20, no. 1 (2002): 26–28.

22. Shailaja Abraham, *Going Nowhere: Trafficking of Women and Children in International Sex Trade* (New Delhi, India: Dominant, 2001); Bridget Anderson and Julia

O'Connell Davidson, *Trafficking—A Demand Led Problem? Part 1: Review of Evidence and Debates* (Stockholm: Save the Children–Sweden, 2004).

23. Therese Caouette, *Need Assessment on Cross-Border Trafficking in Women and Children—The Mekong Sub-region* (Bangkok: UN Working Group on Trafficking in the Mekong Sub-region, 1998).

24. CNN, "Sea Piracy Hits Record High," *World News*, January 28, 2004, http://www.cnn.com/2004/WORLD/asiapcf/01/27/pirates/index.html.

25. Andrew Guest, "Piracy Attacks Hit New High," *Trade Winds*, October 29, 2003.

26. Mark J. Valencia, "International Co-operation in Anti-piracy Efforts in Asia: Some Considerations," *East–West Center, Asia–Pacific Area Network*, February 20, 2001.

27. Dana Dillon, "The War on Terrorism in Southeast Asia: Developing Law Enforcement," *The Backgrounder*, no. 1720 (Washington, DC: Heritage Foundation, January 22, 2004).

28. Ibid.

29. Mark Manyin, Emma Chanlett-Avery, Richard Cronin, Larry Niksch, and Bruce Vaughn, *Terrorism in Southeast Asia* (CSR Report for Congress—RL31672) (Washington, DC: Congressional Research Service, Library of Congress, August 13, 2004), 3, http://fpc.state.gov/documents/organization/35795.pdf.

30. Ibid.

31. Eric Weiner and Michael Sullivan, "Terrorism in Southeast Asia: An NPR Special Report Five-Part Series Traces Spread of Al Qaeda, Militant Islam," NPR news release, February 3–7, 2003, http://www.npr.org/news/specials/mideast/asia/index.html.

32. Ibid.

33. Mark Hosenball, "A Swiss Connection to a Pakistani Bomb Racket?" *Newsweek* 143, no. 9 (March 1, 2004): 8.

34. Weiner and Sullivan, "Terrorism in Southeast Asia."

35. Ibid.

36. Alfonso T. Yuchengco, "Islamist Terrorism in Southeast Asia," *Issues & Insights* 3, no. 1 (2003): 1, http://www.csis.org/pacfor/issues/.

37. Ibid.

38. Ibid.

39. Manyin et al., *Terrorism in Southeast Asia*.

40. Yuchengco, "Islamist Terrorism in Southeast Asia."

41. Terence Hunt, "Bush Visits Bali amid Fears of Terrorism," Associated Press, October 21, 2003, http://web.lexis-nexis.com.

42. APEC, "Bangkok Declaration on Partnership for the Future" (2003 Leaders' Declaration at the 11th APEC Economic Leaders Meeting, Bangkok, Thailand, October 21, 2003), http://www.apecsec.org.sg/apec/leaders_declarations/2003.html.

CHAPTER 9: COMBATING HUMAN SMUGGLING

1. Arian Campo-Flores, "America's Divide," *Newsweek*, March 10, 2006, 28–38.

2. Otis L. Graham Jr., *Unguarded Gates—A History of America's Immigration Crisis*, (New York: Rowman & Littlefield, 2004), xi.

3. Peter Brimelow, *Alien Nation: Common Sense about America's Immigration Disaster* (New York: Random House, 1995), 238.

4. International Labor Organization, *Labor Market Trends and Globalization's Impact on Them*, http://www.itcilo.it/english/actrav/telearn/global/ilo/seura/mains.htm.

5. National Intelligence Council, *Global Trends 2015: Dialogue about the Future with Nongovernment Experts* (NIC 2000-02, December 2000), 8, http://www.cia.gov/nic/NIC_globaltrend2015.html.

6. Michelle Malkin, *Invasion: How America Still Welcomes Terrorists, Criminals, and Other Foreign Menaces to Our Shores* (Washington, DC: Regnery Publishing, 2002).

7. Dan Seligman, "Illegals with Legal Rights," *Forbes*, January 7, 2002, 128.

8. United Nations Population Division, *International Migration 2002* (New York: United Nations, 2002), 5, http://www.un.org/esa/population/.

9. Audrey Singer, *The Rise of New Immigrant Gateways* (Washington, DC: Brookings Institution, 2004), http://www.brookings.edu/metro/publications/20040301_gateways.htm.

10. U.S. Immigration and Customs Enforcement, "Department of Homeland Security Launches Operation 'Ice Storm,'" news release, November 10, 2003, http://www.ice.gov/pi/news/newsreleases/.

11. Douglas S. Massey, Jorge Durand, and Nolan J. Malone, *Beyond Smoke and Mirrors: Mexican Immigration in an Era of Economic Integration* (New York: Russell Sage Foundation, 2002), 156.

12. Ibid., 157.

13. Ibid., 157; Wayne Cornelius, "Controlling 'Unwanted Immigration': Lessons from the United States, 1993–2004," *Journal of Ethnic and Migration Studies* 31, no. 4 (2005): 775.

14. Jeffrey S. Passel, *Size and Characteristics of the Unauthorized Migrant Population in the U.S.* (Washington, DC: Pew Hispanic Center, 2006), i, http://pewhispanic.org/files/reports/61.pdf.

15. Dan Bear, "Secure Our Borders: A Matter of National Defense," *Ether Zone*, October 8, 2003, http://etherzone.com/2003/bear100803.shtml.

16. Michael Doyle, "Immigration Bill Carries Hefty Price Tag," *Sacramento Bee*, May 19, 2006, A14.

17. The National Guard troops are already performing some roles along border regions, mostly in counter-drug operations such as surveillance, intelligence gathering, and other technical support.

18. Naftali Bendavid and Jill Zuckman, "INS Gaffe Prompts Calls for Inquiry," *Chicago Tribune*, March 14, 2002, 1A.

19. Marisa Taylor, "U.S. Struggles to Keep Tabs on Foreign Visitors Leaving," *San Diego Union Tribune*, September 16, 2006, A7.

20. Rachel L. Swarns and Eric Lipton, "U.S. Is Dropping Effort to Track If Visitors Leave," *New York Time*, December 15, 2006, A1.

21. Beverley Lumpkin, "GAO Says Exit Portion of Border Program Will Take 5 to 10 Year to Implement," Associated Press, December 15, 2006, http://web.lexisnexis.com.

22. Personal interview in the summer of 2006.

23. Wayne A. Cornelius, "Thinking Out Loud/IMMIGRATION; There's No Point in Flailing at this Pinata," *Los Angeles Times*, May 29, 2005, M3.

24. Jessa M. Lewis, *Strategies for Survival: Migration and Fair Trade-Organic*

Coffee Production in Oaxaca, Mexico (Center for Comparative Immigration Studies Working Paper No. 118) (San Diego, CA: University of California, San Diego, 2005), http://www.ccis-ucsd.org/PUBLICATIONS/wrkg118.pdf.

25. John Cloud and Mike Allen, "Playing Both Sides of the Fence," *Time*, December 5, 2005, 33.

26. Charles P. Kindleberger, *Europe's Postwar Growth: The Role of Labor Supply* (New York: Oxford University, 1967).

27. Philip L. Martin and Mark J. Miller, "Guestworkers: Lessons from Western Europe," *Industrial and Labor Relations Review* 33 (1980): 315.

28. James Graff, "Why Paris Is Burning," *Time*, November 14, 2005, 36–38.

29. International Organization for Migration, "Foreign Direct Investment, Trade and Aid: An Alternative to Migration," news release no. 781, November 19, 1996, http://www.itcilo.it/english/actrav/telearn/global/ilo/seura/iom2.htm.

30. Thomas L. Friedman, *The World Is Flat: A Brief History of the Twenty-First Century* (New York: Farrar, Straus and Giroux, 2005), 181.

31. Ibid., 335.

32. *Global Poverty Report*, G8 Okinawa Summit Report, July 2000, 6, http://www.adb.org/documents/reports/global_poverty/2000/G8_2000.pdf. The United Nations defines poverty as living at $1 or less a day.

33. Section 7202 of the Intelligence Reform and Terrorism Prevention Act of 2004 authorized the establishment of the Human Smuggling and Trafficking Center. http://www.state.gov/p/inl/41449.htm#sec7202.

34. Kitty Calavita, "Thinking Outside the Box on Immigration," *San Diego Union Tribune*, September 23, 2005, B7.

35. U.S. Immigration and Customs Enforcement (ICE), "U.S. Uncovers Large-Scale Identity Theft Scheme Used by Illegal Aliens to Gain Employment at Nationwide Meat Processor," news release, December 13, 2006, http://www.ice.gov/pi/news/newsreleases/.

36. Roxana Hegeman, "Immigration Raids May Affect Meat Prices," Associated Press, December 15, 2006, http://web.lexis-nexis.com.

37. These strategies are gathered through interviews over the years in the field with federal and local law enforcement officials.

38. Cloud and Allen, "Playing Both Sides of the Fence," 33.

39. Ko-lin Chin, *Smuggled Chinese: Clandestine Immigration to the United States* (Philadelphia: Temple University Press, 1999).

40. It is not the intent of this book to start an ideological debate; however, if the one-child policy can become grounds for asylum, then hundreds of millions of Chinese can qualify and should be offered a safe passage to the United States. At least twenty-five years' worth of generations have been subjected to this family planning policy, under which countless people have been fined, fired, demoted, or coerced into abortion and sterilization, all in the government's effort to control China's population.

41. Based on personal interviews with federal agents in 2005.

42. U.S. Immigration and Customs Enforcement, "Detention, and Removal Operations: Alternatives to Detention," Fact Sheet, July 14, 2004, http://www.ice.gov/pi/dro/factsheets.htm.

43. Leslie Berestein, "Expedited Deportations Loom for More Illegal Border Crossers," *San Diego Union Tribune*, August 11, 2004, A13.

44. Arthur H. Rotstein, "Daily Flights for Illegal Immigrants Resume Friday," Associated Press, June 8, 2005, http://web.lexis-nexis.com.

45. ICE, "Feds Charge 13 Proprietors of Arizona Motels with Using Businesses to Harbor Smuggled Aliens," news release, November 10, 2005, http://www.ice.gov/graphics/news/newsreleases/.

46. Ibid.

47. Ian Bailey and Mark Hume, "Stowaways Land as Anti-smuggling Planning Starts: Seattle-Bound Chinese Discovered When Ship Diverted to Vancouver,' *National Post*, January 5, 2000, A5.

48. U.S. Customs and Border Protection, "Homeland Security Expands Efforts to Combat Human Smuggling in the Los Angeles Area: Initial Phase of Multi-agency Operation Focuses on LAX," press release, July 14, 2004, http://www.cbp.gov/xp/cgov/newsroom/press_releases/.

Glossary of Terms and Acronyms

Alien—A foreign national (e.g., "illegal alien," "resident alien"). A term commonly used in official U.S. documents.

Border Patrol—The mobile, uniformed enforcement arm of the former Immigration and Naturalization Service and current Immigration and Customs Enforcement. Its mission is to maintain control of border regions and ports of entry; it also interdicts narcotics and other contraband.

Coyote—Human smuggler. This term refers to enterprising Mexican agents who guide or smuggle individuals or groups across the border from Mexico into the United States for a fee.

Diaobao (Mandarin)—"Witching the luggage"—in other words, taking on someone else's identity as an imposter.

DOJ—U.S. Department of Justice.

FBI—Federal Bureau of Investigation—undertakes criminal investigations and develops cases for potential prosecution in federal court.

Green card—An identification card that signifies one's legal permanent residency in the United States.

ICE—Immigration and Customs Enforcement, an agency under the recently formed Homeland Security Administration; created in response to the events of September 11, 2001, ICE combines the former law enforcement functions of the Immigration and Naturalization Service under the Department of Justice and U.S. Customs under the Department of Treasury.

Illegal immigrant (alien)—A foreign national who entered the United States without inspection, gained entry through use of fraudulent documents, or who overstayed his/her visa and is residing in the United States unlawfully.

INS—Immigration and Naturalization Service, an agency within the U.S. Department of Justice.

Intensive Supervision Appearance Program (ISAP)—A pilot program that supervises migrants released from detention while they await immigration court proceedings or removal orders. As with parole supervision, participants agree to comply with the conditions of their release. Case specialists monitor these participants in the community by using tools such as electronic monitoring, home visits, work visits, and reporting by telephone.

Operation Gatekeeper—Border enforcement operation, launched in 1994 in San Diego, California.

Operation Hold the Line—Border enforcement operation, launched in 1993 in El Paso, Texas.

Operation Rio Grande—Border enforcement operation, launched in 1997 in Brownsville, Texas.

Operation Safeguard—Border enforcement operation, launched in 1994 in Nogales, Arizona.

Polleros—Mexican slang for human smugglers.

Pollos—"Chicken"; Mexican slang for illegal immigrants.

Release on an appearance bond—Bond posted by detained immigrants who are released after posting bond of not less than $1,500 (typically $5,000). If the immigrant fails to appear in court as required, the bond is forfeited.

Release on Electronic Monitoring Devices (EMD)—A recent ICE program to ensure compliance with appearance at court and removal orders. Immigrants awaiting court hearings or removal orders either wear a monitoring ankle bracelet or report by telephone to a case manager. The EMD program has been implemented nationwide.

Release on an Order of Recognizance (ROR)—Immigrants, mostly non-Mexicans, are released from detention on their promise to appear in immigration court proceedings as scheduled. ROR is usually used when an alien does not possess the financial resources to post a bond but does not pose a threat to the community or national security. If the alien fails to appear for the hearing, he or she will be ordered deported and will be subject to mandatory detention when apprehended.

Resident alien—A foreign national with legal permanent residency in the United States.

RMB—Renminbi (or yuan); Chinese currency. One U.S. dollar is worth approximately 7.80 RMB, as of January 2007.

Shatou (Mandarin)—"Lopping off someone's head"—in other words, replacing the photo in a passport.

Snakehead—A Chinese term for human smuggler; a strict translation from the Mandarin Chinese word *Shetou*, which literally means "the head of a snake" (i.e., someone who leads the rest of the snake's body, slithering through borders without being noticed).

Taitou (Mandarin)—"Lifting one's head"—refers to the takeoff of an airplane (signifying the completion of a smuggling operation).

Bibliography

Abraham, Shailaja. *Going Nowhere: Trafficking of Women and Children in International Sex Trade*. New Delhi, India: Dominant, 2001.

Agbu, Osita. "Corruption and Human Trafficking: The Nigerian Case." *West Africa Review*, 2003. http://www.westafricareview.com/vol4.1/agbu.html.

Amnesty International. Human Rights Concerns in the Border Region with Mexico (AI Index: AMR 51/003/1998), 1998. http://web.amnesty.org/library/Index/engAMR510031998.

Anderson, Bridget, and Julia O'Connell Davidson. *Trafficking—A Demand Led Problem? Part 1: Review of Evidence and Debates*. Stockholm: Save the Children-Sweden, 2004.

Andreas, Peter. *Border Games: Policing the U.S.-Mexico Divide*. Ithaca, NY: Cornell University Press, 2000.

APEC. *Bangkok Declaration on Partnership for the Future: 2003 Leaders' Declaration at 11th APEC Economic Leaders Meeting*. Bangkok, Thailand, October 21, 2003. http://www.apecsec.org.sg/apec/leaders_declarations/2003.html.

Arizona Republic (Online Print Edition), "In Altar, Teeming with Transients, Small Town Shares Arizona's Conflicts over Impact of Illegal Immigration," August 21, 2005. http://www.azcentral.com.

Arnold, Christina, and Andrea M. Bertone. "Addressing the Sex Trade in Thailand: Some Lessons Learned from NGOs." *Gender Issues* 20, no. 1 (2002): 26–52.

Arrillaga, Pauline, and Olga R. Rodriguez. "AP Investigation: Immigrants Smuggled from Lands with Terror Ties." Associated Press, July 2, 2005. http://web.lexis-nexis.com.

Associated Press. "Closer Look at Smuggling from Nations with Terror Ties," July 2, 2005. http://web.lexis-nexis.com.

———. "14 Indicted in Human Smuggling Ring on U.S.-Canada Border," April 13, 2006. http://web.lexis-nexis.com.

———. "Major Child Prostitution Rings Broken: 31 Indicted." *San Diego Union Tribune*, December 17, 2005, A7.

——. "Smuggler Sentenced in Immigrant Deaths," November 22, 2005. http://web.lexis-nexis.com.

——. "Woman Faces Charges of Sex Trafficking." *San Diego Union Tribune*, May 8, 2005, A5.

Bailey, Ian, and Mark Hume. "Stowaways Land as Anti-smuggling Planning Starts: Seattle-Bound Chinese Discovered When Ship Diverted to Vancouver." *National Post*, January 5, 2000, A5.

Bales, Kevin. *Understanding Global Slavery: A Reader*. Berkeley and Los Angeles: University of California Press, 2005.

Bales, Kevin, Laurel Fletcher, and Eric Stover. *Hidden Slaves—Forced Labor in the United States*. Berkeley, CA: Free the Slaves & Human Rights Center, University of California Berkeley, 2004. http://www.hrcberkeley.org/download/hiddenslaves_report.pdf.

Barboza, David. "Meatpackers' Profits Hinge on Pool of Immigrant Labor." *The New York Times*, December 21, 2001, sec. A26.

Barlett, Donald L., and James B. Steele. "Who Left the Door Open?" *Time*, September 20, 2004, 51–66.

Barnes, Edward. "Two-Faced Woman." *Time*, July 31, 2000, 48–50.

Barry, Ellen. "Card-Size Identity Crisis in Tennessee." *Los Angeles Times*, July 27, 2004, A1.

Bazar, Emily. "Arizona, New Mexico, Declare Emergencies." *USA Today*, August 19, 2005, A2.

Bear, Dan. "Secure Our Borders: A Matter of National Defense." *Ether Zone*, October 8, 2003. http://etherzone.com/2003/bear100803.shtml.

Belanger, Francis. *Drugs, the U.S., and Khun Sa*. Bangkok: Duang Kamol, 1989.

Bendavid, Naftali, and Jill Zuckman. "INS Gaffe Prompts Calls for Inquiry." *Chicago Tribune*, March 14, 2002, A1.

Bennetto, Jason. "Gang Held over Smuggling 100,000 Turks into Britain." *Independent* (London), October 12, 2005. http://news.independent.co.uk/uk/crime/article318866.ece.

Berestein, Leslie. "Expedited Deportations Loom for More Illegal Border Crossers." *San Diego Union Tribune*, August 11, 2004, A13.

——. "Immigration Loophole Leads to Spread of Fake-ID Mills." *San Diego Union Tribune*, February 19, 2006, A1.

——. "Migrant Smugglers Drawn to Casinos." *San Diego Union Tribune*, December 19, 2004, A1.

——. "Record Numbers Have Died Trying to Cross Border." *San Diego Union Tribune*, September 4, 2005, 3A.

Bernton, Hal, Mike Carter, David Heath, and James Neff. "A Terrorist Within: The Story of One Man's Holy War against America." *Seattle Times*, June 23–July 7, 2002. http://archives.seattletimes.nwsource.com/.

Bian, Yanjie. "Chinese Social Stratification and Social Mobility." *Annual Review of Sociology* 28 (2002): 91–116.

Brimelow, Peter. *Alien Nation—Common Sense about America's Immigration Disaster*. New York: Random House, 1995.

Calavita, Kitty. "Thinking Outside the Box on Immigration." *San Diego Union Tribune*, September 23, 2005, B7.

Campo-Flores, Arian. "America's Divide." *Newsweek*, March 10, 2006, 28–38.

Caouette, Therese. *Need Assessment on Cross-Border Trafficking in Women and Children—The Mekong Sub-region*. Bangkok: UN Working Group on Trafficking in the Mekong Sub-region, 1998.

Cearley, Anna. "7 Charged with Trafficking Children." *San Diego Union Tribune*, November 26, 2005, B2.

Chalk, Peter. "Southeast Asia and the Golden Triangle's Heroin Trade: Threat and Response." *Studies in Conflict & Terrorism* 23 (2000): 89–106.

Chapa, Sergio. "Mexico Closes Loophole That Gave Brazilians Springboard for Illegal U.S. Entry." *The Brownsville Herald*, September 13, 2005. http://www.brownsvilleherald.com/.

Chin, Ko-lin. *Chinatown Gangs: Extortion, Ethnicity, & Enterprise*. New York: Oxford University Press, 1996.

———. *Smuggled Chinese: Clandestine Immigration to the United States*. Philadelphia: Temple University Press, 1999.

Chin, Ko-lin, Sheldon Zhang, and Robert Kelly. "Transnational Chinese Organized Crime Activities." *Transnational Organized Crime* 4, no. 3&4 (1998): 127–54.

Chin, Tung Pok, and Winifred C. Chin. *Paper Son—One Man's Story*. Philadelphia: Temple University, 2000.

Cloud, John, and Mike Allen. "Playing Both Sides of the Fence." *Time*, December 5, 2005, 33–35.

CNN. "Sea Piracy Hits Record High." *World News*, January 28, 2004. http://www.cnn.com/2004/WORLD/asiapcf/01/27/pirates/index.html.

Cockburn, Andrew. "21st Century Slaves." *National Geographic Magazine*, September 2003. http://magma.nationalgeographic.com/ngm/0309/feature1/.

Cornelius, Wayne A. "Controlling 'Unwanted Immigration': Lessons from the United States, 1993–2004." *Journal of Ethnic and Migration Studies* 31, no. 4 (2005): 775–94.

———. "Death at the Border: The Efficacy and Unintended Consequences of U.S. Immigration Control Policy, 1993–2000." Working Paper No. 27, Center for Comparative Immigration Studies, University of California, San Diego, 2000. http://www.ccis-ucsd.org/PUBLICATIONS/wrkg27new.pdf.

———. "Thinking Out Loud/IMMIGRATION; There's No Point in Flailing at This Pinata." *Los Angeles Times*, May 29, 2005, M3.

Damask, James A. "Cigarette Smuggling: Financing Terrorism?" Mackinac Center for Public Policy, Midland, Michigan, July 1, 2002. http://www.mackinac.org/article.aspx?ID=4461.

Diaz, Madeline Baro. "Cuban Mails Herself to Miami, and to Freedom Airport: Workers Find Woman Alive in Crate." *South Florida Sun-Sentinel*, August 26, 2004, 1A.

Dillon, Dana. "The War on Terrorism in Southeast Asia: Developing Law Enforcement." *The Backgrounder*, no. 1720. Washington, DC: Heritage Foundation, January 22, 2004.

Dobinson, Ian. "Pinning a Tail on the Dragon: The Chinese and the International Heroin Trade." *Crime & Delinquency* 39, no. 3 (1993): 373–84.

Doyle, Michael. "Immigration Bill Carries Hefty Price Tag." *Sacramento Bee*, May 19, 2006, A14.

Economic and Social Commission for Asia and the Pacific (ESCAP). *Sexually Abused and Sexually Exploited Children and Youth in the Greater Mekong Subregion.* New York: United Nations, 2000.

Economist. "Migrants in Mexico: Waiting to Cross," August 10, 2006. http://www.economist.com/.

Eschbach, Karl, Jacqueline M. Hagan, and Nestor P. Rodriguez. "Deaths during Undocumented Migration: Trends and Policy Implications in the New Era of Homeland Security." *In Defense of the Alien* 26 (2003): 37–52. New York: Center for Migration Studies.

Espenshade, Thomas J., and Charles A. Calhoun. "An Analysis of Public Opinion toward Undocumented Immigration." *Population Research and Policy Review* 12 (1993): 189–224.

Espenshade, Thomas J., and Katherine Hempstead. "Contemporary American Attitudes toward U.S. Immigration." *International Migration Review* 30 (1996): 535–670.

Federal Bureau of Investigation. "Suspected Hezbollah Cell Disrupted." *Terrorism 2000/2001,* July 21, 2000. http://www.fbi.gov/publications/terror/terror2000_2001.htm.

———. "Under the Cover of Romance: Breaking the Heart of Chinese Immigration Fraud." News release, July 29, 2003. http://www.fbi.gov/page2/july03/072903chinaimm.htm.

Feingold, David A. "Think Again: Human Trafficking." *Foreign Policy Issue* 150 (2005): 26–32.

Friedman, Thomas L. *The World Is Flat: A Brief History of the Twenty-First Century.* New York: Farrar, Straus and Giroux, 2005.

Gambetta, Diego. *The Sicilian Mafia: The Business of Private Protection.* Cambridge, MA: Harvard University Press, 1993.

Gaudette, Karen. "Missing Chinese Girl Turns Up on East Coast with Kin." *San Diego Union-Tribune,* August 4, 2002, A3.

Gaylord, Mark. "City of Secrets: Drugs, Money and the Law in Hong Kong." *Crime, Law & Social Change* 28 (1997): 91–110.

Geffray, Christian. "Introduction: Drug Trafficking and the State." *International Social Science Journal* 53, no. 3 (2001): 421–26.

Glaberson, William. "Sex-Trafficking Pleas Detail Abuse of Mexican Women." *New York Times,* April 6, 2005, B3.

Global Commission on International Migration. *Migration in an Interconnected World: New Directions for Action,* October 2005. http://www.gcim.org.

Global Poverty Report. Collectively issued at G8 Okinawa Summit, July 2000, by African Development Bank, Asian Development Bank, European Bank for Reconstruction and Development, Inter-American Development Bank, International Monetary Fund, and World Bank. http://www.adb.org/documents/reports/global_poverty/2000/G8_2000.pdf.

Gonzalez, Daniel, and Sergio Bustos. "'Coyotes': Criminals to the U.S. but Heroes to Many Immigrants." *USA Today,* November 30, 2003, 19A.

Government Accounting Office. *State Department—Improvements Needed to Strengthen U.S. Passport Fraud Detection Efforts.* Report to the Committee on Homeland Security and Governmental Affairs, U.S. Senate, May 2005. http://www.gao.gov/new.items/d05477.pdf.

Gozdziak, Elzbieta M., and Elizabeth A. Collett. "Research on Human Trafficking in North America: A Review of Literature." *International Organization for Migration* 43, no. 1/2 (2005): 99–128.

Graff, James. "Why Paris Is Burning." *Time*, November 14, 2005, 36–38.

Graycar, Adam. "Human Smuggling." A speech delivered to the Symposium on Human Smuggling at the Center for Criminology, University of Hong Kong, February 19, 2000. http://www.aic.gov.au/conferences/other/graycar_adam/2000-02-humansmuggling.html.

Grieco, Elizabeth. "Immigrant Women," *Migration Information Source*. Washington, DC: Migration Policy Institute, 2002. http://migrationinformation.org/USFocus/display.cfm?ID=2.

Guest, Andrew. "Piracy Attacks Hit New High." *Trade Winds*, October 29, 2003.

Harns, Charles. "Improved Travel Documents in the Context of the Overall Migration Management in Africa." A keynote speech at the International Travel Documents and Issuance Systems: Technical Review of Standards and Systems for East and Central African Governments, and Participating West African Governments, Nairobi (Kenya), February 6–8, 2006.

Harris, John R., and Michael P. Todaro. "Migration, Unemployment, and Development." *American Economic Review* 60, no. 1 (1970): 126–42.

Hegeman, Roxana. "Immigration Raids May Affect Meat Prices." Associated Press, December 15, 2006. http://web.lexis-nexis.com.

Hervocek, Sam Howe. "Deadly Choice of Stowaways: Ship Containers." *New York Times*, January 12, 2000, A1.

Hood, Marlowe. "The Taiwan Connection." *Los Angeles Times Magazine*, October 9, 1994.

Hosenball, Mark. "A Swiss Connection to a Pakistani Bomb Racket?" *Newsweek*, March 1, 2003, 8.

Human Smuggling and Trafficking Center. *Fact Sheet: Distinctions between Human Smuggling and Human Trafficking*, 2005. http://www.usdoj.gov/crt/crim/smuggling_trafficking_facts.pdf.

Hunt, Terence. "Bush Visits Bali amid Fears of Terrorism." Associated Press, October 21, 2003. http://web.lexis-nexis.com.

International Crime Threat Assessment. A U.S. government interagency working group report in support of and pursuant to the President's International Crime Control Strategy, December 2000. http://clinton4.nara.gov/WH/EOP/NSC/html/documents/pub45270/pub45270index.html.

International Labor Organization. "A Global Alliance against Forced Labor." *International Labor Conference 93rd Session*, 2005. http://www.ilo.org/.

———. *Labor Market Trends and Globalization's Impact on Them*. http://www.itcilo.it/english/actrav/telearn/global/ilo/seura/mains.htm.

International Organization for Migration. "Foreign Direct Investment, Trade and Aid: An Alternative to Migration." News release no. 781, November 19, 1996. http://www.itcilo.it/english/actrav/telearn/global/ilo/seura/iom2.htm.

Jablon, Robert. "30 Chinese Arrested for Illegal Entry to U.S." *San Diego Union Tribune*, December 30, 1999, A3.

Jamieson, Robert L., Jr. "Illegal Entry into U.S. Has a Long, Dangerous History." *Seattle Post-Intelligencer*, January 11, 2000. http://seattlepi.nwsource.com/local/dang11.shtml.

Jones, James A. "The Immigration Marriage Fraud Amendments: Sham Marriages or Sham Legislation?" *Florida State University Law Review* 24, no. 3 (1997): 679–701.

Jones, Maldwyn Allen. *American Immigration.* Chicago: University of Chicago, 1992.

Kaplan, David E. "Paying for Terror—How Jihadist Groups Are Using Organized-Crime Tactics—and Profits—to Finance Attacks on Targets around the Globe." *U.S. News & World Report,* December 5, 2005, 41–54.

Kindleberger, Charles P. *Europe's Postwar Growth: The Role of Labor Supply.* New York: Oxford University, 1967.

Kochhar, Rakesh. *Survey of Mexican Migrants—Part Three.* Washington, DC: The Pew Hispanic Center, December 6, 2005. http://pewhispanic.org/files/reports/58.pdf.

Kossoudji, Sherrie. "Playing Cat and Mouse at the U.S.-Mexico Border." *Demography* 29, no. 2 (1992): 159–80.

LaFraniere, Sharon. "Many Women Snared in Fake Marriages in South Africa." *New York Times,* September 5, 2004, A3.

Lambsdorf, Johann G. *Corruption Perceptions Index: Global Corruption Reports.* Ann Arbor, MI: Transparency International, 2005.

Lau, Angela, and Sandra Dibble. "Illegal Chinese Immigrants Found in Baja—At Least 82 Have Been Detained." *San Diego Union Tribune,* August 25, 1999, A3.

Lee, Erika. *At America's Gates: Chinese Immigration during the Exclusion Era, 1882–1943.* Chapel Hill: University of North Carolina, 2003.

Lee, Rose Hum. *The Chinese in the United States of America.* Hong Kong: Hong Kong University Press, 1960.

Lewis, Jessa M. *Strategies for Survival: Migration and Fair Trade-Organic Coffee Production in Oaxaca, Mexico.* Center for Comparative Immigration Studies Working Paper No. 118, University of California, San Diego, 2005. http://www.ccis-ucsd.org/PUBLICATIONS/wrkg118.pdf.

Lumpkin, Beverley. "GAO Says Exit Portion of Border Program Will Take 5 to 10 years to Implement." Associated Press, December 15, 2006. http://web.lexis-nexis.com.

MacLeod, Scott. "New Zealand Plans Law Switch on Stolen Passports." *New Zealand Herald,* May 2, 2003, A4.

Mahler, Sarah. *American Dreaming: Immigrant Life on the Margins.* Princeton: Princeton University, 1995.

Malkin, Michelle. *Invasion: How America Still Welcomes Terrorists, Criminals, and Other Foreign Menaces to Our Shores.* Washington, DC: Regnery, 2002.

Mansfield, Duncan. "Tennessee Driver Certificates Lure Illegal Immigrants from Other States." Associated Press, January 29, 2006. http://web.lexis-nexis.com.

Manyin, Mark, Emma Chanlett-Avery, Richard Cronin, Larry Niksch, and Bruce Vaughn. *Terrorism in Southeast Asia* (CSR Report for Congress—RL31672). Washington, DC: Congressional Research Service, Library of Congress, August 13, 2004. http://fpc.state.gov/documents/organization/35795.pdf.

Martin, John L. *Can We Control the Border? A Look at Recent Efforts in San Diego, El Paso and Nogales.* Washington, DC: Center for Immigration Studies, 1995. http://www.cis.org/articles/1995/border/index.html.

———. *Operation Blockade: Bullying Tactic or Border Control Model?* Washington, DC: Center for Immigration Studies, 1993. http://www.cis.org/articles/1993/back993.html.

Martin, Philip L., and Mark J. Miller. "Guestworkers: Lessons from Western Europe." *Industrial and Labor Relations Review* 33 (1980): 315–30.

Masci, David. "Human Trafficking and Slavery: Are the World's Nations Doing Enough to Stamp It Out?" *CQ Researcher* 14, no. 12 (2004): 273–96.

Massey, Douglas S. "Foreword." In *Smuggled Chinese: Clandestine Immigration to the United States*, by Ko-lin Chin, ix–xiii. Philadelphia: Temple University, 1999.

Massey, Douglas S., Joaquin Arango, Graeme Hugo, Ali Kousaouci, Adela Pellegrino, and J. Edward Taylor. "Theories of International Migration: A Review and Appraisal." *Population and Development Review* 19, no. 3 (1993): 431–66.

———. *Worlds in Motion—Understanding International Migration at the End of the Millennium.* Oxford: Clarendon, 1998.

Massey, Douglas S., Jorge Durand, and Nolan J. Malone. *Beyond Smoke and Mirrors: Mexican Immigration in an Era of Economic Integration.* New York: Russell Sage Foundation, 2002.

Mata Press Service. "Mother of All 'Snakeheads' Gets 35 years in Jail." *Asian Pacific Post*, March 27, 2006. http://www.asianpacificpost.com.

McCoy, Alfred. "Requiem for a Drug Lord: State and Commodity in the Career of Khun Sa." In *States and Illegal Practices*, edited by Josiah Heyman, 129–67. Oxford, UK: Berg, 1999.

McGrory, Daniel. "Lithuanian Gangs Forge Ahead in Britain." *Times*, February 21, 2005. http://www.timesonline.co.uk/article/0,,2-1493053,00.html.

McIllwain, Jeffrey S. "From Tong War to Organized Crime: Revising the Historical Perception of Violence in Chinatown." *Justice Quarterly* 14, no. 1 (1997): 25–52.

———. *Organizing Crime in Chinatown: Race and Racketeering in New York, 1890–1910.* Jefferson, NC: McFarland & Company, 2003.

Migrants Rights International. *Background on U.S. Border Militarization: Failed Immigration Enforcement Strategy Is Causing More Migrant Deaths*, July 2003. http://www.migrantwatch.org/mri/background_doc_to_press_statement.htm.

Miko, Francis T. *Trafficking in Women and Children: The U.S. and International Response.* A Congressional Research Service Report, 98-649C, Foreign Affairs, Defense, and Trade Division, 2004. http://digitalcommons.ilr.cornell.edu/key workplace/57.

Miko, Francis T., and Grace (Jea-Hyun) Park. *Trafficking in Women and Children: The U.S. and International Response.* Washington, DC: The Library Congress, Congressional Research Service, 2002.

Morawska, Ewa. "The Sociology and Historiography of Immigration." In *Immigration Reconsidered: History, Sociology, and Politics*, edited by Virginia Yans-McLaughlin, 187–239. New York: Oxford University, 1990.

Moreno, Sylvia. "Flow of Illegal Immigrants to U.S. Unabated— Mexicans Make Up Largest Group; D.C. Area Numbers Up 70 Percent since 2000." *Washington Post*, March 22, 2005, A2.

Myers, Willard. "Transnational Ethnic Chinese Organized Crime: A Global Challenge to the Security of the United States, Analysis and Recommendations." A testimony in Senate Committee on Foreign Affairs, Subcommittee on Terrorism, Narcotics and International Operations, on April 21, 1994.

National Intelligence Council. *Global Trends 2015: Dialogue about the Future with Nongovernment Experts* (NIC 2000-02). Washington, DC: NIC, 2000. http://www.cia.gov/nic/NIC_globaltrend2015.html.

Ngai, Mae M. "Legacies of Exclusion: Illegal Chinese Immigration during the Cold War Years." *Journal of American Ethnic History* 18, no. 1 (1998): 3–35.

Offley, Ed, and Joel Connelly. "U.S., Canada Casting High-Tech Net to Catch Smugglers of Chinese." *San Diego Union Tribune*, October 8, 1999, A29.

O'Neil, Kevin, Kimberly Hamilton, and Demetrios Papademetriou. "Migration in the Americas." A paper prepared for the Policy Analysis and Research Program of the Global Commission on International Migration. Washington, DC: Migration Policy Institute, 2005. http://www.gcim.org/en/ir_experts.html.

Orrenius, Pia M. "Illegal Immigration and Border Enforcement along the U.S.-Mexico Border: An Overview." *Economic & Financial Review* 1 (2001): 2–11.

Otis L. Graham, Jr. *Unguarded Gates—A History of America's Immigration Crisis.* New York: Rowman & Littlefield, 2004.

Outshoorn, Joyce. "The Political Debates on Prostitution and Trafficking of Women, Social Politics." *International Studies in Gender, State and Society* 12, no. 1 (2005): 141–55.

Ovalle, David. "Stowaway Found on Plane at Miami International Airport." *Miami Herald*, March 5, 2004. http://www.latinamericanstudies.org/dominican-republic/stowaway.htm.

Passel, Jeffrey S. *Size and Characteristics of the Unauthorized Migrant Population in the U.S.* Washington, DC: Pew Hispanic Center, 2006. http://pewhispanic.org/files/reports/61.pdf.

Phongpaichit, Pasuk, Sungsidh Piriyarangsan, and Nualnoi Teerat. *Guns, Girls, Gambling, and Ganja: Thailand's Illegal Economy and Public Policy.* Bangkok: Silkworm Books, 1998.

Pieke, Frank N. "Introduction: Chinese Migrations Compared." In *Internal and International Migration—Chinese Perspectives*, edited by Frank N. Pieke and Hein Mallee, 1–26. Surrey, UK: Curzon, 1999.

Pieke, Frank N., Pal Nyiri, Mette Thuno, and Antonella Ceccagno. *Transnational Chinese: Fujianese Migrants in Europe.* Stanford, CA: Stanford University, 2004.

Piore, Michael J. *Birds of Passage: Migrant Labor in Industrial Societies.* New York: Cambridge University, 1979.

Porter, Eduardo. "Social Security Numbers Offered for Rent." *San Diego Union Tribune*, June 7, 2005, A1.

Potter, Gary W. *Criminal Organizations: Vice, Racketeering, and Politics in an American City.* Prospect Heights, IL: Waveland, 1994.

Price, Susannah. "Sri Lanka's Human Smuggling Rings." *BBC News*, February 10, 2000. http://news.bbc.co.uk/1/hi/world/south_asia/637825.stm.

Program Against Corruption and Organized Crime (PACO). *Trafficking in Human Beings and Corruption.* Portoroz, Slovenia: Program against Corruption and Organized Crime in South Eastern Europe, Economic Crime Division, 2002.

Rathgeber, Corene. "The Victimization of Women through Human Trafficking—An Aftermath of War?" *European Journal of Crime, Criminal Law & Criminal Justice* 10, no. 2/3 (2002): 152–63.

Reuters. "China Refugees Found on Canadian Island." *San Diego Union Tribune*, August 13, 1999, A17.

Rhoads, Edward J. M. "White Labor vs. Coolie Labor: The Chinese Question in Pennsylvania in the 1870s." *Journal of American Ethnic History* 21, no. 2 (2002): 3–32.

Rice, Condoleezza. *Release of the Fifth Annual Department of State Trafficking in Persons Report*. U.S. State Department, June 3, 2005. http://www.state.gov/secretary/rm/2005/47193.htm.

Ritter, John. "Finding Labor for the Fields a Trying Task—California's Building Boom Is Pulling Workers Away from Agriculture." *USA Today*, October 10, 2005, 3A.

Rodriguez, Olga R. "Mexico Falls Short on Crack-Down Promise." Associated Press, July 26, 2004. http://web.lexis-nexis.com.

———. "Migrants Forgo Smugglers to Enter U.S." Associated Press, May 19, 2006. http://web.lexis-nexis.com.

Rotstein, Arthur H. "Cell Phones Sometimes Provide a Lifeline for Illegal Immigrants Stranded in Desert." Associated Press, May 27, 2005. http://web.lexis-nexis.com.

———. "Daily Flights for Illegal Immigrants Resume Friday." Associated Press, June 8, 2005. http://web.lexis-nexis.com.

San Diego Union Tribune. "Abu Sayyaf Claims It Is Responsible in Ferry Fire," February 29, 2004, A22.

Saulny, Susan. "Here Comes the Bride. Again, and Again..." *New York Times*, July 10, 2003, A1.

Seligman, Dan. "Illegals with Legal Rights." *Forbes*, January 7, 2002, 128.

Shah, Anup. *Poverty Facts and Stats*, June 11, 2005. http://www.globalissues.org/TradeRelated/Facts.asp.

Shelley, Louise. "Russian and Chinese Trafficking: A Comparative Perspective." In *Human Traffic and Transnational Crime: Eurasian and American Perspectives*, edited by Sally Stoecker and Louise Shelley, 63–77. New York: Rowman & Littlefield, 2005.

Shirk, David, and Alexandra Webber. "Slavery without Borders: Human Trafficking in the U.S.-Mexican Context." *Hemisphere Focus* XII, no. 5 (2004): 1–5. San Diego, CA: Center for Strategic and International Studies, Americas Program Newsletter. http://www.csis.org/index.php?option=com_csis_pubs&task=view&id=603.

Simpson, Glenn R. "Tiny Pacific Island Is Big Worry for U.S." *Wall Street Journal*, May 16, 2003, A4.

Singer, Audrey. *The Rise of New Immigrant Gateways*. Washington, DC: Brookings Institution, 2004. http://www.brookings.edu/metro/publications/20040301_gateways.htm.

Siobhan, Morrissey. "Sinister Industry." *ABA Journal* 92, no. 3 (2006): 59–60.

Skeldon, Ronald. *Myths and Realities of Chinese Irregular Migration*. IOM Migration Research Series, No. 1. Geneva, Switzerland: International Organization for Migration, 2000.

Smith, Paul J. "The Terrorists and Crime Bosses behind the Fake Passport Trade."
    Jane's Intelligence Review, no. 13 (July 2001): 42–44.
Snow, Anita. "Cuban Authorities Shoot Suspected Smuggler." Associated Press,
    April 7, 2006. http://web.lexis-nexis.com.
Soto, Onell R. "Case against 2 Sailors Detailed—Document Say Old Port of Entry
    was Used to Smuggle Immigrants." *San Diego Union-Tribune*, February 3,
    2006, B2.
———. "Four Men Linked to Immigrant Smuggling Arrested in County." *San
    Diego Union-Tribune*, December 7, 2004, B2.
Stark, Oded. "Migration Incentives, Migration Types, the Role of Relative Depri-
    vation." *Economic Journal* 101 (1991): 1163–78.
Stark, Oded, and David Bloom. "The New Economics of Labor Migration." *American
    Economic Review* 75 (1985): 173–78.
Stevens, Todd. "Tender Ties: Husbands' Rights and Racial Exclusion in Chinese
    Marriage Cases, 1882–1924." *Law & Social Inquiry* 27, no. 2 (2002): 271–305.
Stevenson, Mark. "Mexico a Portal to U.S. for Fake-Passport Users." *San Diego
    Union Tribune*, August 8, 2005, A25.
Stone, Robyn I., and Joshua M. Wiener. *Who Will Care for Us?—Addressing Long
    Term Care Workforce Crisis*. Washington, DC: Urban Institute, 2001.
    http://www.urban.org/url.cfm?ID=310304.
Swarns, Rachel L., and Eric Lipton. "U.S. Is Dropping Effort to Track If Visitors
    Leave." *New York Times*, December 15, 2006, A1.
Sweeney, Jason. "FBI's Operation Gilded Cage Includes Knollwood Drive Raid."
    Saratoga News, July 27, 2005. http://www.svcn.com/archives/saratoga
    news/20050727/index.html.
Tang, Alisa. "Thailand Emerges as Fake Passport Capital." Associated Press,
    September 8, 2005. http://web.lexis-nexis.com.
Taylor, Marisa. "U.S. Struggles to Keep Tabs on Foreign Visitors Leaving." *San
    Diego Union Tribune*, September 16, 2006, A7.
Thompson, Roger. *Fukienese Alien Smuggling*. A paper presented at the Second
    Annual Southeast Regional Asian Crime Symposium, Clearwater, FL, 2000.
Thoumi, Francisco E. "Illegal Drugs in Colombia: From Illegal Economic Boom to
    Social Crisis." *Annals of the American Academy of Political & Social Science* 582
    (2002): 102–16.
Tsai, Shih-shan Henry. *China and the Overseas Chinese in the United States
    1868–1911*. Fayetteville: University of Arkansas Press, 1983.
United Nations. *International Migration Report 2002*. New York: United Nations,
    Department of Economic and Social Affairs Population Division, 2002.
———. *Living Arrangements of Older Persons around the World*. New York: United
    Nations, Department of Department of Economic and Social Affairs, Popula-
    tion Division, 2005. http://www.un.org/esa/population/publications/living
    arrangement/report.htm.
———. *Protocol against the Smuggling of Migrants by Land, Sea and Air, Supplement-
    ing the United Nations Convention against Transnational Organized Crime*,
    2000. http://www.unodc.org/pdf/crime/final_instruments/383e.pdf.
———. *Protocol to Prevent, Suppress and Punish Trafficking in Persons, Especially
    Women and Children, Supplementing the United Nations Convention against
    Transnational Organized Crime*, 2000. http://www.unodc.org/pdf/crime/
    final_instruments/383e.pdf.

United Nations' Commission on Population and Development. *Concise Report on World Population Monitoring, 1997: International Migration and Development*. Report of the Secretary-General, 13th Session, February 24–28, 1997. http://www.itcilo.it/english/actrav/telearn/global/ilo/seura/migwod2.htm.

United Nations Development Program. *Human Development Report 1999*. Oxford: Oxford University Press, 1999.

United Nations International Drug Control Program. *World Drug Report*. New York: Oxford University Press, 1997.

United Nations Population Division. *International Migration 2002*. New York: United Nations, 2002. http://www.un.org/esa/population/.

U.S. Attorney General. *Assessment of U.S. Activities to Combat Trafficking in Persons*, August 2003. http://www.usdoj.gov/ag/.

———. *Assessment of U.S. Activities to Combat Trafficking in Persons*, September 2005. http://www.usdoj.gov/ag/.

———. "California Man Pleads Guilty to Marriage Fraud Charges." News release, February 23, 2004. http://www.state.gov/m/ds/rls/29972.htm.

———. *An Investigation of Travel Reimbursements in Connection with the INS's Operation Safeguard* (December). Washington, DC: U.S. Department of Justice, Office of the Inspector General, 2002. http://www.usdoj.gov/oig/special/0301/index.htm.

———. "More Charges in Operation Gilded Case: Man Charged with Alien Harboring and Money Laundering Offenses in Operating San Francisco Brothel." Press release, March 1, 2006. http://www.usdoj.gov/usao/can/press/.

———. "Operation Gatekeeper: An Investigation into Allegations of Fraud and Misconduct." *USDOJ/OIG Special Report* (July). Washington, DC: U.S. Department of Justice, Office of Inspector General, 1998. http://www.usdoj.gov/oig/special/9807/.

———. "29 Charged in Connection with Alien Harboring Conspiracy." Press release, July 1, 2005. http://www.usdoj.gov/usao/can/press/.

U.S. Border Patrol. "Freight Train Apprehensions Dramatically Reduced." News release, January 15, 2003. Washington, DC: U.S. Department of Justice, Border Patrol (McAllen Sector). http://www.cbp.gov/.

———. "McAllen Border Patrol Sector Initiates Operation 'Door Stop.'" News release, January 15, 2003. http://www.cbp.gov/.

U.S. Customs and Border Protection. "CBP Launches Operation Desert Safeguard Aimed at Preventing Migrant Deaths: Effort Focuses on Dangerous Sonoran Desert Area." Press release, June 3, 2003. http://www.cbp.gov.

———. "Homeland Security Expands Efforts to Combat Human Smuggling in the Los Angeles Area: Initial Phase of Multi-agency Operation Focuses on LAX." Press release, July 14, 2004. http://www.cbp.gov/xp/cgov/newsroom/press_releases/.

———. "On a Typical Day..." *Fact Sheet*, 2006. http://www.cbp.gov/.

———. "22 Smuggled Chinese Arrested at the Seattle Seaport: ICE Launches Probe into Human Smuggling Scheme." News release, April 5, 2006. http://www.cbp.gov/xp/cgov/newsroom/news_releases/.

U.S. Department of Homeland Security. "Fact Sheet: Arizona Border Control Initiative—Phase II." News release, March 30, 2005. http://www.dhs.gov/xnews/releases/press_release_0646.shtm.

————. "Homeland Security Agencies Thwart Unusual Human Smuggling Scheme Involving Luxury Sailing Yacht." News release, September 1, 2004. http://www.uscg.mil/pacarea/News/newsreleases/index04.htm.

U.S. Department of Justice. "Inspector General Announces Arrest of INS Official in Alien Smuggling Ring." Press release, July 16, 1996. http://www.usdoj.gov/opa/pr/1996/July96/339ig.htm.

————. "Reno Announces New Agents and Resources to Boost Operation Safeguard and Cut Illegal Immigration." News release, January 5, 1995. http://www.usdoj.gov/opa/pr/Pre_96/January95/.

U.S. General Accounting Office (GAO). *Human Trafficking: Better Data, Strategy, and Reporting Needed to Enhance U.S. Antitrafficking Efforts Abroad* (GAO-06-825). Washington, DC: U.S. Government Accountability Office, 2006. http://www.gao.gov/.

————. *Illegal Immigration: Status Report of Southwest Border Strategy Implementation.* A report to Congressional Committees (GAO/GGD-99-44). Washington, DC: U.S. General Accounting Office, 1999. http://www.gao.gov.

U.S. Immigration and Customs Enforcement (ICE). "Counterfeit Document Ringleader Sentenced to 5 Years." News release, December 8, 2003, 14. http://www.ice.gov/pi/news/newsreleases/.

————. "Department of Homeland Security Launches Operation 'Ice Storm.'" News release, November 10, 2003. http://www.ice.gov/pi/news/newsreleases/.

————. "Detention and Removal Operations: Alternatives to Detention." *Fact Sheet*, July 14, 2004. http://www.ice.gov/pi/dro/factsheets.htm.

————. "Driver Charged in Deadly Smuggling Car Crash." News release, March 11, 2005. http://www.ice.gov/pi/news/newsreleases.

————. *Fact Sheet: Operation ICE Storm*, July 11, 2005. http://www.ice.gov/graphics/news/factsheets/icestorm20040812.htm.

————. "Federal Grand Jury Indicts 12 for Marriage Fraud, International Alien Smuggling." News release, September 15, 2005. http://www.ice.gov/pi/news/newsreleases/.

————. "Feds Charge 13 Proprietors of Arizona Motels with Using Businesses to Harbor Smuggled Aliens." News release, November 10, 2005. http://www.ice.gov/graphics/news/newsreleases/.

————. "Feds Vow to Use '*Ice Storm*' Tactics in Other Cities as Phoenix Sees Progress in Human Smuggling Crackdown." News release, May 18, 2004. http://www.ice.gov/pi/news/newsreleases/.

————. "55 Charged in Federal Probe Targeting Large-Scale Human Smuggling Network." News release, October 11, 2006. http://www.ice.gov/pi/news/newsreleases.

————. "Four Arrested in Counterfeit Document Scheme—An Array of Fake Documents and Sophisticated Machinery Uncovered." News release, November 14, 2003. http://www.ice.gov/pi/news/newsreleases/.

————. "ICE Agent Testifies before Congress on Growing Threat of Human Trafficking." News release, June 24, 2003. http://www.ice.gov/pi/news/newsreleases/.

————. "ICE Arrests Men Who Forced Women to Work as Strippers—Ukrainian Women Were Tricked into Traveling to the U.S., Then Forced to Work at Strip Club." News release, February 17, 2005. http://www.ice.gov/pi/news/newsreleases/.

———. "Landmark Marriage Fraud Case Nets 44 in California." *Inside ICE* 2, no. 25 (2005). http://www.ice.gov/pi/news/insideice/articles/insideice_122105_web1.htm.

———. "Laredo Marine Corps Recruiter Convicted of Alien Smuggling." News release, October 14, 2005. http://www.ice.gov/pi/news/newsreleases/.

———. "Sister Ping Sentenced to 35 years in Prison for Alien Smuggling, Hostage Taking, Money Laundering and Ransom Proceeds Conspiracy." News release, March 16, 2006. http://www.ice.gov/graphics/news/newsreleases/.

———. "South Bay Man Pleads Guilty to Smuggling Aliens and Tropical Fish into United States." News release, September 9, 2005. http://www.ice.gov/pi/news/newsreleases/.

———. "10 Charged in International Human Smuggling Ring That Lured Young Honduran Women to U.S. for Forced Labor." News release, July 21, 2005. http://www.ice.gov/pi/news/newsreleases/.

———. "24 Indicted in Korean Human Smuggling Scheme That Brought Prostitutes into the United States." News release, July 14, 2005. http://www.ice.gov/pi/news/newsreleases/.

———. "26 Unauthorized Workers Arrested at Northrop Grumman Facility." News release, June 1, 2005. http://www.ice.gov/pi/news/newsreleases/.

———. "2 Criminally Charged with Alien Smuggling." News release, May 6, 2005. http://www.ice.gov/pi/news/newsreleases/.

———. "Two Sentenced for Smuggling Operation That Left Eleven Dead in Iowa Railcar." News release, November 21, 2005. http://www.ice.gov/pi/news/newsreleases/.

———. "U.S. Uncovers Large-Scale Identity Theft Scheme Used by Illegal Aliens to Gain Employment at Nationwide Meat Processor." News release, December 13, 2006. http://www.ice.gov/pi/news/newsreleases/.

———. "Wisconsin Couple Indicted on Human Trafficking Charges: Brookfield Pair Is Charged with Holding a Woman in Servitude for 19 Years." News release, March 16, 2005. http://www.ice.gov/pi/news/newsreleases/.

U.S. State Department. *Fact Sheet: Distinctions between Human Smuggling and Human Trafficking*. Washington, DC: U.S. State Department, Human Smuggling and Trafficking Center, 2005. http://www.state.gov/p/inl/rls/fs/49768.htm.

———. *International Narcotics Control Strategy Report (INCSR)*. Washington, DC: U.S. Department of State, Bureau for International Narcotics and Enforcement Affairs, 2005. http://www.state.gov/p/inl/rls/nrcrpt/.

———. *International Narcotics Control Strategy Report (INCSR)*. Washington, DC: U.S. Department of State, Bureau for International Narcotics and Enforcement Affairs, 2006. http://www.state.gov/p/inl/rls/nrcrpt/.

———. *Trafficking in Persons Report*. Washington, DC: U.S. Department of State, Office to Monitor and Combat Trafficking in Persons, 2001. http://www.state.gov/g/tip/rls/.

———. *Trafficking in Persons Report*. Washington, DC: U.S. Department of State, Office to Monitor and Combat Trafficking in Persons, 2002. http://www.state.gov/g/tip/rls/.

———. *Trafficking in Persons Report*. Washington, DC: U.S. Department of State, Office to Monitor and Combat Trafficking in Persons, 2003. http://www.state.gov/g/tip/rls/.

————. *Trafficking in Persons Report.* Washington, DC: U.S. Department of State, Office to Monitor and Combat Trafficking in Persons, 2004. http://www. state.gov/g/tip/rls/.

————. *Trafficking in Persons Report.* Washington, DC: U.S. Department of Justice, Office to Monitor and Combat Trafficking in Persons, 2005. http://www.state.gov/g/tip/rls/.

————. *Trafficking in Persons Report.* Washington, DC: U.S. Department of State, Office to Monitor and Combat Trafficking in Persons, 2006. http://www.state.gov/g/tip/rls/.

Valencia, Mark J. "International Co-operation in Anti-piracy Efforts in Asia: Some Considerations." *East–West Center, Asia–Pacific Area Network*, February 20, 2001.

Van Derbeken, Jaxon, and Ryan Kim. "Alleged Sex-Trade Ring Broken Up in Bay Area—Police Say Koreans in Massage Parlors Were Smuggled In." *San Francisco Chronicle*, July 2, 2005, A1.

Verhovek, Sam Howe. "22 Chinese Stowaways Found at Cargo Facility in Seattle." *Los Angeles Times*, April 6, 2006, A5.

Wadhwani, Anita. "Driving Certificates Turning into IDs." *Tennessean.com*, June 25, 2004. http://www.tennessean.com/government/archives/04/06/53319732.shtml.

Wagner, Dennis. "Illegals Dying at Record Rate in Arizona Desert." *USA Today*, August 19, 2005, 1A.

Wardell, Jane. "British Panel: Raise Retirement Age to 69." *San Diego Union Tribune*, December 1, 2005, A3.

Watson, Julie. "More Women Risking Rape, Death, Capture to Cross Desert into U.S." Associated Press, April 28, 2006. http://web.lexis-nexis.com.

Weiner, Eric, and Michael Sullivan. "Terrorism in Southeast Asia: An NPR Special Report Five-Part Series Traces Spread of Al Qaeda, Militant Islam." NPR news release, February 3–7, 2003. http://www.npr.org/news/specials/mideast/asia/index.html.

Weitzer, Ronald. "The Growing Moral Panic over Prostitution and Sex Trafficking." *Criminologist* 30, no. 5 (2005): 1–5.

Wong, K. Scott. "Introduction: Paper Lives." In *Paper Son: One Man's Story*, by Tung Pok Chin and Winifred C. Chin, xi–xx. Philadelphia: Temple University, 2000.

World Bank, *Poverty in Mexico: An Assessment of Conditions, Trends and Government Strategy.* Mexico: The World Bank (Report No. 28612-ME), 2004.

Yuchengco, Alfonso T. "Islamist Terrorism in Southeast Asia." *Issues & Insights* 3, no. 1 (2003): 1–11. http://www.csis.org/pacfor/issues/.

Zhang, Sheldon, and Ko-lin Chin. "The Declining Significance of Triad Societies in Transnational Illegal Activities—A Structural Deficiency Perspective." *British Journal of Criminology* 43, no. 3 (2003): 469–88.

————. "Enter the Dragon: Inside Chinese Human Smuggling Organizations." *Criminology* 40, no. 4 (2002): 737–68.

Zhao, Shi-lung, and Ke Su-ya. *Golden Triangle: A Future without Heroin?* Beijing: Economic Daily Publishing Company, 2003.

Zhu, Liping. *A Chinaman's Chance—The Chinese on the Rocky Mountain Mining Frontier.* Niwot, CO: University of Colorado, 1997.

Index

About the Author

SHELDON X. ZHANG is Professor of Sociology at San Diego State University. He is coauthor of *Criminology: A Global Perspective*. His research revolves around two main themes—transnational organized crime and community-based corrections. His articles have appeared in journals such as *Criminology, British Journal of Criminology, Criminology and Social Policy, Journal of Research in Crime and Delinquency,* and *Crime and Delinquency.* He has given numerous conference presentations and keynote speeches to academic as well as law enforcement audiences.

DATE DUE

DE 28 07			

WITHDRAWN

DEMCO 38-296